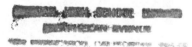

JM

DANTE ALIGHIERI
His Life and Works

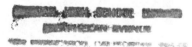

BRONZE BUST OF DANTE
In the possession of Whitworth Wallis, Esq., Birmingham

DANTE ALIGHIERI
His Life and Works

Paget Toynbee

Introduction by
Robert Hollander

Dover Publications, Inc.
Mineola, New York

Bibliographical Note

This Dover edition, first published in 2005, is an augmented republication of
the 1910 "Revised and Considerably Enlarged" fourth edition of the work originally published by Methuen & Co. Ltd., London, in 1900. Robert Hollander has
written a new Introduction specially for the Dover edition.

Library of Congress Cataloging-in-Publication Data

Toynbee, Paget Jackson, 1855–1932.
    Dante Alighieri : his life and works / Paget Toynbee ; introduction by Robert
Hollander.
        p. cm.
    Originally published: London : Methuen, 1900.
    Includes bibliographical references and index.
    ISBN 0-486-44340-X (pbk.)
    1. Dante Alighieri, 1265–1321. 2. Authors, Italian—To 1500—Biography.
I. Title.

PQ4335.T7 2005
851'.1—dc22
[B]

2005045176

Manufactured in the United States of America
Dover Publications, Inc., 31 East 2nd Street, Mineola, N.Y. 11501

INTRODUCTION TO THE DOVER EDITION

Robert Hollander

IN the first twenty years of the last century, Paget Jackson Toynbee (1855–1932) made a lasting mark on Dante studies. (His main contributions will be mentioned below.) This book, published as a short monograph in 1899 (with less detailed descriptions of the works being the most notable difference with respect to the present volume), was much revised in the fourth edition of 1910 (the third edition had already been paid the rare– at that time–compliment, for a book about Dante, of an Italian translation).

What distinguishes Toynbee's work is its meticulous attention to detail, bringing a gift for clear-headed analysis into play in an attempt to get the life and works "right," since both are sur-rounded by uncertainty that results from the near-total absence of any corroborating record for the "facts" about Dante and his work that have come down to us. It is also distinguished by a judicious turn of mind in dealing with most of these thorny prob-lems (some nearly inevitable, given that uncertainty).

We want to remember (as Toynbee himself demonstrates in his later volume *Dante in English Literature*) that, until the Romantic era, with the imposing exception of Chaucer, rarely were English poets excited to the level of imitation by Dante's great poem, as were, to name but two, Byron and Shelley. Thus Toynbee's enthu-siasm is part of a second British "Dante moment," this one cen-tered in Oxford (where both he and Edward Moore taught) and involving literary critics more than poets. The most important of these figures was the first of them, Moore (1835–1916), one of the great textual editors of the *Comedy*, his work used and admired even by Italian scholars, who did not hesitate to employ the texts that he edited as the new standard. In addition, and among his other contributions, were his "Studies in Dante," collected in four volumes, useful even today. A great scholar himself, Toynbee, who collaborated with Moore on the collection of Dante's works known as "The Oxford Dante" (1924), frequently acknowledges his debt to Moore in the footnotes at the bottom of these pages. Another brilliant Dantean presence on the scene was that of Philip Wicksteed (1844–1927), a clergyman, a prolific student of economics, and a man who raised an amateur's interest in the Italian poet to the highest levels of scholarship, as is evident, for instance, in his *Dante and Aquinas* (1913). A sometime collaborator of Wicksteed was the much younger Edmund Gardner (1869–1935), whose two important book-length contributions are *Dante's Ten Heavens* (1898) and *Dante and the Mystics* (1913). These four men were the flower of this period in English Dante studies, but several other scholars also contributed to making this time extraordinary for Dante studies in Great Britain.

Toynbee's own other major contributions include *A Dictionary of Proper Names and Notable Matters in the Works of Dante* (1898; second edition, Charles Singleton, 1968); *Dante in English Literature from Chaucer to Cary* (1909), an effort to gather every instance of the occurrence of references to Dante in English literature up to 1840; important articles collected in *Dante Studies and Researches* (1902) and *Dante Studies* (1921); and at that point the best critical edition of Dante's letters (1920). It is a record of accomplishment in Dante studies that is difficult to match.

This particular book was the first of its kind and obviously filled a need; it is a concise, straightforward presentation of Dante's life and works written for the general reader but useful for the specialist as well. One is impressed, reading through it, at how it has not become dated in a field of study in which the essential bibliography changes in major respects every quarter century. Only one present issue concerning the Dantean canon is not broached here, the question of the attribution of *Il fiore* and *Il Detto d'amore*, a question that divides its contemporary students but was not even an issue in Toynbee's day; indeed, the first editions of Dante's complete works containing these two extended poetic exercises saw the light of day only after the First World War.

Toynbee's judgments hold up remarkably well, even his hedging on the date of composition of the *Monarchia* (while leaving the question open, he decidedly prefers a date sometime between 1310 and 1313, while most contemporary students of the problem, after Pier Giorgio Ricci's intervention in his edition [1965], date it later, and no earlier than 1317). A century and more after he decided to dedicate himself to this task, forty years after Charles Singleton republished the then out-of-print text (1965), this book remains one of the best guides to someone trying to find an orientation in the world that Dante manufactured.

Hopewell, New Jersey
31 December 2004

PREFACE TO FIRST EDITION

THIS little book lays no claim to originality, and makes no pretence to learning or research. It is addressed rather to the so-called general reader than to the serious Dante student. The narrative is taken largely from the pages of Villani, Boccaccio, and from other similar sources. The reader will find fiction (at any rate from the critic's point of view) as well as fact in these pages, but he will, I hope, be at no loss to distinguish between the two. The legends and traditions which hang around the name of a great personality are a not unimportant element in his biography, and may sometimes serve to place him as well as, if not better than, the more sober estimates of the serious historian. I have not, therefore, thought it outside the scope of this sketch of Dante's life to include some of the anecdotes which at an early date began to be associated with his name, though certain of them demonstrably belong to a far earlier period.

Again, when a thing has been well said by a previous writer, I have been content to let him speak, instead of saying the same thing less well in my own words.

The translations for the most part are my own. I

have, however, been indebted for an occasional turn or phrase to Selfe and Wicksteed's *Selections from Villani*, and to the latter's versions of the *Early Lives of Dante*.

The illustrations are reproduced, by permission, from photographs by Messrs. Alinari and Messrs. Brogi of Florence.

May, 1900

PREFACE TO FOURTH EDITION

A FOURTH edition of this book (the third edition of which has lately been translated into Italian by Professor Balsamo-Crivelli, of Turin) having been called for, I have, at the suggestion of the publishers, availed myself of the opportunity to make considerable additions to it (as well as to rectify sundry mistakes and omissions), which will, I trust, increase its value to students, without at the same time diminishing its interest for the general reader.

The present edition differs from its predecessors chiefly in respect of the much fuller treatment (in Part V) of Dante's works, of which brief analyses have now been supplied, together with information as to MSS. and critical editions, and, in the case of the *Divina Commedia* commentaries, as well as *data*, of special interest to the English reader, as to the various editions and translations of each work published in this country. Many additional details will also be found in some of the other sections, especially in the more strictly biographical portions of the work.

Further, in the present edition I have made a point of supplying copious references to authorities (generally at the foot of the page), which will serve at once as an acknowledgment of my own obligations, and as a means whereby the reader may, if desired, check the information furnished in the text.

The bibliographical and biographical notes in the original Appendix have been considerably amplified, and four Appendices have been added. The first of these consists of a Genealogical Table of the family of Dante, with references to Dante's own allusions to members of his family. The others contain respectively, a translation of the letter of Frate Ilario to Uguccione della Faggiuola, to which renewed attention has been directed of late ; extracts from some interesting letters of Seymour Kirkup to Gabriele Rossetti concerning the discovery of the Giotto portrait of Dante in the Bargello, and Kirkup's drawing from it (further information about which, supplied by Kirkup himself to the late owner of the original sketch, will be found in the body of the book) ; and, lastly, a Chronological List of early (cent. xiv-xvi) commentaries on the *Divina Commedia*.

The index, which of necessity has been entirely recast, has been made as full as possible in order to render the varied contents of the book easily accessible to the student for purposes of reference, and dates have been inserted as a convenient means of " orientation ".

Sundry illustrations have been added, among them

one of a fine bronze bust of Dante (supposed to be the work of a French artist at the beginning of the seventeenth century) in the possession of Mr. Whitworth Wallis, Director of the Birmingham Museum and Art Gallery, who kindly supplied a photograph (hitherto unpublished) for the purpose of reproduction in this book.

PAGET TOYNBEE

20 *January*, 1910
(*the* 590*th anniversary of the disputation*
" *De Aqua et Terra* " *at Verona*)

*** In the numbering of the poems in the *Canzoniere*, and the line references in the prose works, the arrangement of the Oxford Dante has been followed.

" Se Dio ti lasci, Lettor, prender frutto
Di tua lezion."

Inf. xx. 19

CONTENTS

PART I

GUELFS AND GHIBELLINES

PART II

DANTE IN FLORENCE

CONTENTS

LIST OF ILLUSTRATIONS

Thou know'st perchance how Phœbus' self did guide
Our Tuscan DANTE up the lofty side
Of snow-clad Cyrrha; how our Poet won
Parnassus' peak, and founts of Helicon;
How with Apollo, ranging wide, he sped
Through Nature's whole domain, and visited
Imperial Rome, and Paris, and so passed
O'er seas to BRITAIN's distant shores at last.

(*Boccaccio to Petrarch*)

"the gretë poete of Ytaille
That hightë Dant."

CHAUCER, *Monk's Tale*

DANTE ALIGHIERI
His Life and Works

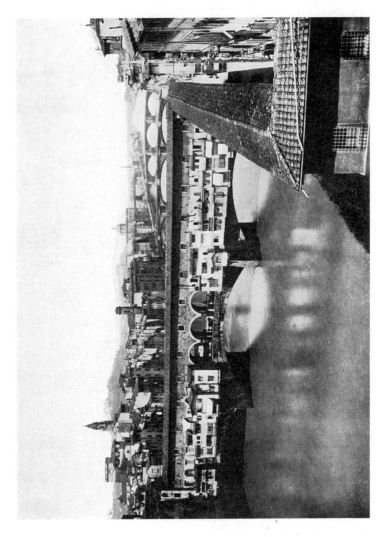

FLORENCE AND THE ARNO

PART I

GUELFS AND GHIBELLINES

CHAPTER I

1215–1250

Origin of the names—Distinguishing principles of the two parties in Italy—Introduction of the parties into Florence—The Ghibellines with the aid of Frederick II expel the Guelfs from Florence—Return of the Guelfs after the Emperor's death, and pacification between the two parties.

NORTHERN ITALY in the middle of the thirteenth century, at the time of Dante's birth,[1] was divided into two great political parties, of which the one, known by the name of Guelfs, looked to the Pope as their head, while the others, the Ghibellines, looked to the Emperor. The distinctive titles of these two parties were of German origin, being merely Italianized forms (*Guelfo* and *Ghibellino*) of the two German names *Welf* and *Weiblingen*. The former of these was the name of an illustrious family, several members of which had successively been Dukes of Bavaria in the tenth and eleventh centuries. The heiress of the last of these intermarried with a younger son of the house of Este; and from them sprang a second line of Guelfs, from whom the royal house of Brunswick is descended.

[1] May, 1265.

Weiblingen was the name of a castle in Franconia, belonging to Conrad the Salic, who was Emperor from 1024
to 1039, and was the progenitor, through the female line,
of the Swabian emperors.   By the election of Lothair in
1125 in succession to Henry V (Emperor from 1106 to
1125) the Swabian family were ousted from what they
had come to regard almost as an hereditary possession ;
and at this time a hostility appears to have commenced
between them and the house of Welf, who were nearly
related to Lothair.   In 1071 the Emperor Henry IV had
conferred the Duchy of Bavaria upon the Welfs; and in
1080 the Duchy of Swabia had been conferred upon the
Counts of Hohenstaufen, who represented the Franconian
line.

The accession in 1138 of Conrad III of Swabia to the
Imperial throne, and the rebellion of Henry the Proud,
the Welf Duke of Bavaria, gave rise to a bloody struggle
between the two houses; and at the battle of Weinsberg,
fought on 21 December, 1140, in which the Welf Duke
was defeated by Conrad, the names *Welf* and *Weiblingen*
were for the first time, it is said, adopted as war-
cries.

These names, which in Germany, as we have seen, distinguished the two sides in the conflict between the Welfs
and the Imperial Swabian or Hohenstaufen line, in Italy
acquired a different meaning, and became identified respectively with the supporters of the Church and the
supporters of the Empire.   Their first appearance in
Italy seems to have been quite at the beginning of the
thirteenth century, when they were adopted by the two
leading parties which divided the towns of Lombardy
during the struggle for the Imperial throne between
Philip, Duke of Swabia (brother of the Emperor Henry
VI), and the Welf Otto of Brunswick, many important

Italian towns sympathizing with the latter, who after his rival's death in 1208 became Emperor as Otto IV.

The division between the opposing factions rapidly deepened, till not only rival towns, but also the leading families within the towns themselves, became involved in party strife, the citizens ranging themselves, ostensibly at least, under the chiefs on either side.

The main outlines of the principles which actuated the two parties in Italy, during the period covered by this book, have been ably sketched by the late Dean Church. " The names of Guelf and Ghibelline," he writes, " were the inheritance of a contest which, in its original meaning, had been long over. The old struggle between the priesthood and the Empire was still kept up traditionally, but its ideas and interests were changed. It had passed over from the mixed region of the spiritual and temporal into the purely political. The cause of the Popes was that of the independence of Italy—the freedom and alliance of the great cities of the north, and the dependence of the centre and south on the Roman See. To keep the Emperor out of Italy, to create a barrier of powerful cities against him south of the Alps, to form behind themselves a compact territory, rich, removed from the first burst of invasion, and maintaining a strong body of interested feudatories, had now become the great object of the Popes. The two parties did not care to keep in view principles which their chiefs had lost sight of. The Emperor and the Pope were both real powers, able to protect and assist; and they divided between them those who required protection and assistance. Geographical position, the rivalry of neighbourhood, family tradition, private feuds, and above all private interest, were the main causes which assigned cities, families, and individuals to the Ghibelline or Guelf party. One party called themselves

the Emperor's liegemen, and their watchword was authority
and law; the other side were the liegemen of Holy
Church, and their cry was liberty; and the distinction as
a broad one is true. But a democracy would become
Ghibelline, without scruple, if its neighbour town was
Guelf; and among the Guelf liegemen of the Church and
liberty the pride of blood and love of power were not a
whit inferior to that of their opponents.

"The Ghibellines as a body reflected the worldliness,
the licence, the irreligion, the reckless selfishness, the
daring insolence, and at the same time the gaiety and
pomp, the princely magnificence and generosity and large-
ness of mind of the house of Swabia; they were the men
of the court and camp, imperious and haughty from ancient lineage, or the Imperial cause, yet not wanting in the
frankness and courtesy of nobility; careless of public
opinion and public rights, but not dead to the grandeur
of public objects and public services. The Guelfs, on the
other hand, were the party of the middle classes; they
rose out of and held to the people; they were strong by
their compactness, their organization in cities, their com-
mercial relations and interests, their command of money.
Further, they were professedly the party of strictness and
religion, a profession which fettered them as little as their
opponents were fettered by the respect they claimed for
Imperial law. But though by personal unscrupulousness
and selfishness, and in instances of public vengeance, they
sinned as deeply as the Ghibellines, they stood far more
committed as a party to a public meaning and purpose—
to improvement in law and the condition of the poor, to
a protest against the insolence of the strong, to the encouragement of industry. The genuine Guelf spirit was
austere, frugal, independent, earnest, religious, fond of its
home and Church, and of those celebrations which bound

together Church and home; but withal very proud, very intolerant; in its higher form intolerant of evil, but intolerant always to whatever displeased it." [1]

"Speaking generally," as another writer [2] puts it, "the Ghibellines were the party of the Emperor, and the Guelfs the party of the Pope: the Ghibellines were on the side of authority, or sometimes of oppression; the Guelfs were on the side of liberty and self-government. Again, the Ghibellines were the supporters of a universal Empire, of which Italy was to be the head; the Guelfs were on the side of national life and national individuality."

The introduction of the Guelf and Ghibelline factions into Florence is said by the old Florentine chroniclers to have taken place in the year 1215, on the occasion of a blood-feud which arose out of the murder of one of the Buondelmonti by one of the Amidei, both of them noble Florentine families, on Easter Sunday in that year. The story of this murder, and of the incident which led to it, is related as follows by Giovanni Villani in his *New Chronicle of the City of Florence*, which he began to write in 1300, the year of the first Jubilee of the Roman Church.

"In the year of Christ 1215," he says, "Messer Gherardo Orlandi being Podestà of Florence,[3] one Messer Buondelmonte dei Buondelmonti, a noble citizen of Florence, having promised to take to wife a damsel of the house of the Amidei, honourable and noble citizens; as the said M. Buondelmonte, who was a very handsome and

---

[1] *Dante: An Essay.* By R. W. Church.

[2] O. Browning, in *Guelfs and Ghibellines.*

[3] The Podestà was the chief magistrate of the city, who was appointed for one year. With a view to securing impartiality in the administration of justice the office of Podestà was always held by a stranger—never by a native of Florence.

fine cavalier, was riding through the city, a lady of the house of the Donati called to him, and found fault with him on account of the lady to whom he had betrothed himself, as being neither fair enough nor a fitting match for him, and saying: I had kept my daughter here for you—whom she showed to him, and she was very beautiful. And he straightway, at the prompting of the Evil One, becoming enamoured of her, was betrothed to her and took her to wife; for which cause the kinsfolk of the lady to whom he was first betrothed, being assembled together and smarting under the shame which M. Buondelmonte had put upon them, were filled with the accursed rage, whereby the city of Florence was laid waste and divided against herself; for many families of the nobles swore together to put shame on the said M. Buondelmonte in revenge for these wrongs. And as they were in council among themselves as to how they should retaliate on him, either by beating him or by stabbing him, Mosca de' Lamberti spoke the evil word: A thing done has an end—that is, that he should be slain. And so it was done; for on the morning of Easter Day they assembled in the house of the Amidei of Santo Stefano, and M. Buondelmonte coming from beyond Arno, bravely arrayed in new garments all white, and on a white palfrey, when he reached the foot of the Ponte Vecchio on this side, just at the foot of the pillar where stood the statue of Mars, the said M. Buondelmonte was thrown from his horse on to the ground by Schiatta degli Uberti, and set on and stabbed by Mosca Lamberti and Lambertuccio degli Amidei, and his throat cut by Oderigo Fifanti, and an end made of him; and with them was one of the Counts of Gangalandi. On these doings the city rushed to arms in tumult; and this death of M. Buondelmonte was the cause and beginning of the accursed Guelf and Ghibelline parties in Florence, albeit that before this time there had been many factions among the nobles of the city, and parties as aforesaid, by reason of the quarrels and disputes between the Church and the Empire; but on account of the death of the said M. Buondelmonte all the families of the nobles and other citizens of Florence took sides, and some held with the Buondelmonti, who joined the Guelf party and became its leaders, and some with the Uberti, who became the leaders of the Ghibellines. And from this followed great evil and ruin to our city, which is like never to have an end, unless God bring it to an end."[1]

Villani then proceeds to give a list of the noble families in Florence who joined either side, the Guelfs, as he has already explained, under the leadership of the Buondelmonti, and the Ghibellines under that of the Uberti. "And this," he repeats, "is how these accursed parties took their origin in Florence, albeit at first not very openly, there being division among the nobles of the city, in that some loved the rule of the Church, and some that of the Empire, nevertheless as to the good estate and well-being of the commonwealth all were at one."

The conflict between the Guelfs and Ghibellines in Florence, thus commenced by the murder of Buondelmonte, continued, with varying fortune to either side, for a period of fifty-two years, from 1215 to 1267, when the Guelf party finally remained masters of the situation. In 1248 the Emperor Frederick II, wishing to retaliate upon the Papacy for the unjust sentence of deposition pronounced against him by Innocent IV three years before at the Council of Lyons, and anxious to weaken the Church party, made offers to the Uberti, the leaders of the Florentine Ghibellines, to help them to expel from their city his enemies and their own. His offer being accepted, he des-

[1] Villani, bk. v. ch. 38.

patched a force of German horsemen under his son, Frederick of Antioch, by whose aid, after a fierce struggle, the Guelfs were driven out.

Villani gives a vivid account of the street-fighting which took place on this occasion. Being a Guelf, he naturally has no sympathy with Frederick and his allies. " In these times," he writes, " Frederick being in Lombardy, after his deposition from the title of Emperor by Pope Innocent, set himself, so far as he was able, to destroy in Tuscany and Lombardy the faithful sons of Holy Church in every city where he had power. And inasmuch as our city of Florence was not among the least notable and powerful of Italy, he desired to pour out his venom upon her, and to breed further strife between the accursed parties of the Guelfs and Ghibellines, which had begun some time before through the murder of Buondelmonte, and even earlier, as we have already related. But although since then the said parties had continued among the nobles of Florence, and they had at sundry times been at war among themselves on account of their private enmities, and were divided by reason of the said parties and held to their several sides, those who were called Guelfs preferring the government of the Pope and Holy Church, and those who were called Ghibellines favouring the Emperor and his following, nevertheless the people and commonwealth of Florence were steadfast in unity, to the well-being and honour and good estate of the republic.

" But now the Emperor sending letters and ambassadors to the family of the Uberti, who were the heads of his party, and to their following who called themselves Ghibellines, invited them to drive from the cities their enemies the Guelfs, offering some of his horsemen to help them. And thus he caused the Uberti to begin dissension and civil warfare in Florence, whereby the city fell into great disorder, and the nobles and all the people were divided, some holding to one side and some to the other; and in several quarters of the city there was fighting for a long time. The chief of it was among the houses of the Uberti, where the great palace of the people now stands; there they gathered with their followers and fought against the Guelfs of San Piero Scheraggio; and the Guelfs from beyond Arno crossed over by the river dams and came and helped to fight the Uberti. The next place was in Porte San Piero, where the Tedaldini were the chief Ghibellines, as having the strongest buildings, palaces, and towers; and they and their allies fought against the Donati, the Adimari, and others. And the third fight took place in Porte del Duomo, by the tower of Messer Lancia de' Cattani of Castiglione, with the Brunelleschi and other Ghibelline leaders, and many of the populace on the same side, against the Tosinghi and others. And another was in San Brancazio, where the Lamberti were the Ghibelline leaders, with many of the people on their side, against the Guelfs of that quarter. And the Ghibellines in San Brancazio made their stand at the tower of the Soldanieri, where a bolt from the tower struck the Guelf standard-bearer (their standard being a crimson lily on a white field) in the face, so that he died. And on the day the Guelfs were driven out they came in arms and buried him in San Lorenzo; and when they were gone the canons of San Lorenzo removed the body, for fear the Ghibellines should dig it up and do it violence, inasmuch as this M. Rustico Marignolli was a great captain among the Guelfs. And the Ghibellines made another attack in the Borgo, where the Soldanieri and Guidi were their leaders, against the Buondelmonti, Cavalcanti, and others. And there was fighting between the two sides beyond Arno as well, but here it was chiefly among the populace.

" So it came about that this warfare went on for some time, as they fought at the barriers or barricades, from one quarter to another, and from one tower to another (for there were many towers in Florence in those days, a hundred cubits and more in height), and they used mangonels and other engines of war, and kept up the fighting day and night. In the midst of the struggle the Emperor sent his bastard son Frederick to Florence, with sixteen hundred of his German horsemen. And when the Ghibellines heard that they were at hand, they took heart and fought more stoutly and with greater boldness against the Guelfs, who had no other help, and looked for none, seeing that the Pope was at Lyons on Rhone, beyond the mountains, and that the power of Frederick was far too great in every part of Italy. And at this time the Ghibellines made use of a device of war, for they collected the greater part of their force at the house of the Uberti, and when the fighting began in the quarters named above, they went in a body to oppose the Guelfs, and by this means overpowered them in nearly every part of the city, save in their own quarter, against the barricade of the Guidalotti and Bagnesi, who held out for a time ; and to that place the Guelfs repaired, and the whole force of the Ghibellines against them. At last the Guelfs, finding themselves hard pressed, and learning that the Emperor's horsemen were already in Florence (King Frederick having arrived with his men on the Sunday morning), after holding out until the Wednesday, abandoned the defence, the force of the Ghibellines being too strong for them, and fled from the city on Candlemas night (2 February), in the year 1248." [1]

Villani goes on to describe how the Ghibellines made use of their victory, ruthlessly destroying their enemies' property, and even attempting to wreck the beautiful Bap-

[1] Villani, bk. vi. ch. 33.

tistery of San Giovanni, which the Guelfs used as a meeting
place, by throwing down upon it the neighbouring Tower
of the "Guardamorto,"—so called because the bodies of
those taken to be buried in San Giovanni rested there.
In this attempt fortunately they failed, and the Baptistery,
which before the erection of the present Duomo served as
the Cathedral of Florence, stands to this day.

"The Ghibellines, who now remained masters of Florence," continues the chronicler, "set to work to refashion
the city after their own manner, razing to the ground
thirty-six strongholds of the Guelfs, both palaces and great
towers, among them being the noble residence of the
Tosinghi in the old Market Place, known as the Palace,
which was ninety cubits high, built with marble columns,
and had a tower above of a hundred and thirty cubits.
And still greater wickedness were the Ghibellines guilty
of; for inasmuch as the Guelfs used to come together often
to the Church of San Giovanni, and all the good people
went there every Sunday morning, and were married
there, when the Ghibellines came to destroy the towers of
the Guelfs, among the rest was a very tall and beautiful
one, which stood upon the Piazza of San Giovanni, at the
entrance of the Corso degli Adimari, and it was called the
'Torre del Guardamorto,' because anciently all the good
folk who died were buried in San Giovanni, and the foot
of this tower the Ghibellines caused to be cut away, and
props to be inserted in such wise that when fire was set to
the props, the tower might fall upon the Church of San
Giovanni.[1]   And this was done; but as it pleased God,

[1] According to Vasari, this method of throwing down high towers,
which is employed to this day for the demolition of disused factory-
chimneys, was invented by the famous architect, Niccola Pisano.   He is
said to have contrived it on this very occasion of the destruction of the
Guardamorto tower, which he was commissioned to carry out.   There is

by a miracle of the blessed St. John, when the tower, which was a hundred and twenty cubits high, began to fall, it appeared clearly that it would miss the church, and turning round it fell right across the Piazza, whereat all the Florentines marvelled greatly, and the people were much rejoiced. Now mark this," concludes the indignant Villani, "that from the day Florence was rebuilt there had not been a single house destroyed, and this accursed wickedness of destruction was first begun by the Ghibellines at this time."

When later on the turn of the Guelfs came, they retaliated on their foes by building the walls of the city with the stones of Ghibelline palaces.[1] Such was their hatred of the Uberti, the Ghibelline leaders, that it was decreed that the site on which their houses had stood should never again be built on, and it remains to this day the Great Square (Piazza della Signoria) of Florence. When in 1298 the architect Arnolfo di Lapo was commissioned to build the Palazzo della Signoria (now known as the Palazzo Vecchio), he was obliged to sacrifice the symmetry of his plans, and place it awry, the Guelfs insisting in spite of his repeated protests, that not a stone of the foundations should rest on the accursed ground once occupied by the Uberti.[2]

On the death of the Emperor Frederick (13 December, 1250) the Guelfs were allowed to return to Florence, and a pacification between the two parties took place.

"On the very night," says Villani, "that the Emperor died, the Podestà who held for him in Florence, as he was

a tradition that what Villani attributes to a miracle was in reality due to design on the part of Niccola, who, wishing to spare the Baptistery, purposely contrived that the tower should fall wide of it.

[1] Villani, bk. vi. ch. 65.

[2] Villani, bk. viii. ch. 26; Vasari, *Vita di Arnolfo di Lapo.*

THE CITY OF FLORENCE

sleeping in his bed in the house of the Abati, was killed by the fall of the vaulting of his chamber. And this was a sure sign that the Emperor's power was to come to an end in Florence; and so it came to pass very soon, for there being a rising among the people by reason of the violence and excesses of the Ghibelline nobles, and the news of the Emperor's death reaching Florence, a few days afterwards the people recalled and restored the Guelfs who had been driven out, and made them make their peace with the Ghibellines. And this took place on the seventh day of January, in the year of Christ 1250." [1]

[1] Villani, bk. vi. ch. 42.

CHAPTER II

1251–1260

Renewed hostilities—Adoption of distinctive banners by the two parties in Florence—The Ghibellines intrigue with Manfred and are forced to leave Florence—They retire to Siena and persuade Manfred to send them help—Great Ghibelline victory at Montaperti.

THE peace concluded between the Guelfs and Ghibellines in Florence after the Emperor Frederick's death was not fated to be of long duration. Already in the very next year several prominent Ghibelline families were expelled from the city on account of their opposition to a Florentine expedition against the neighbouring Ghibelline stronghold of Pistoja. The Pistojans were defeated, and on their return the Florentines, flushed with victory, turned upon their factious opponents at home, and drove them into banishment (July, 1251). It was at this time that the two parties definitely adopted distinctive standards, and thus openly ranged themselves in opposite camps, as Villani relates.

" After the banishment of the Ghibelline leaders, the people and the Guelfs who remained masters of Florence changed the arms of the commonwealth of Florence; and whereas of old they bore a white lily on a red field, they now reversed them, making the field white and the lily red; and the Ghibellines retained the former ensign. But the ancient ensign of the commonwealth, half white, half red, that is the standard which went to battle on the Carroccio,[1] was never changed." [2]

Six or seven years later than this (in 1258) the Florentines found it necessary to expel the rest of the important Ghibelline families, in consequence of their having entered into a conspiracy, at the head of which were the Uberti, the Ghibelline leaders, with the aid of Manfred, son of the Emperor Frederick, to break up the popular government of Florence, which was essentially Guelf.

"When this plot was discovered," writes the Florentine chronicler, "the Uberti and their Ghibelline following were summoned to appear before the magistrates, but they refused to obey, and violently assaulted and wounded the retinue of the Podestà; for which cause the people rose in arms and in fury made for the houses of the Uberti, where is now the Piazza of the Palace of the People and of the Priors, and slew there one of the Uberti family and several of their retainers; and another of the Uberti and one of the Infangati were taken and, after they had confessed as to the conspiracy, were beheaded in Orto San Michele. And the rest of the Uberti, together with the leading Ghibelline families, fled from Florence, and went to Siena, which was under a Ghibelline Government, and was hostile to Florence; and their palaces and towers, which were many in number, were destroyed, and with the stones were built the walls of San Giorgio beyond Arno, which were begun at this time on account of war with Siena."[3]

In illustration of the temper of the Government at this time, and of their loyalty and uprightness towards the

---

[1] The Carroccio was a large waggon drawn by oxen which carried the standard of the Florentines, and usually accompanied them on the field. See Villani's description given below (pp. 17-18).

[2] Villani, bk. vi. ch. 45.

[3] Villani, bk. vi. ch. 65.

commonwealth, Villani relates how one of their number, who appropriated and sent to his country house a grating which had belonged to the lion's den, and was lying in the mud in the Piazzi of San Giovanni, was fined a thousand lire, as having defrauded the State.[1]

The exiled Ghibellines, who had taken refuge in Siena, without loss of time made preparations for an attempt to win their way back to Florence. Failing to obtain the necessary support from the Sienese, they determined to apply for help to Manfred, who was now King of Sicily, and they sent envoys to the king in Apulia for that purpose. "And when the envoys arrived, being the best captains and leaders among them, there was a long delay, for Manfred neither despatched the business, nor gave audience to their request, on account of the many affairs he had on hand. At last when, being anxious to depart, they took leave of him very ill-content, Manfred promised to furnish them a hundred German horsemen for their aid. The envoys, much disturbed at this offer, withdrew to take counsel as to their answer, being minded to refuse such a sorry aid, and ashamed to return to Siena, for they had hoped that Manfred would give them a force of at least fifteen hundred horsemen. But Farinata degli Uberti said: Be not dismayed, let us not refuse his aid in any wise, be it never so little; but let us beg as a favour that he send with them his standard, and when they are come to Siena we will set it in such a place that he will needs have to send us more men. And so it came to pass that following Farinata's wise counsel they accepted Manfred's offer, and prayed him as a favour to send his standard to be at their head; and he did so. And when they returned to Siena with this scanty force, there was great scorn among the Sienese, and great dismay among the Florentine exiles,

[1] Villani, bk. vi. ch. 65.

who had looked for much greater help and support from King Manfred."[1]

An opportunity for carrying out Farinata's scheme soon offered itself, for in May, 1260, the Florentines fitted out a great host and advanced against Siena, with their standard flying from the Carroccio, and their great war-bell tolling. Villani takes occasion in his account of this expedition to give a full description of the pomp observed by the Florentines when they went to war in those days.

"The people and commons of Florence gathered a general host against the city of Siena, and led out the Carroccio. And you must know that the Carroccio which the Florentines led out to war was a car upon four wheels all painted red, and on it were raised two great masts also red, upon which was spread to the wind the great standard with the arms of the commonwealth, half white and half red, as is to be seen to this day in San Giovanni; and it was drawn by a pair of oxen of great size, covered with cloth of red, which were kept solely for this purpose, and the driver was a freeman of the commonwealth. This Carroccio was used by our forefathers in triumphal processions and on high occasions; and when it went out with the host, the lords and counts of the country round, and the noble knights of the city, fetched it from its quarters in San Giovanni, and brought it on to the Piazza of the Mercato Nuovo; and having stationed it beside a boundary-stone, carved like the Carroccio, which is still there, they handed it over to the keeping of the people. And it was escorted to the field of battle by the best and bravest and strongest of the foot-soldiers of the people of the city, who were chosen to guard it, and round it was mustered the whole force of the people. And when war was declared, a month before they were to set out, a bell was hung on

[1] Villani, bk. vi. ch. 74.

the archway of the gate of Santa Maria, which was at the
end of the Mercato Nuovo, and it was rung without ceas-
ing night and day; and this was done out of pride, in
order that the enemy against whom war was declared
might have time to prepare himself. And this bell was
called by some the Martinella, and by others the Asses'
Bell.[1] And when the Florentine host set out, the bell was
taken down from the archway and was hung in a wooden
tower on a waggon, and the toll of it guided the host on
its march. And by this pomp of the Carroccio and the
bell was maintained the masterful pride of the people of
old and of our forefathers when they went to battle.

" And now we will leave that matter and will return to
the Florentines and their expedition against Siena. After
they had taken three castles of the Sienese, they sat down
before the city, hard by the entrance-gate to the monastery of Santa Petronella, and there on a high mound which
could be seen from the city they erected a tower, wherein
they kept their bell. And in contempt of the Sienese, and
as a record of victory, they filled it with earth, and planted
an olive tree in it, which was still there down to our
days." [2]

It was in the course of these operations before Siena
that Farinata's scheme for forcing Manfred to send further
assistance to the Ghibelline exiles was put into execution.

" It came to pass during the siege of Siena that one day
the exiled Florentines gave a feast to King Manfred's
German horsemen, and having plied them well with wine
till they were drunk, they raised a shout and instantly
urged them to arm and get to horse and attack the Flor-

[1] This bell was afterwards hung in the campanile of the Palazzo della
Signoria, and was used to summon the magistrates and people to
meetings.
[2] Villani, bk. vi. ch. 75.

entine host, promising them large gifts and double pay;
and this was craftily devised in accordance with the
counsel given by M. Farinata degli Uberti when in Apulia.
The Germans, flushed with wine and excitement, sallied
out from Siena, and made a vigorous attack on the camp
of the Florentines, who were unprepared, and had only a
small guard, as they made little account of the enemy's
forces; and the Germans, though they were only few in
number, in their sudden assault wrought great havoc
among the Florentines, numbers of whom, both horse and
foot, behaved very ill, and fled in a panic, supposing their
assailants to be in much greater force.   But presently,
seeing their mistake, they took to their arms, and made a
stand against the Germans, and of all who came out from
Siena not a single one escaped alive, for they overpowered
and slew them every one; and King Manfred's standard
was captured and dragged through the camp, and taken
to Florence; and shortly afterwards the Florentine host
returned to Florence." [1]

The Ghibellines lost no time in sending the news to
Manfred of how his Germans had nearly put to flight the
whole Florentine army, and they represented that if there
had been more of them they would undoubtedly have
been victorious; owing, however, to their small number
they had all been left dead upon the field, and the royal
standard had been captured, and insulted, and dragged in
the mire through the Florentine camp, and afterwards in
the streets of Florence.   In this manner they used the
arguments which they knew would most strongly appeal
to Manfred, who, now that his honour was involved, engaged to send into Tuscany, under the command of Count
Giordano, 800 more of his German horsemen, their services
to be at the disposal of the Ghibellines for the space of

[1] Villani, bk. vi. ch. 75.

three months, the cost being borne half by Manfred and half by the Sienese and their allies. This force reached Siena at the end of July, 1260, and was welcomed with great rejoicings not only by the Sienese and the Florentine exiles, but by the whole of the Ghibellines throughout Tuscany. "And when they were come to Siena, immediately the Sienese sent out an expedition against the castle of Montalcino, which was subject to the commonwealth of Florence, and they sent for aid to the Pisans and to all the Ghibellines of Tuscany, so that what with the horsemen of Siena, and the exiles from Florence, together with the Germans, and their other allies, they had eighteen hundred horsemen in Siena, of whom the Germans were the best part." [1]

The great anxiety of the Sienese and their allies now was to draw the Florentines into the field, before the three months expired during which the services of King Manfred's Germans were at their disposal. Farinata degli Uberti, therefore, with the connivance of the Sienese, entered into secret negotiations with the Florentines, pretending that the exiled Ghibellines were dissatisfied with the Sienese, and longed for peace, and that many of the Sienese themselves were anxious to shake off the government of their arrogant leader, Provenzano Salvani. He consequently proposed to the Florentines that, under pretext of relieving Montalcino, which was being besieged by the Sienese, they should despatch a strong force to the Arbia, in readiness for an attack on Siena, one of the gates of which he promised should be opened to them. The majority of the Florentines, completely deceived, were for accepting Farinata's proposal, and acting on it without delay. But the wiser heads among them were not so sanguine. The great Guelf nobles, with the re-

[1] Villani, bk. vi. ch. 76.

nowned Guido Guerra[1] at their head, and with Tegghiaio
Aldobrandi[2] as their spokesman, knowing more of the
conditions of warfare, and being aware that their enemies
had been reinforced by a body of German mercenaries,
looked upon the undertaking with grave misgivings, and
counselled delay, until the Germans, whose term of three
months had already half expired, should be disbanded.
But the minds of the others were made up, and they ob-
stinately refused to listen to reason—one of them even
going so far as to taunt Tegghiaio, who was acknowledged
as a brave and valiant knight, with cowardice, to which he
replied by challenging his opponent to adventure himself
on the day of battle wherever he himself should go.

" And so, through the proud and headstrong people, the
worse counsel prevailed, namely, that the host should set
forth immediately and without delay.   And the people of
Florence having taken the ill resolve to send the expedition, asked their allies for help ; and there came foot and
horse from Lucca, and Bologna, and Pistoja, and Prato,
and Volterra, and San Miniato, and San Gemignano, and
from Colle in the Valdelsa, all of which were in league
with the commonwealth and people of Florence ; and in
Florence there were eight hundred horsemen belonging to
the city, and more than five hundred mercenaries.   And
when all these were assembled in Florence, the host set out
at the end of August, with the Carroccio and the bell called
Martinella, and with them went out nearly all the people,
with the banners of the guilds, and there was scarce a house
or a family in Florence which did not send, on foot or
mounted, at least one, or two, or more, according as they
were able.

" And when they arrived in the Sienese territory, at the

[1] *Inferno*, xvi. 38.
[2] *Inferno*, vi. 79 ; xvi. 41-2.

place agreed upon on the Arbia, called Montaperti,[1] together with the men of Perugia and of Orvieto, who there joined the Florentines, there were in all assembled more than three thousand horsemen, and more than thirty thousand foot.

" And while the Florentine host was thus making ready, the Ghibelline conspirators in Siena, to make sure of the success of their plot, sent other messengers to Florence to concert treason with certain of the Ghibellines who had not been exiled from Florence, and who were obliged to join in the common muster of the Florentines. With these it was agreed that, when they were drawn up for battle, they should desert from their companies in every quarter, and come over to the other side, so as to throw the Florentines into a panic; for to the Ghibellines their own force appeared to be small compared with that of the Florentines. And this was agreed upon. Meanwhile the Florentine host was on the hills of Montaperti, and the leaders who had entered into the secret negotiations with M. Farinata degli Uberti, as has already been told, were waiting for the traitors within Siena to open one of the gates to them, as had been promised.

" And one of the Ghibellines in the Florentine host, named Razzante, having got wind of what the Florentines were waiting for, with the consent of the Ghibellines in the camp who were meditating treason, galloped out from the camp into Siena, in order to make known to the Florentine exiles how the city of Siena was to be betrayed, and how the Florentine host was well equipped, with great force of horse and foot, and to urge those inside not to hazard battle. And when he was come into Siena and had laid these things before M. Farinata and the others who were in the secret, they said to him : It will be the

---

[1] *Inferno*, x. 85-6; xxxii. 81.

death of us if you spread this news abroad in Siena, inasmuch as every one will be panic-struck; but do you say the contrary, for if we do not fight while we have these Germans, we are all dead men, and shall never see Florence again; death and defeat would be better for us, than to go moping about the world any longer. And they decided to adventure the fortune of battle.

"So Razzante, being primed by them, promised to speak after their mind; and with a garland on his head, and with great show of joy, accompanied on horseback by M. Farinata and M. Gherardo de' Lamberti, he came to the assembly in the palace where were all the people of Siena, with the Germans, and their other allies. And here, with a joyful countenance, he told great news from the Ghibellines and traitors in the enemy's camp, how the Florentine host was ill-ordered, and badly led, and disunited; and how, if they were boldly attacked, they would of a certainty be routed. Having heard this false account from Razzante, at the cry of the people they all rushed to arms, shouting: To battle, to battle. And the Germans demanded a promise of double pay, which was granted; and their troop led the way to the attack by the gate of San Vito, which was to have been given over to the Florentines; and the rest of the horse and foot marched out behind them.

"When those among the Florentine host who were waiting for the gate to be opened to them, saw the Germans and the rest of the horse and foot coming out from Siena against them, as for battle, they wondered greatly, and were in no small alarm, at the sight of their sudden advance and unexpected attack; and they were still further dismayed, when a number of the Ghibellines who were in their camp, both on horse and on foot, seeing the enemy's troops advance, treacherously deserted to the

other side, as had been previously arranged. Nevertheless the Florentines and their allies did not neglect to
draw up their ranks and await the onset.

" And as the troop of Germans charged headlong into
the body of Florentine horsemen, where was the standard
of the commonwealth cavalry, which was carried by M.
Jacopo del Nacca of the Pazzi family of Florence, a man
of great valour, the traitor, M. Bocca degli Abati,[1] who
was in his troop and close to him, struck M. Jacopo with
his sword, and cut off the hand with which he was holding
the standard.   And when this was done, both horse and
foot, seeing the standard down, and finding that there
were traitors among them, and that they were being
furiously attacked by the Germans, very soon turned and
fled.   But owing to the Florentine horsemen being the
first to discover the treachery, there were but thirty-six
men of note among them taken or killed.   The greatest
number of killed and prisoners was among the Florentine
foot, and those of Lucca and of Orvieto, inasmuch as they
shut themselves up in the castle of Montaperti, and were
all taken ; but more than two thousand five hundred of
them were left dead on the field, and more than fifteen
hundred were taken prisoners of the flower of the people
of Florence, of every family, and of Lucca, and of the rest
of the allies who took part in the battle.

" And thus was abased the arrogance of the ungrateful
and overbearing people of Florence.   And this took place
on Tuesday, the fourth of September, in the year of Christ
1260.   And there was taken the Carroccio,[2] and the Martinella, and an immense booty, of the baggage of the Florentines and their allies.   And on this day was broken and

[1] *Inferno*, xxxii. 78-111.
[2] Two flagstaffs, said to be those of the Florentine Carroccio captured
at Montaperti, are preserved in the Cathedral of Siena.

destroyed the ancient people of Florence, which had continued in so great power and estate, and with so great
victories, for the space of ten years." [1]

The victorious Sienese returned into their city "with
great triumph and glory, to the utter shame and disgrace
and confusion of the dogs of Florentines," the procession
being headed by the Florentine envoy seated on an ass,
with his face to its tail, which he held as a bridle, and
dragging behind him in the mud the standard of the
commonwealth of Florence. [2]

[1] Villani, bk. vi. ch. 78.
[2] From a contemporary account by a Sienese chronicler.

CHAPTER III

1261–1267

THE news of the terrible disaster at Montaperti was received in Florence with the utmost consternation, "and there arose so great a lamentation both of men and women that it reached to the heavens, inasmuch as there was not a house in the city that had not one killed or a prisoner".[1] The Guelfs did not wait to be driven out, but hastily fled with their families to Lucca, abandoning the city of Florence to its fate. "And for this desertion the Guelfs were greatly to be blamed, seeing that the city of Florence was strongly fortified with walls and with moats full of water, and might well have been defended and held. But the judgment of God must needs run its course without let in the punishment of wickedness; and to whom God intends ill, him He deprives of wisdom and forethought. And the Guelfs having departed on the Thursday, on the Sunday following, being the sixteenth day of September, the exiles from Florence who had taken part in the battle at Montaperti, together with Count Giordano and his German troops, and the other soldiers of the

[1] Villani, bk. vi. ch. 79.

FARINATA DEGLI UBERTI
From the painting by Andrea del Castagno, in the Museo Nazionale at Florence

Tuscan Ghibellines, laden with the spoils of the Florentines and other Guelfs of Tuscany, entered into the city of Florence without hindrance of any kind; and immediately they appointed Guido Novello, of the Counts Guidi, Podestà of Florence for King Manfred, for the term of two years from the following January." [1]

The whole of Tuscany, with the exception of Lucca, was now in the hands of the Ghibellines, who proceeded to hold a great council of their party at Empoli, about twenty miles from Florence, for the purpose of establishing a Ghibelline league. At this council it was proposed by the deputies from Siena and Pisa, the two most bitter enemies of Florence, that in order effectually to secure the ascendancy of the Ghibelline party, and to put an end once and for all to the power of the Florentines, the city of Florence should be razed to the ground. To this savage proposal, which was approved by the majority of the assembly, Farinata degli Uberti offered the most determined opposition, declaring that he would defend his native city with his own sword as long as he had breath in his body, even though he should have to do it single-handed. [2] In consequence of this vehement protest the proposal was abandoned, Count Giordano fearing lest Farinata and his following should withdraw from the league and so lead to the break up of the Ghibelline party in Tuscany. " And thus by one good man and citizen," says Villani, " our city of Florence escaped so great fury, and destruction, and ruin." [3]

After their great victory at Montaperti the Ghibellines remained in undisputed possession of Florence, and of all

[1] Villani, bk. vi. ch. 79.
[2] Villani, bk. vi. ch. 81; *Inferno*, x. 91-3.
[3] Villani, bk. vi. ch. 81.

the other cities of Tuscany, save Lucca alone, which now
became the stronghold of the exiled Guelfs. The latter,
however, were not allowed to remain long in their place of
refuge. The Florentine Ghibellines, finding them trouble-
some neighbours, and learning that they were intriguing
with the young Conradin, King Manfred's nephew, sent
two successive expeditions with the forces of the Tuscan
league, under Count Guido Novello, against Lucca, and
forced the Lucchese to expel the refugees from their city
(1263). The unhappy Guelfs, deprived of their last foot-
hold in Tuscany, fled across the Apennines to Bologna,
and with their departure "there remained neither town
nor castle, little or great, throughout Tuscany but was subject to the Ghibellines".[1]

The period of Ghibelline ascendancy, however, was
not destined to be a long one. Within a few years the
tide of fortune had once more turned against them. Their
champion and protector, King Manfred, to whose assistance
they owed their triumph at Montaperti, while at the height
of his power was suddenly overthrown, and the Ghibelline
party was involved in his ruin.

In the spring of 1265 Charles of Anjou, brother of the
French king, entered Italy at the invitation of the Pope
(Clement IV), as the champion of Holy ¡Church and of
the Guelf cause, to take possession of the kingdom of
Sicily, which the Pope declared to have been forfeited by
Manfred. Having collected a large force, Charles in the
following January was crowned King of Sicily and Apulia
at Rome, and immediately afterwards set out to invade
Manfred's dominions. Manfred was prepared to make a
stubborn resistance, and on 26 February, 1266,[2] the two

[1] Villani, bk. vi. ch. 85.
[2] According to the reckoning of the Florentines, whose year began on
25 March, this was 26 February, 1265. See p. 36, note 3.

armies met at Benevento, about thirty miles north-east from Naples. Manfred's force was in three divisions, consisting of his Saracen archers, German cavalry, and a reserve of Apulian barons. The French army was in four divisions, one of which was composed of the Guelf exiles from Florence and other Tuscan cities, under the leadership of Guido Guerra. At the sight of these last Manfred is said to have exclaimed bitterly: Where are the Ghibellines for whom I have done so much?" His Germans and Saracens fought with desperate valour, but were outnumbered by the French. Manfred accordingly ordered the Apulian barons to charge, but they, either through cowardice or treachery, instead of obeying, turned and fled from the field. With a handful of troops who still remained faithful, Manfred resolved to die rather than seek safety in flight, and plunging into the thickest of the fight, he fell dead in the midst of the enemy.[1]

The defeat and death of Manfred was a crushing blow to the Ghibelline cause, and the effects of it soon began to be felt throughout Tuscany, and in Florence in particular. "When the news came to Florence and the rest of Tuscany of the discomfiture of Manfred, the Ghibellines began to lose heart and to be afraid in every part. And the Guelf exiles from Florence, who were outlawed, everywhere began to grow stronger and to take heart and courage; and they drew close to the city, and, in concert with their friends inside who had an understanding with them, they made plots for a change and for a new state of affairs within the city, for they had hopes from the Guelfs who had taken part in King Charles' victory, whom they looked for to come to their aid together with some of the French. Wherefore the people of Florence, who were at heart more Guelf than Ghibelline, by reason of the losses

[1] Villani, bk. vii. ch. 9.

they had received, one of his father, another of his son, and another of his brothers, at the defeat at Montaperti, likewise began to take courage; and they murmured and complained throughout the city of the expenses and heavy burdens which were laid on them by Count Guido Novello and by the others who were ruling the city.

" Seeing this, and hearing the tumult and murmuring throughout the city, the rulers, for fear the people should rise against them, in order to content them and by way of compromise elected two knights of the Jovial Friars of Bologna to hold the office of Podestà in Florence,[1] one of whom was a Guelf, and the other a Ghibelline. And they ordained thirty-six good men, merchants and handicraftsmen of the greatest and best in the city, the which were to give counsel to the said two, and were to make provision for the expenses of the commonwealth; and, of this number were both Guelfs and Ghibellines, both of the people and of the trusty nobles, such as had remained in Florence when the Guelfs were driven out. And the said thirty-six met together every day to take counsel for the good estate and common weal of the city; and they made many good ordinances for the welfare of the commonwealth, among the which they ordained that each of the seven greater Arts[2] in Florence should have a college and consuls, and that each should have its own banner and ensign, in order that, if there were any rising in the city with force of arms, they might assemble under their banners for the defence of the people and of the commonwealth.

[1] Hitherto the office had always been filled by a single individual. The names of the two were Catalano de' Malavolti and Loderingo degli Andalò, the former a Guelf, the latter a Ghibelline. Cf. *Inferno*, xxiii. 103-8.

[2] These were, the judges and notaries; the merchants of Calimala, i.e. of French cloths; the money-changers; the wool-workers; the physicians and apothecaries; the silk-workers and mercers; and the furriers.

"Now by reason of these changes which were made in the city of Florence by the two Podestà and the said thirty-six, the noble Ghibelline houses of Florence, to wit the Uberti, and the Lamberti, and the rest of the Ghibelline nobles, began to fear for their party; for it seemed to them that the thirty-six supported and favoured the Guelfs of the people who had remained in Florence, and that every change was against the Ghibelline party. By reason of this fear, and because of the news of the victory of King Charles, Count Guido Novello sent for help to all their allies near at hand, namely to Pisa, and Siena, and Arezzo, and Pistoja, and Prato, and Volterra, and Colle, and San Gemignano, so that, together with six hundred Germans, they mustered in Florence fifteen hundred horsemen in all. And it came to pass that in order to pay the German troops which were with Count Guido Novello, as captain of the league, he demanded that a levy should be made of ten per cent.; but the thirty-six looked for some other means of finding the money, which should be less of a burden to the people. For this cause, when they had delayed some days longer than seemed good to the Count and the other Ghibelline nobles of Florence, by reason of the suspicion they felt concerning the ordinances made by the people, the said nobles determined to raise a tumult in the city, and to do away the office of the thirty-six, with the help of the great body of horsemen which the Count had in Florence.

"And when they had taken arms, the first who began were the Lamberti, who with their men-at-arms came out from their houses in the Calimala [1] shouting: Where are the thirty-six, the robbers, that we may cut them all in pieces? And the said thirty-six were at that time in

---

[1] The Calimala was the street which connected the Mercato Vecchio with the Mercato Nuovo. In it were located the cloth-merchants.

council in the warehouse where the consuls of the Calimala administered justice, below the house of the Cavalcanti in the Mercato Nuovo ; and hearing this they broke up the council, and in a moment the whole city was in a tumult, and the shops were shut, and every one rushed to arms. The people all assembled together in the wide street of Santa Trinita, in very great numbers, and they took their stand by the house of the Soldanieri, and put up barricades at the foot of the tower the Girolami. Count Guido Novello, with all the horsemen, and the Ghibelline nobles of Florence, was in arms and mounted in the Piazza of San Giovanni; and they moved out against the people, and drew up in front of the barricade and made some show and attempt at fighting, but the people held their ground, defending themselves with crossbows, and shooting from the towers and houses. And Count Guido, seeing that they could not dislodge the people, gave the signal to retire, and went back with all the horsemen to the Piazza of San Giovanni ; and from there he went to the palace of the Podestà and demanded the keys of the city-gates in order that they might get out of the city. And the two Podestà cried out from the palace to those who were with the Count that he should return to his house and not depart from the city, and that they would quiet the people and would see that the soldiers were paid. But the Count, being in great dread and suspicion of the people, would not listen, but would have only the keys of the gates. And this was a proof that it was the work of God, and no other cause ; for this great and powerful body of horsemen had not been attacked, nor driven out, nor disbanded, nor was there any force to oppose them ; for although the people were armed and collected together, this was more from fear than to attack the Count and his horsemen, and they would soon have been quieted, and would have returned to their homes and have laid down their arms. But when the judgment of God is ripe, the occasion is ever at hand. And after the Count had received the keys, he went out with all his horsemen by the old ox-gate, and made for Prato, where they came in the evening; and this was on St. Martin's Day, the eleventh of November, in the year of Christ 1266." [1]

When Count Guido and his forces were safe in Prato they began to realize that they had committed an act of folly in leaving Florence without striking a blow, and they determined to return the next day. But the Florentines were in no mood to throw away their advantages and risk exposing themselves once more to the Count's vengeance; so that when he and his horsemen presented themselves in the morning at the gate of the Carraja bridge, and demanded admission to the city, they were met with a refusal; and when they made an attempt to force the gate they were shot at and many of them wounded; and at last, neither threats nor persuasions being of any avail, they were obliged to retreat. " And when they reached Prato they bitterly reproached one another; but after a thing ill-advised and worse done, repentance is in vain." [2]

The Florentines now dismissed the two Bolognese from the office of Podestà, and sent to Orvieto for a Podestà and Captain of the People, who arrived with a guard of a hundred horsemen for the protection of the city. " And by a treaty of peace in the following January both Guelfs and Ghibellines were restored to Florence, and many marriages and alliances were made between them, among which these were the chief: Bonaccorso Bellincioni degli Adimari gave for wife to M. Forese, his son, the daughter of Count Guido Novello; and M. Bindo, his brother, took one of the Ubaldini; and M. Cavalcante de'

---

[1] Villani, bk. vii. ch. 13-14.   [2] Villani, bk, vii, ch. 15.

Cavalcanti gave for wife to Guido, his son, the daughter of
M. Farinata degli Uberti;[1] and M. Simone Donati gave
his daughter to M. Azzolino, son of M. Farinata degli
Uberti.

"But by reason of these alliances the other Guelfs of
Florence held all these as doubtful members of the party;
wherefore this peace lasted but a short time, for when the
Guelfs had returned to Florence, feeling themselves
powerful, and emboldened by the victory which they and
King Charles had gained over Manfred, they sent secretly
into Apulia to the said King Charles for troops and for a
captain. And the king sent Count Guy of Montfort, with
eight hundred French horsemen, who arrived in Florence
on Easter Day in the year of Christ 1267. And when
the Ghibellines heard of his coming, the night before,
they departed out of Florence without stroke of sword,
and went, some to Siena, some to Pisa, and some to other
places. And the Florentine Guelfs gave the lordship of
their city to King Charles for ten years; and he accepted
it; and for the exercise thereof he sent year by year his
vicars, that together with twelve good men, citizens of
Florence, his vicar should govern the city. And be it
noted that the expulsion of the Ghibellines at this time
was on the same day, namely Easter Day, whereon they
had committed the murder of M. Buondelmonte dei
Buondelmonti, from which arose the factions of the Guelfs
and Ghibellines in Florence, and laid waste the city; and
it seemed to be a judgment from God, for never more did
the Ghibellines return to power in Florence."[2]

---

[1] Farinata had died in Florence about two years before. The name of
his daughter was Beatrice; the actual date of her marriage to Guido
Cavalcanti, by which they had two children, is unknown. Guido at the
time of the betrothal cannot have been more than seventeen, at the outside.

[2] Villani, bk. vii. ch. 15.

"And at the same time that the city of Florence came into the hands of the Guelfs, and the Ghibellines were driven out, and King Charles' vicar came into Tuscany, many of the cities of Tuscany likewise returned to the Guelf party and drove out the Ghibellines, namely, the cities of Lucca, and of Pistoja, and Volterra, and Prato, and San Gemignano, and Colle ; and they made a league with the Florentines, whereof the head was King Charles' vicar, with eight hundred French horsemen ; and there remained to the Ghibelline party only the cities of Pisa and of Siena. And in so short space of time, by reason of the defeat of King Manfred and of the victory of King Charles, was the state of affairs changed in Tuscany and in many cities of Lombardy, which from being on the side of the Ghibellines and of the Empire passed over to the side of the Guelfs and of the Church." [1]

[1] Villani, bk. vii. ch. 20.

PART II

DANTE IN FLORENCE

CHAPTER I

1265–1290

Dante's birth and ancestry—His father and mother—Cacciaguida—
Geri del Bello—Beatrice Portinari—Episodes in the *Vita Nuova*—
Folco Portinari—Death of Beatrice—Poetical correspondence with Cino
da Pistoja, Guido Cavalcanti, and Forese Donati.

DANTE ALIGHIERI [1] was born in Florence in
May, [2] 1265, a few months before, and, according
to the Florentine reckoning, [3] in the same year as, the
great victory of Charles of Anjou over King Manfred at
Benevento, which ruined the Ghibelline cause, and once
more restored the Guelf supremacy in Florence and
throughout Tuscany. Dante's family were Guelfs. [4] This

[1] See Genealogical Table at end of volume (*Appendix* A).

[2] From the reference in *Paradiso*, xxii. 110 ff. it follows that Dante
must have been born towards the end of the month, at any rate later than
the 21st (see Casini, *in loc.*).

[3] The battle of Benevento, according to our reckoning, was fought on
26 February, 1266; but as the Florentine year began on 25 March, according to their reckoning it was fought on 26 February, 1265. The date
according to both styles is indicated by writing 26 February, 126⅚, where
the *lower* figure represents the *modern*, and the *upper* figure the *old*, method
of reckoning.

[4] It may be noted that Dante's intimacies were for the most part among
the Guelfs: his mentor, Brunetto Latino, was a Guelf; his friend, Guido

36

DANTE'S HOUSE IN FLORENCE

he himself tells us in the *Divina Commedia*, in his account of his conversation with the Ghibelline Farinata degli Uberti in Hell. Dante having answered Farinata's question as to who were his forefathers, Farinata says: "They were fierce foes of me and of my fathers and of my party, so that twice we scattered them" (i.e. in 1248 and 1260). To which Dante retorts: " If my side were driven out twice from Florence both times they returned (i.e. in 1251 and 1266), which your side have not been able to do".[1]

Dante's father, whose name was Alighiero, lived in the quarter of San Martino del Vescovo;[2] he was the son of Bellincione degli Alighieri, and was descended, as is supposed, from the ancient and noble family of the Elisei, who lived in the Sesto di Porta San Piero in Florence. Boccaccio goes so far as to trace Dante's descent from the noble Frangipani family of Rome, but of this connection

Cavalcanti, was a Guelf; his wife, Gemma Donati, was a Guelf; and his uncle Burnetto fought on the Guelf side at the battle of Montaperti. Further, according to Filippo Villani (in the preface to his Latin commentary on the first canto of the *Inferno*, cap. xxii.), Dante was intimate with Filippo's uncle, Giovanni Villani, the chronicler, who was a staunch Guelf: " Patruus meus Johannes Villani hystoricus . . . Danti fuit amicus et sotius." On the other hand, his mother is conjectured to have belonged to the Ghibelline family of the Abati ; while his stepmother was one of the Guelf Cialuffi.

[1] *Inferno*, x. 42-51.

[2] See p. 38, note 3. The house in which Dante is supposed to have been born is still preserved. It is situated in what is now known as the Via Dante Alighieri, a continuation of the Via Tavolini, which starts from the Via Calzaioli, a little above Or San Michele, and leads at right angles into the Via de' Cerchi, on the opposite side of which begins the Via Dante. Doubts have been raised of late as to whether this could be the house in which Dante was born. M. Barbi, however, shows that the " case degli Alighieri." were certainly situated on the spot indicated, and he holds that the traditional site of the actual house of Dante may be accepted as practically correct (see *Bullettino della Società Dantesca Italiana*, N.S. (1904), xi. 258-60 ; and (1905), xii. 314-20).

we have no evidence. His connection with the Elisei, on the other hand, seems hardly doubtful. Several names occur among Dante's ancestry which are common among the Elisei, and one of his ancestors, who is mentioned in the *Divina Commedia*, actually bore the name of Eliseo.[1]

The name of Dante's mother was Bella, but it is not known for certain to what family she belonged. There are grounds for believing that she was the daughter of Durante, son of Scolaio degli Abati (a Ghibelline family); in which case there can be little doubt that Dante's Christian name (a contraction of Durante) was derived from his maternal grandfather. Dante's father was a notary.[2] He was twice married, and died when his son was about eighteen.[3] Bella, who died in or before 1278, was Alighiero's first wife, and Dante was their only child. By his second wife, Lapa, daughter of Chiarissimo Cialuffi,[4] Alighiero had three children, a son Francesco,[5] who survived his half-brother Dante more than twenty years, a daughter Tana (i.e. Gaetana),[6] and another daughter,[7]

---

[1] *Paradiso*, xv. 136. Eliseo was the brother of Dante's great-great-grandfather, Cacciaguida, who had another brother called Moronto, one of the Elisei names.

[2] His name occurs at the foot of three documents, one dated 1239, the other two 1256, as "Alagerius ymperiali auctoritate iudex atque notarius" (see Scherillo, *Alcuni Capitoli della Biografia di Dante*, p. 11).

[3] Dante is mentioned in a document dated 1283 as "the heir of his father, the late Alighieri" ("Dante del già Alighieri del popolo di S. Martino del Vescovo, come herede del padre, vende," etc.) (see *Bullettino della Società Dantesca Italiana*, No. 5-6 (1891), p. 40).

[4] Both Lapa and Bella are mentioned in a document relating to the Alighieri family, dated 16 May, 1332, at which date Lapa was still alive (see Scherillo, *Alcuni Capitoli della Biografia di Dante*, p. 29).

[5] See p. 39, note 2.   [6] See p. 39, note 2.

[7] This half-sister of Dante's is supposed to be the "donna giovane e gentile, la quale era meco di propinquissima sanguinità congiunta" of *Vita Nuova*, § 23, ll. 86, 95-6.

name unknown, who married one Leon Poggi. A son of this Leon Poggi, called Andrea, was an intimate friend of Boccaccio, who says that he bore a remarkable resemblance to his uncle Dante both in face and figure. From Andrea Poggi Boccaccio learned many details about Dante's habits and manner of life.

Dante's father can hardly have been a person of much consequence in Florence; otherwise, as a Guelf, he would have shared the exile of his party after the disastrous defeat of the Florentine Guelfs at Montaperti (4 September, 1260), which, from the fact that Dante was born in Florence in 1265, it would appear that he did not do. At any rate if he did leave Florence on that occasion he must have returned before the rest of his party, since the restoration of the Guelfs did not take place, as has been related in a former chapter, until January, 1267.[1] The only contemporary references to Alighiero occur in a poetical (and not very edifying) correspondence (or *tenzone*)[2] between Dante and his friend Forese Donati, from whose expressions it is difficult to avoid the conclusion that Dante's father was either a personal coward or of little moral worth.

Judging from the position of their house in the heart of the city, and from Dante's own allusions in the *Divina Commedia*,[3] the Alighieri would seem to have been a noble family, as nobility went in those days. The fact that they are not mentioned by Giovanni Villani in his several lists of the important Guelf families of Florence[4]

[1] Villani, bk. vii. ch. 15. See above, p. 33.

[2] Dante's half-brother and sister, Francesco and Tana, are also mentioned by Forese in this *tenzone*, which is printed in the third edition of the Oxford Dante (1904), pp. 179-80.

[3] *Paradiso*, xv. 40-5; *Inferno*, xv. 74-8.

[4] Villani, bk. v. ch. 39; bk. vi. ch. 33, 79.

may be accounted for on the ground that though of "ancient and honourable lineage,"[1] they were neither wealthy nor numerous.

Nothing is known for certain of any of Dante's ancestors further back than his great-great-grandfather, Cacciaguida, whose existence is attested by a document dated 9 December, 1189, in which his two sons, Preitenitto and Alighiero,[2] bind themselves to remove a fig tree growing against the wall of the Church of San Martino. In another document recently discovered, and dated 28 April, 1131, appears the name of a Cacciaguida, son of Adamo,[3] who on plausible grounds has been identified with Dante's ancestor; in which case our knowledge of Dante's ancestry goes back one generation further. Cacciaguida's history, in so far as we are acquainted with it, is related in the *Divina Commedia*,[4] where we are told that he was born in Florence in the Sesto di Porta San Piero about the year 1090; that he belonged (as is supposed) to the Elisei, one of the old Florentine families which boasted Roman descent; that he was baptized in the Baptistery of San Giovanni in Florence; that he had two brothers, Moronto and Eliseo; that his wife came from the valley of the Po (probably from Ferrara), and that from her, through his son, Dante got his surname of Alighieri; that he followed the Emperor Conrad III on the Second Crusade, and was knighted by him; and finally that he fell fighting against the infidel about the year 1147. Cacciaguida indicates[5] the situation of the house in which he and his ancestors lived in Florence as being "in the place where

---

[1] Villani, bk. ix. ch. 136.

[2] "Preitenittus et Alaghieri fratres, filii olim Cacciaguide" (see E. Frullani e G. Gargani, *Della Casa di Dante*, p. 29).

[3] "Cacciaguide filii Adami" (see Davidsohn, *Geschichte von Florenz*, i. 440 n.).

[4] *Paradiso*, xv. 19–xvi. 45.　　　　　[5] *Paradiso*, xvi. 40-2.

the last sextary is first attained by him who runs in the yearly horse-race," i.e. on the boundary of the district known later as the Sesto di Porta San Piero.[1]

By his wife, Alighiera degli Alighieri, Cacciaguida had two sons, already mentioned, namely, Preitenitto and Alighiero. The latter (who it seems, according to Pietro di Dante,[2] Dante's eldest son, married a sister of "la buona Gualdrada " of *Inferno*, xvi. 37, and daughter of Bellincion Berti of *Paradiso*, xv. 112; xvi. 99) in his turn had two sons, one of whom, Bellincione, was Dante's grandfather; while the other, Bello (i.e. Gabriello), was the father of the Geri del Bello, in connection with whom Dante alludes in the *Divina Commedia*[3] to a piece of family history, which shows that the *Vendetta* was a recognized institution in Florence in those days, and moreover that it was approved by Dante. It appears that Geri was a turbulent and quarrelsome person, and had

---

[1] The house of the Elisei stood not far from the junction of the Mercato Vecchio and the Corso, apparently just at the angle formed on the north side of the present Via de' Speziali by its intersection with the Via Calzaioli. The Sesto di Porta San Piero appears to have been the last of the city divisions to be traversed by the competitors in the yearly horse-race, who entered the city probably at the Porta San Pancrazio, close to where the Palazzo Strozzi now stands, crossed the Mercato Vecchio, and finished in the Corso, which was thence so called.

[2] In the later recension of his commentary on the *Commedia* in a note on *Paradiso*, xvi. 97-9, he writes: " de quibus Ravegnanis descenderunt, scilicet de dicto domino Bellincione de dicta domo, comites Guidones, . . . ex domina Gualdrada ejus filia ; cujus tres alie filie nupte sunt una in domo illorum de Donatis, alia in domo illorum de Adimaribus, alia in domo hujus auctoris, scilicet illorum de Alagheriis. Que tres domus jam multos habuerunt a dicto domino Bellincione nominatos Bellintiones " (see L. Rocca : *Del commento di Pietro di Dante alla D. C. contenuto nel codice Ashburnham* 841, in *Giornale Storico della letteratura italiana*, vii. 366-85). Pietro's statement is confirmed by the fact that one of Alighiero's sons, Dante's grandfather, was named Bellincione (see *Table* in *Appendix* A).

[3] *Inferno*, xxix. 3-36.

stirred up bad blood among certain members of the Sacchetti family of Florence, one of whom retaliated by killing
him. His murder had not been avenged at the time
Dante wrote, and consequently Dante represents him as
regarding himself, when they met in Hell, with a threaten-
ing and indignant mien because of this neglect on the part
of his kindred. Subsequently, more than thirty years
after the event, and quite possibly as a result of Dante's
allusion to the incident, Geri's death was avenged by his
nephews, who murdered one of the Sacchetti in his own
house. This blood-feud between the Alighieri and the
Sacchetti lasted till 1342, when an act of reconciliation [1]
was entered into between the two families at the instance
of the Duke of Athens, the guarantor on the part of the
Alighieri being Dante's half-brother, Francesco, who appeared on behalf of himself, and his two nephews, Dante's
two sons, Pietro and Jacopo.

Bellincione, the son of Alighiero, had four sons, of
whom the eldest, Alighiero, was Dante's father; the
youngest, Brunetto, took part in the battle of Montaperti,
where he was in charge of the Florentine Carroccio.

That Dante was born in Florence we know from his
own statements several times repeated in his works, the
most explicit of which occurs in the *Divina Commedia* [2]
where he says: " I was born and bred up in the great city
on the fair river Arno ". We know from himself too that,
like his ancestor Cacciaguida, he was baptized in the
ancient Baptistery of San Giovanni. [3] Years afterwards,
he tells us, [4] he was instrumental in breaking the font for

---

[1] The record of this act is still preserved (see *Dante Dictionary*,
s.v. Bello, Geri del).

[2] *Inferno*, xxiii. 94-5. In the *Convivio* (i. 3, ll. 21-5), he speaks
of " that most beautiful and most famous daughter of Rome, Florence,
where I was born and bred up until the climax of my life ".

[3] *Paradiso*, xxv. 8-9. [4] *Inferno*, xix. 17-21.

BAPTISTERY OF SAN GIOVANNI AT FLORENCE

the purpose of rescuing from suffocation a small boy [1] who had fallen into one of the circular spaces at the side, where the officiating priest stood during baptisms in order to escape the pressure of the crowd.[2]

Of the history of Dante's early years we know little beyond the episode of his love for Beatrice, which is narrated in the *Vita Nuova*. Dante says that he first saw Beatrice when she was at the beginning of her ninth year, and he had nearly completed his ninth year, that is to say in the spring of 1274. " Her dress on that day," he narrates,[3] "was of a most noble colour, a subdued and goodly crimson, girdled and adorned in such sort as best suited her very tender age." At the moment when he saw her Dante's heart was possessed by a passionate love for her, which from that time forward, he declares, completely mastered his soul. Boccaccio, who probably had the information from one of the Portinari family,[4] and (quite independently) Dante's own son, Pietro, tell us that this Beatrice was the daughter of Folco Portinari, a highly respected and influential citizen of Florence. Boccaccio gives the following description of the scene of their

[1] The name of the boy is given by one of the early commentators as Antonio di Baldinaccio de' Cavicciuli, a member of a branch of the Adimari family which was especially hostile to Dante. The font which Dante broke is said to have been removed in 1576, by the Grand Duke Francesco I de' Medici, on the occasion of the baptism of his son Philip. The present font was placed where it stands in 1658, but it is the work of an earlier period.

[2] As baptisms used to take place only on two days in the year, on the eves of Easter and Pentecost, and in the Baptistery alone, the crowd on these occasions must have been very great. Villani, Dante's contemporary, says (bk. xi. ch. 94) that in his time the yearly baptisms averaged between five and six thousand; the numbers were checked by means of beans—a black one for every male, a white one for every female.

[3] *Vita Nuova*, § 2, ll. 15-18.

[4] See Del Lungo, *Beatrice nella Vita e nella Poesia del Secolo xiii.* pp. 49-52.

first meeting, as he, with his intimate knowledge of
Florence and of Florentine ways, imagines it to have
taken place :—

"In that season of the year when the tender heavens
clothe the earth once more with its adornments, and make
it everywhere smile with many-coloured flowers mingled
with green leaves, it was the custom in our city for the
men and women of the several districts to hold festival
together in companies, each in his own.[1]   Wherefore it
came to pass that, among the rest, Folco Portinari, a man
much in honour at that time among his fellow-citizens, had
on the first of May assembled his neighbours for a festival
at his own house.   Among the company was the Alighiero
of whom we have spoken, attended (as children are wont
to attend their parents, especially on festal occasions) by
Dante, who had not yet completed his ninth year.   And
it befell that mingling here with the others of his own age,
both boys and girls, of whom there were many in the
house of the giver of the feast, after the first course had
been served, in childish fashion he began to play with the
others in such wise as befitted his tender years.   Among
the crowd of children was a daughter of the aforesaid
Folco, whose name was Bice (although Dante always
called her by her full name Beatrice), and who was then
about eight years old.   She was very graceful and pretty
in her girlish way, and very gentle and pleasing in her
manners, and more grave and modest in her demeanour
and speech than might have been expected of her years.
Besides this the features of her face were very delicate
and regular, and full not only of beauty but of such comeliness and charm that by many she was held to be little
short of an angel.   She then, such as I describe her, or,
it may be, far more beautiful, appeared at this feast, not as

---

[1] Cf. Villani, bk. vii. ch. 132 (*ad fin.*).

I suppose for the first time, but for the first time with the power to kindle love, before the eyes of our Dante, who, though still a boy, received into his heart the beauteous image of her with so great affection that from that day forward, so long as he lived, it never departed from him." [1]

Nine years later, when they were both in their eighteenth year, that is to say in 1283, Dante saw Beatrice dressed all in pure white, walking in the street between two ladies older than herself. On this occasion she turned her eyes upon Dante, and saluted him. After this greeting, which, he says, seemed to reveal to him the utmost limits of happiness, Dante retired to the solitude of his own chamber and sat himself down to think of Beatrice. And as he sat thinking he fell asleep, and had a marvellous vision, whereon he composed a sonnet beginning

" To every captive soul, and gentle heart," [2]

which is his earliest known composition. This sonnet he sent to various famous poets of the day, and among those. from whom he received replies was Guido Cavalcanti, who from this time became Dante's most intimate friend.[3]

Later on, Dante meanwhile, in order to conceal his love for Beatrice, having paid attentions to another lady, Beatrice denied him her salutation, which plunged him into the deepest grief.[4] The next time he saw her was at a wedding-feast, whither he had been taken by a friend, and on this occasion his emotion so overcame him that his confusion was remarked, and the ladies, including Beatrice herself, whispered and mocked at him, whereupon his friend,

[1] *Vita di Dante*, ed. Macri-Leone, § 3, pp. 13-15. This work was probably written between 1357 and 1362 (see O. Hecker, *Boccaccio-Funde*, p. 154 *n.*).

[2] " A ciascun' alma presa e gentil core."

[3] *Vita Nuova*, § 3.   [4] *Vita Nuova*, § 10.

perceiving his distress, led him from the house.[1] This episode may perhaps be connected with the marriage of Beatrice Portinari, to which Dante never directly refers in the *Vita Nuova*, but which is known to have taken place before the year 1288, her husband being Simone de' Bardi,[2] a member of one of the great banking-houses of Florence.[3]

Not long after this Dante learned of the death of Beatrice's father, Folco Portinari, whom he describes as a man " of exceeding goodness," [4] and who was a personage of no little importance in Florence, for he had held high office in the city, and had several times served as Prior.[5]

[1] *Vita Nuova*, § 14.

[2] This marriage (which Del Lungo thinks took place as early as 1283), like many others of that period, was probably political, that is to say, it was a " matrimonial alliance," not in any sense a marriage of affection (see Del Lungo, *op. cit.* pp. 13-14, 66-7).

[3] The Bardi, who were Guelfs, were of European celebrity as bankers. They had extensive relations with Edward III, through whose default they failed, together with several other important Florentine houses, in 1345, twenty-four years after Dante's death. Edward's debt to the Bardi amounted to nearly a million gold florins.

[4] *Vita Nuova*, § 22, ll. 1-18.

[5] Folco Portinari had been one of the fourteen " Buonomini " instituted in 1281 by Cardinal Latino; and he subsequently three times (in 1282, 1285, and 1287) held the office of Prior. He died on 31 December, 1289, and was buried in the chapel of the hospital founded by himself, his funeral being honoured by the official attendance of the Signoria of Florence. The monument erected over his tomb is still preserved, though not in its original site. The inscription on it runs as follows:—

" Hic iacet Fulchus de Portinariis qui fuit fundator et edificator uius ecclesie et ospitalis S. Marie Nove et decessit anno MCCLXXXIX die XXXI decembris. Cuius anima pro Dei misericordia requiescat in pace" (Del Lungo, *op. cit.* pp. 8-9).

Folco married Cilia di Gherardo de' Caponsacchi of Florence, and had by her ten children (five sons and five daughters) besides Beatrice, who are all mentioned by name in his will (dated 15 January, 128$\frac{7}{8}$). To the four unmarried daughters, Vanna, Fia, Margarita, and Castoria, he left eighty Florentine pounds each for a dowry. To the son of his daughter Ravig-

He was also a great public benefactor, for in June, 1288, the same year in which he made his will, he had founded the well-known hospital of Santa Maria Nuova in Florence.[1] Folco's death, and the grief of Beatrice for him, brought into Dante's mind the thought that one day Beatrice herself too must die; and in a very short time his forebodings were realised. Beatrice died, within six months of her father, in June, 1290, just on the completion of her twenty-fourth year.[2] Dante was for a time over-

nana, wife of Bandino Falconieri, he left fifty Florentine pounds; and he left the like sum to "mistress Bice, his daughter, the wife of Simone de' Bardi" (*Item domine Bici etiam filie sue, et uxori domini Simonis de Bardis, legavit de bonis suis libras L ad florenos*). His five sons, Manetto, Ricovero, Pigello, Gherardo, and Jacopo (of whom the last three were minors) were named as residuary legatees. Manetto (d. 1334), Beatrice's eldest brother, was most probably the near relation of Beatrice who is mentioned by Dante in the *Vita Nuova* as being his dearest friend after Guido Cavalcanti (*Vita Nuova*, § 33, ll. 2-7: "Si venne a me uno, il quali, secondo li gradi dell' amistade, è amico a me immediatamente dopo il primo: e questi fu tanto distretto di sanguinità con questa gloriosa, che nullo più presso l' era"). Manetto, it appears, was also a friend of Guido's, who addressed a sonnet to him, which has been preserved among Guido's poems (see Ercole, *Guido Cavalcanti e le sue Rime*, pp. 145-6, 353, 355).

[1] The endowment of this hospital is said to have been suggested to Folco by the then Bishop of Florence, Andrea de' Mozzi (whose name appears in the deed of foundation)—the same Bishop who is branded by Dante in the *Inferno* (xv. 112-14) as an unclean liver. The deed of foundation is printed by L. Passerini in *Storia degli Stabilimenti di Beneficenza . . . della Città di Firenze* (1853), pp. 835-9.

[2] The exact date on which Beatrice died was 8 June, as follows from what Dante says in § 30 of the *Vita Nuova*. His aim is to prove that the number *nine* was intimately connected with the day, the month, and the year of Beatrice's death. As regards the year his statement (ll. 7-13) presents no difficulty—she died in 1290. In order to bring in the number nine in the case of the month and the day Dante has recourse to the Syrian and Arabian calendars ("io dico che, secondo l' usanza d' Arabia, l' anima sua nobilissima si partì nella prima ora del nono giorno del mese; e secondo l' usanza di Siria, ella si partì nel nono mese dell' anno; perchè il primo mese è ivi Tisrin primo, il quale a noi è Ottobre"). He says Beatrice died in the ninth month according to the Syrian reckoning, which

whelmed with grief,[1] but after a while he devoted himself to the study of philosophy, and having thereby regained his peace of mind, he made the resolve, which is recorded at the conclusion of the *Vita Nuova*, that, should his life be spared, he would write of Beatrice what had never yet been written of any woman, a resolve which was carried into execution in the *Divina Commedia*.

A beautiful canzone on the death of Beatrice was addressed to Dante by his friend Cino da Pistoja,[2] one of the

(as he learned from Alfraganus, his astronomical authority) corresponds to our sixth month, namely June. The difficulty, therefore, as to her having died in June, the sixth month according to our reckoning, is got over by saying that she died in the ninth month according to the Syrian reckoning. As regards the day, Dante says that she died in the first hour of the ninth day of the month, according to Arabian usage. Now Alfraganus explains that according to the Arabian usage the day begins, not at sunrise, as with the Romans and others, but at sunset. If, then, Dante, in order to get the required connexion between the number nine and the day of the month on which Beatrice died, was obliged to have recourse to the Arabian usage, in the same way as he fell back upon the Syrian usage in the case of the month itself, we are forced to the conclusion that the actual date of Beatrice's death was not, as has been too hastily assumed, the ninth of the month, but *the evening of the eighth*, which according to the Arabian reckoning would be the beginning of the ninth day (see Paget Toynbee, *Dante Studies and Researches*, pp. 61-4).

[1] Perhaps it was at this period that Dante, if the tradition mentioned by Buti (in his comment on *Inf.* xvi. 106, and *Purg.* xxx. 42) is to be accepted, joined for a time the Franciscan Order. This tradition is held by some to be confirmed by Dante's reference in the *Inferno* (xvi. 106-8) to the cord with which he was girt, the cord being one of the distinctive marks of the Franciscans, who were hence known as *Cordeliers*. Some see a further confirmation of the tradition in the facts that Dante speaks of the Sun as the "image of God" (*Convivio*, iii. 12, l. 54) as did St. Francis; and that Statius, on meeting Dante and Virgil in Purgatory, gives them the Franciscan salutation, to which Virgil returns the recognized countersign (*Purg.* xxi. 12-15). It has also been suggested in the same connexion that Dante derived his explanation of the fall of the rocks in Hell (*Inf.* xii. 1-45; xxi. 112-14) from the Franciscan legend, that the chaotic rocks of La Vernia, where St. Francis received the *stigmata*, were upheaved by the earthquake at the Crucifixion.

[2] Born in 1270 at Pistoja, where he died in 1336 or 1337.

"famosi trovatori," to whom Dante had sent his earliest
sonnet.[1]   In this canzone, from which it appears that
Dante in his despair had been tempted to seek death,
Cino strives to console him with the thought that Beatrice
is glorified in heaven, where she watches over him and
recalls his devotion to her on earth :—

> How ever shouldst thou see the lovely face
> If any desperate death should once be thine ?
>   From justice so condign
> Withdraw thyself even now : that in the end
>   Thy heart may not offend
> Against thy soul, which in the holy place,
> In Heaven, still hopes to see her and to be
> Within her arms.   Let this hope comfort thee.
>
> Look thou into the pleasure wherein dwells
>   Thy lovely lady who is in Heaven crown'd,
>   Who is herself thy hope in Heaven, the while
> To make thy memory hallowed she avails ;
>   Being a soul within the deep Heaven bound,
>   A face on thy heart painted, to beguile
>   Thy heart of grief, which else should turn it vile.
>
> Even as she seemed a wonder here below,
>   On high she seemeth so,—
> Yea, better known, is there more wondrous yet.
>   And even as she was met
>   First by the angels with sweet song and smile,
> Thy spirit bears her back upon the wing,
> Which often in those ways is journeying.
>
> Of thee she entertains the blessed throngs,
>   And says to them : " While yet my body thrave
>   On earth, I gat much honour which he gave,
> Commending me in his commended songs ".
>   Also she asks alway of God our Lord
>   To give thee peace according to His word.[2]

[1] See pp. 45, 159.
[2] The whole canzone is translated by D. G. Rossetti in *Dante and his
Circle* (pp. 184-6), whose version of the concluding portion is printed
above. The original is printed by Carducci in *Rime di M. Cino da
Pistoja*, Florence, 1862 (pp. 9-12).

Cino, who subsequently wrote a canzone on the death of Dante himself,[1] was one of several friends of his youth with whom Dante held a poetical correspondence. As in the case of Guido Cavalcanti,[2] this friendship doubtless owed its origin to the fact of Dante's having sent to him the sonnet referred to above, the first in the *Vita Nuova*, to which Cino returned a sonnet in reply.[3] At least five other sonnets addressed by Cino to Dante have been preserved,[4] and two of Dante's to him,[5] besides a Latin letter on a subject connected with love.[6]

Guido Cavalcanti,[7] one of the most distinguished poets of the day, and Dante's earliest friend, addressed five sonnets to Dante[8] (including his reply to Dante's first sonnet), mostly on the subject of love; but one of them contains a severe reproof to Dante for falling away from his former high standard of life:—

> I come to thee by daytime constantly,
> > But in thy thoughts too much of baseness find :
> > Greatly it grieves me for thy gentle mind,
> And for thy many virtues gone from thee.
> It was thy wont to shun much company,
> > Unto all sorry concourse ill inclin'd :
> > And still thy speech of me, heartfelt and kind,
> Had made me treasure up thy poetry.
> But now I dare not, for thine abject life,
> > Make manifest that I approve thy rhymes ;
> > > Nor come I in such sort that thou mayst know.
> > Ah ! prythee read this sonnet many times :
> So shall that evil one who bred this strife
> > Be thrust from thy dishonoured soul and go.[9]

[1] See below, p. 107.   [2] See above, p. 45.

[3] Printed by Carducci, *op. cit.* pp. 4-5; translated by Rossetti, *op. cit.* p. 183.

[4] See Carducci, *op. cit.* pp. 103, 106, 108, 116, 117.

[5] *Sonnets* xxxiv, xlvi, in the Oxford Dante.

[6] *Epist.* iv. (see below, p. 248).   [7] C. 1255-1300.

[8] See P. Ercole : *Guido Cavalcanti e le sue Rime*, Livorno, 1885 (pp. 313, 318, 319-20, 322, 324-5).

[9] Translated by Rossetti, *op. cit.* p. 161. For the original, see Ercole, *op. cit.* pp. 324-5.

It is supposed that Guido is here referring to some moral lapse on Dante's part, consequent on his alleged faithlessness to the memory of Beatrice;[1] but it is possible that what Guido had in mind was Dante's degrading intercourse with such company as Forese Donati,[2] his poetical correspondence with whom (written probably within a year or two of the death of Beatrice) has been already mentioned.[3] The tone of this correspondence, the authenticity of which has been questioned, but which in the face of the evidence it is difficult not to accept,[4] gives an unpleasing impression both of Forese and of Dante, teeming as it does with personalities and abusive recriminations. In after years, we gather, Dante recalled this episode of his early career with bitter shame. "If thou bring back to mind," he says to Forese when they meet in Purgatory,

> "If thou bring back to mind
> What thou wast once with me, and I with thee,
> The recollection will be grievous yet." [5]

It was to Guido Cavalcanti, while Beatrice was yet alive, that Dante addressed that charming sonnet (known to English readers as "The Boat of Love")[6] in which he imagines Guido, Lapo Gianni, and himself wafted overseas in a boat with their respective ladies :—

> Guido, I wish that Lapo, thou, and I,
>   Could be by spells conveyed, as it were now,
>   Upon a barque, with all the winds that blow
> Across all seas at our good will to hie.
> So no mischance nor temper of the sky

[1] See below, p. 71.   [2] Forese died in July, 1296.   [3] See above, p. 39.

[4] On this *tenzone*, which is printed in the third edition (1904) of the Oxford Dante (pp. 179-80), see Del Lungo, *Dante ne' tempi di Dante*, pp. 437 ff. A translation of four sonnets of the *tenzone* is given by Rossetti, *op. cit.* pp. 243-5.

[5] *Purgatorio*, xxiii, 115-17.

[6] From the title of D. G. Rossetti's picture of the subject.

Should mar our course with spite or cruel slip;
But we, observing old companionship,
To be companions still should long thereby.
And Lady Joan, and Lady Beatrice,
    And her the thirtieth on my roll with us
        Should our good wizard set, o'er seas to move
        And not to talk of anything but love:
And they three ever to be well at ease
    As we should be, I think, if it were thus.[1]

---

[1] *Son.* xxxii.; translated by Rossetti, *op. cit.* p. 143.

CHAPTER II

1289–1290

OF Dante's life outside the limits of the *Vita Nuova*, during his first twenty-five years, we get occasional glimpses, which show that, however deeply absorbed he may have been in his devotion to Beatrice, he was yet no "love-sick idler". We find him taking his share in the active duties of family life, and as a patriotic citizen bearing the burden of military service in the field on behalf of the State. In a document dated 1283 (the same year in which he records his first public salutation from Beatrice) his name appears, as the representative of the Alighieri family, in a matter of business which had been left unsettled at the death of his father.[1] Dante at this time was eighteen, and, both his father and mother being dead, according to Florentine usage was of age. Six years later, we are told, he took part in the war which had broken out in 1287 between Florence and Arezzo, and was present, fighting on the side of the Florentine Guelfs, at their great victory over the Aretines at Campaldino on 11 June, 1289. If we are to accept as authentic the fragment of a

[1] See *Bullettino della Società Dantesca Italiana*, No. 5-6 (1891), pp. 39-45.

letter preserved by one of his biographers,[1] this was not Dante's first experience in the field ; he confesses, nevertheless, that he was at first greatly afraid, but at the end felt the greatest elation, according to the shifting fortunes of the day.

This battle of Campaldino was an event of no little importance in the history of Florence. If the Aretines had been victorious the position of the Florentine Guelfs would have been seriously endangered. As it was, the result was a crushing blow to the Ghibellines of Tuscany, who had made Arezzo their headquarters, whence during the past few years they had repeatedly raided the Florentine territory. In June, 1287, the Aretines, with the help of the exiled Ghibellines from Florence, expelled the Guelfs from their city, whereupon the Florentines, in alliance with the other Guelfs of Tuscany, declared war against Arezzo, and in June of the following year sent a strong expedition into their territory, which ravaged the country right up to the city walls. The Sienese contingent of this expedition, however, rashly allowed themselves to be intercepted by the Aretines, who surprised them and cut them to pieces, the Sienese losing more than 300 killed and wounded. This success greatly elated the Aretines, and proportionately discouraged the Florentine Guelfs and their allies,

[1] Leonardo Bruni of Arezzo, who was secretary of the Florentine Republic from 1427 till his death in 1444. In his *Vita di Dante* he claims to have seen several letters of Dante in the poet's own handwriting, which he describes as being " fine and slender and very accurate " (" era la lettera sua magra e lunga e molto corretta, secondo io ho veduto in alcune epistole di sua mano propria scritte ";—elsewhere, in his *Dialogus ad Petrum Histrum*, speaking of Dante, he says: " Legi nuper quasdam eius litteras, quas ille videbatur peraccurate scripsisse : erant enim propria manu atque eius sigillo obsignatae "—quoted by Bartoli, *Storia della Letteratura Italiana*, v. 89). In this letter Dante is represented as saying that at the battle of Campaldino he was present " not as a child in arms " (" non fanciullo nell' armi ").

who were still further discomfited by the news of the expulsion of the Guelfs from Pisa, and of the imprisonment
of the Guelf leader, Ugolino della Gherardesca, who in
the following March ($128\frac{8}{9}$) was put to death in the Tower
of Famine.[1] Not long after this (at the beginning of May)
Charles II of Anjou passed through Florence on his way
to Rome to be crowned King of Naples in succession to
his father. After spending three days in Florence, amid
great rejoicings, he set out to continue his journey towards Siena. "And when he was departed news came to
Florence that the Aretine forces were making ready to
enter the Sienese territory in order either to intercept or
to bring shame upon Prince Charles, who had only a small
escort of men-at-arms. Immediately the Florentines sent
out their cavalry, consisting of the flower of the citizens
of Florence and of the mercenaries who were in the city,
to the number of eight hundred horsemen, together with
three thousand foot, to escort the said Prince; and when
the Aretines heard of it they did not dare to go against
them. And the Florentines asked the Prince to appoint
them a captain of war, and to allow them to carry the
royal standard to battle, and the Prince granted it, and he
knighted Aimeri of Narbonne, a man very noble and brave,
and cunning in war, and gave him to them for their captain.
And Aimeri, with his troop of about one hundred horsemen, returned to Florence together with the Florentine
force." [2]

No sooner were the Florentines returned home than it
was decided without loss of time to send a strong force to
attack the Aretines, in order to exact retribution for their
continued ravages in the territories of Florence and of the
allied Guelfs. On 2 June, 1289, the host marched out,

[1] Villani, bk. vii. ch. 128; *Inferno*, xxxiii.
[2] Villani, bk. vii. ch. 130.

with the Guelf banners and the royal standard of King
Charles flying, and the bells sounding; "and there were
assembled sixteen hundred horsemen and ten thousand
foot, whereof six hundred horsemen were citizens of
Florence, the best armed and the best mounted that ever
went out even from Florence, and four hundred mercenaries
together with the men-at-arms of the captain, M. Aimeri,
in the pay of the Florentines; and from Lucca there were
an hundred and fifty horsemen; and from Prato forty horse
and foot; from Pistoja sixty horse and foot; and from
Siena an hundred and twenty horsemen; and from Volterra forty horsemen; and from Bologna their envoys with
their men-at-arms; and from San Miniato and from San
Gemignano, and from Colle, there came horse and foot
from each place; and Maghinardo of Susinana,[1] a good
and wise captain of war, came with his men from Romagna.
And the said host being assembled, they descended into
the plain of Casentino, laying waste the lands of Count
Guido Novello, who was Podestà of Arezzo. And when
the Bishop of Arezzo heard of this, he and the other
Ghibelline captains, among whom were many of renown,
determined to come with all their force to Bibbiena to prevent its being laid waste; and they were eight hundred
horsemen and eight thousand foot, all picked men; and
among them were many wise captains of war, the flower
of the Ghibellines of Tuscany, and of the March,[2] and of
the Duchy,[3] and of Romagna, all of them experienced in
arms and warfare. And they challenged the Florentines
to battle, having no fear, although the Florentines had
twice as many horsemen as they, but they despised them,

[1] Maghinardo, though a Ghibelline by birth, supported the Florentine
Guelfs. His political inconsistency is alluded to by Dante, *Inferno*,
xxvii. 51.
[2] Of Ancona. [3] Of Spoleto.

saying that they tricked themselves out and combed their tresses like women, laughing at them and holding them of no account. And the Florentines having joyfully accepted the gage of battle, the two hosts by common consent drew up their ranks and faced each other in battle array, more perfectly ordered on both sides than ever were hosts in Italy before this time; and the field of battle was on the plain at the foot of Poppi, in the district called Certomondo, for so the place is named, and a church of the Franciscans which is close by, and the plain is called Campaldino. And this was Saturday morning, the eleventh of June, on the day of St. Barnabas the Apostle." [1]

Among the Florentine horsemen, according to the account of Leonardi Bruni,[2] was Dante, " who fought vigorously on horseback in the front rank, where he was exposed to very grave danger; for the first shock of battle was between the opposing troops of horse, in which the Aretine cavalry charged the Florentine horsemen with such fury, that they were borne down, broken and routed, and driven back upon the foot-soldiers." This rout of the Florentine cavalry was the cause of the defeat of the Aretines, whose victorious horsemen pursued the fugitives so far that their own foot-soldiers were left unsupported; consequently the Florentines, having rallied their horse, were enabled to crush first the Aretine cavalry and then their foot. Villani gives a detailed account of this important battle—important to us, owing to Dante's presence, in a manner in which no one at that time could have foreseen—and of the miraculous way in which the tidings of the victory were brought to Florence.

[1] Villani, bk. vii. ch. 131.

[2] Bruni says that Dante in his letter gave an account of the battle, together with a plan: " Questa battaglia racconta Dante in una sua epistola, e dice esservi stato a combattere, e disegna la forma della battaglia," *Vita di Dante*, ed. Brunone Bianchi, 1883, p. xv.

"M. Aimeri and the other captains of the Florentines drew up their troops in good order, setting an hundred and fifty of the best in the host to fight in the front,[1] of whom twenty were new-made knights, dubbed on the field. And M. Vieri de' Cerchi being one of the captains, and being lame of his leg, he would not on that account be excused from fighting in the front: and it falling to him to make the choice for his Sesto,[2] he would not lay this burden on any who did not desire it of his own free will, but chose himself and his son and his nephews. And this thing was counted to him as of great merit; and after his good example, and for very shame, many other noble citizens set themselves in the fore-front of the host. And when this was done they flanked each wing with light-armed infantry, and crossbow-men, and foot-soldiers with long lances; and the main body to the rear of the fore-front was also flanked by foot-soldiers; and in the rear of all was the baggage drawn up so as to support the main body, outside of which were stationed two hundred horse and foot of the Lucchese and the Pistojans and other allies; the captain of these was M. Corso Donati, at that time Podestà of Pistoja, whose orders were, if needful, to take the enemy in flank.

"The Aretines on their side ordered their troops skilfully, inasmuch as they had, as we have said, good captains of war among them; and they set a strong body to fight in the front, to the number of three hundred, among whom were chosen twelve of the chief leaders, whom they styled the twelve paladins.[3] And each side having adopted

[1] It is probable from what Leonardo Bruni says that Dante was among these.

[2] One of the six divisions into which the city of Florence was at this time divided.

[3] Doubtless in allusion to the fact that they were opposed to Aimeri de Narbonne, a name familiar in the old *Chansons de Geste* as at one time a foe of Charlemagne and afterwards as one of his doughtiest warriors.

their war-cry, the Florentines 'Nerbona' and the Aretines 'San Donato,' the fore-front of the Aretine horsemen advanced with great daring at full speed to charge
the host of the Florentines, and their remaining ranks
followed close behind, except that Count Guido Novello,
who was in command of a troop of an hundred and fifty
horse for a flank attack, did not venture to join battle, but
stood his ground, and then took to flight to his own territory.[1] And the charge and attack of the Aretines
against the Florentines was to the end that, being con-
fident in their prowess, they might by their bold stroke
break the Florentines at the first onset, and put them to
flight. So great was the shock that the most part of the
Florentine fore-front were unhorsed, and the main body
was thrust back some way across the field, but for all that
they were not dismayed nor thrown into confusion, but
received the enemy steadily and bravely; and with the
foot-soldiers drawn up on either flank they closed in on
the enemy, fighting desperately for a good while. And
M. Corso Donati, who was in charge of the reserve of
Lucchese and Pistojans, and had been ordered to stand fast,
and not to attack, under pain of death, when he saw the
battle begun, said like a brave man: If we lose, I will
die in the battle with my fellow-citizens; and if we win,
let him come who will to Pistoja and exact the penalty;
and he boldly moved out his troop, and took the enemy
in flank, and was the main cause of their rout.

"After this, as it pleased God, the Florentines had the
victory, and the Aretines were routed and defeated; and
there were killed more than seventeen hundred, horse and
foot, and more than two thousand taken prisoners, whereof
many of the best were got away secretly, some by their

---

[1] This was the second time that Guido Novello distinguished himself
by running away. The first occasion was when he abandoned Florence
after the defeat of Manfred at Benevento (see above, pp. 32-3).

friends, and others for ransom; but seven hundred and forty of them were brought into Florence in bonds. Among the slain was M. Guglielmino degli Ubertini, Bishop of Arezzo, who was a great warrior, and M. Guglielmo de' Pazzi of Valdarno and his nephews, who was the best and most crafty captain of war of his time in Italy; and there was killed too Buonconte, son of Guido da Montefeltro, and three of the Uberti, and one of the Abati, and many other exiles from Florence. On the side of the Florentines scarce one man of note was slain, but many both of the Florentines and of their allies were wounded.

"The news of this victory came to Florence that very day, at the very hour it took place; for the Priors being gone to sleep and rest after their meal, by reason of their anxiety and watching the night before, suddenly there was a knocking on the door of their chamber, with the cry: Arise, for the Aretines are defeated; and having risen and opened the door, they found no one, and their servants outside had heard nothing, wherefore it was held to be a great and notable wonder, inasmuch as it was the hour of vespers before any one came from the host with the news. And this was the truth, for I heard it and saw it; and all the Florentines marvelled whence this could have come, and waited in suspense. But when the messengers from the host were come, and brought back the news to Florence, there was great gladness and rejoicing; as well there might be, for at this defeat were left dead many captains and brave men of the Ghibelline party, enemies of the commonwealth of Florence, and the arrogance and pride, not of the Aretines only, was brought down, but of the whole Ghibelline party and of the Empire." [1]

[1] Villani, bk. vii. ch. 131.

Of those who fought on the same side as Dante in this
battle two, Vieri de' Cerchi and the impetuous Corso
Donati, were destined to play an important part in the
fortunes of Florence, and incidentally in those of Dante
himself.

One of the leaders on the opposite side, the Ghibelline
Buonconte da Montefeltro, forms the subject of one of
the most beautiful episodes in the *Divina Commedia*.
Buonconte's body, it seems, was never found after the
battle, and Dante, when he meets him in the confines of
Purgatory, asks him : " What violence, or what chance,
carried thee so far astray from Campaldino, that thy
burial-place was never known ? "   Buonconte replies :
" At the foot of the Casentino crosses a stream, named
the Archiano ; at the place where its name becomes void
(i.e. at its junction with the Arno) I arrived, pierced in
the throat, flying on foot, and staining the plain with
blood.   There I lost my sight, and my speech finished
with the name of Mary, and there I fell, and my flesh remained alone.   I will tell the truth, and do thou repeat
it among the living.   The Angel of God took me, and he
of Hell cried out : ' O thou from heaven, why dost thou
rob me ?   Thou bearest away for thyself the eternal part
of this one, for one little tear which takes him from me ;
but of the other part I will make other governance.'   Then,
when the day was spent, he covered the valley with cloud,
from Pratomagno to the great ridge (of the Apennine),
and made overcast the heaven above, so that the teeming
air was turned to water.   The rain fell, and to the trenches
came so much of it as the earth did not endure ; and as
it gathered in great streams it rushed so swiftly towards
the royal river that nothing held it back.   The swollen
Archiano found my body, cold, near its outlet, and thrust
it into the Arno, and loosed on my breast the cross which

I made of myself when the pain overcame me. It rolled me along its banks, and along the bottom, then with its spoil it covered me and girt me."[1]

Dante's military experiences did not end, as probably they did not begin, with the battle of Campaldino. In the following August, in consequence of the death of the unhappy Count Ugolino, and of the expulsion of the Guelfs from Pisa, the Tuscan Guelfs, headed by the Florentines and Lucchese, invaded the Pisan territory, and ravaged it for the space of twenty-five days. During this time they laid siege to the castle of Caprona, about five miles from Pisa, which after eight days capitulated. By the terms of the surrender the garrison were allowed to march out under a safe-conduct from the besieging force. Dante tells us in the *Divina Commedia* that he was present on this occasion, and witnessed the alarm of the beleaguered foot-soldiers, as they filed out between their enemies, lest the latter should not keep their compact.[2]

There are other reminiscences in the *Commedia* of Dante's campaigning days. One of these passages, in which he speaks of how "at times a horseman goes out at a gallop from his troop during the charge and seeks to win the honour of the first assault,"[3] is pretty certainly a recollection of what took place at the beginning of the battle of Campaldino. In another passage he gives a vivid picture of the various scenes he must have witnessed during the hostilities between Florence and Arezzo, including the running of the horse-races under the enemy's walls, as the Florentines did before Arezzo the year before Campaldino:[4]—"I have seen ere now horsemen change their ground, and set out to charge, and make their muster, and sometimes fall back in their retreat; I have seen

[1] *Purgatorio*, v. 91-129.   [2] *Inferno*, xxi. 93-6.
[3] *Purgatorio*, xxiv. 94-6.   [4] Villani, bk. vii. ch. 120.

skirmishers overrun your land, men of Arezzo, and I have
seen raiders go out, tourneys held, and jousts run, now
with trumpets, now with bells, and with drums and with
signals from castle-walls".[1]   And elsewhere he describes
a troop of soldiers manœuvring on the field, how they
wheel with the banner at their head, as they change front
under cover of their shields.[2]

All these are indications that Dante's military experiences were a very real part of his life, even though they
occurred at the very time when, as we know from his own
confession in the *Vita Nuova*, his mind was most deeply
occupied with the thought of Beatrice and of his love for
her.   In less than a year after the triumphant return from
Campaldino the loss of " his most gentle lady" was to turn
gladness into mourning, so that, while all the world in
Florence was feasting and rejoicing, to Dante, as he sat
weeping in his chamber, the city was desolate—"How
doth the city sit solitary," he cries with Jeremiah, "she
that was full of people! how is she become a widow, she
that was great among the nations!"[3]

[1] *Inferno*, xxii. 1-8.   [2] *Purgatorio*, xxxii. 19-24.
[3] *Vita Nuova*, §§ 29, 31 ; Lamentations, i. 1.

CHAPTER III

1291-1300

Early studies—Brunetto Latino—Classical acquirements—Marriage—Gemma Donati—Children—Public life—Embassy to San Gemignano—Priorate.

OF Dante's studies during his early years we know but little for certain. From a misunderstanding of an expression in the *Divina Commedia* [1] it has been assumed that he was a pupil of Brunetto Latino, a Florentine notary and statesman, who was the author of a book called the *Trésor*, a sort of encyclopædia of the knowledge of the day, written in French. Brunetto could hardly have been Dante's master, in the ordinary acceptation of the term, inasmuch as he was about fifty-five when Dante was born; besides which he was too constantly occupied with the affairs of the commonwealth to allow of his having leisure for teaching during the years of Dante's boyhood.

Already, when he was only eighteen, Dante had acquired the art of versifying, as he tells us in the *Vita Nuova*.[2]

---

[1] When he meets Brunetto in Hell Dante says to him: "In my mind is fixed the dear and kind fatherly image of you, when in the world you from time to time taught me how man becomes eternal" (*Inferno*, xv. 82-5). This probably means nothing more than that Dante learned much from Brunetto's *Trésor*, and especially from the compendium of the *Ethics* of Aristotle which it contains.

[2] *Vita Nuova*, § 3, ll. 69-71: "I had already learned of myself the art of setting words in rime".

And from the same source we know that he was to some extent practised in drawing, for he relates how on the first anniversary of Beatrice's death, "remembering me of her as I sat alone, I betook myself to draw the resemblance of an angel upon certain tablets. And while I did thus, chancing to turn my head, I perceived that some were standing beside me to whom I should have given courteous welcome, and that they were observing what I did : also I learned afterwards that they had been there a while before I perceived them. Perceiving whom, I arose for salutation, and said : Another was with me. Afterwards, when they had left me, I set myself again to mine occupation, to wit, to the drawing figures of angels." [1]

In letters also, as may be gathered from the *Convivio*, Dante was largely his own instructor. After the death of Beatrice, he says, " I remained so overwhelmed with grief that no comfort availed me. Howbeit, after some time, my mind, which was striving to regain its health, resolved (since neither mine own nor others' consolation was of any avail) to have recourse to the plan which a certain other disconsolate one had adopted for his consolation. And I set myself to read that book of Boëthius,[2] whose contents are known but to few, wherewith, when a prisoner and in exile, he had consoled himself. And hearing also that Cicero too had written a book, in which, treating of friendship, he had spoken of the consolation of Laelius, that most excellent man, on the death of his friend Scipio, I set myself to read that.[3] And although at first it was hard for me to understand the meaning of them, yet at length I succeeded so far as such knowledge of Latin as I possessed, and somewhat of understanding on my part, enabled me to do. And as it befalls that a man who is in

---

[1] *Vita Nuova*, § 35, ll. 4-15 (trans. by Rossetti).
[2] The *De Consolatione Philosophiae*.　　　[3] The *De Amicitia.*

search of silver sometimes, not without divine ordinance, finds gold beyond his expectations, so I, who sought for consolation, found not only healing for my grief, but instruction in the terms used by authors in science and other books." [1]

At the time referred to in this passage Dante was past his twenty-fifth year. It is evident, therefore, that in his early manhood he was by no means far advanced in his classical studies. With Provençal literature, on the other hand, it is probable that he was early familiar, not only from the references in the *Vita Nuova*, but from the fact that the work itself was composed more or less after a Provençal model. From the authors quoted in the *Vita Nuova* (which was written between 1292 and 1295, at any rate when Dante was not more than thirty) it is possible to form a pretty accurate estimate of the extent of his classical acquirements at that period. He shows some familiarity with the *Ethics* and *Metaphysics* of Aristotle (not of course in the original Greek—a language he never knew—but through the medium of Latin translations), and quotes Homer twice, once from the *Ethics* of Aristotle, and once from the *Ars Poëtica* of Horace. Ovid, Lucan, Horace, and Virgil are all quoted directly, the last several times, but there is not much trace of intimate acquaintance with any one of them. Dante also displays a certain knowledge of astronomy in the *Vita Nuova*, Ptolemy being quoted by name, while to the Arabian astronomer,

---

[1] *Convivio*, ii. 13, ll. 5-36. The "scuole de' religiosi," which Dante further on in this same passage (ll. 47-8) says he attended at this time, were doubtless those of the Dominicans of Santa Maria Novella, to which laymen were admitted. Here Dante would have received instruction in the seven liberal arts of the *Trivium* (grammar, logic, rhetoric) and *Quadrivium* (music, arithmetic, geometry, astronomy), and in natural and moral philosophy (see G. Salvadori, *Sulla Vita Giovanile di Dante*, pp. 106 ff.).

Alfraganus, he was certainly indebted for some of his *data* as to the motions of the heavens, and for his details as to the Syrian and Arabian calendars. If we add to these authors the Bible, which is quoted four or five times, and the works of Cicero and Boëthius already mentioned, we have practically the range of his reading up to about his thirtieth year, at any rate so far as may be gathered from his writings, which in Dante's case is a fairly safe criterion.

Some of his biographers state that Dante during his early manhood studied at the universities of Bologna and Padua, but there is no evidence to support this statement, which is probably little more than a conjecture.

Within a few years of the death of Beatrice, certainly not later than 1298, Dante married. His wife, whose name was Gemma,[1] was the daughter of Manetto and Maria Donati, of the same ancient and noble Guelf family to which belonged Dante's friend Forese,[2] and the impetuous Corso Donati, who, as we have seen,[3] distinguished himself at the battle of Campaldino. Boccaccio states that Dante's marriage was brought about by his relations in order to console him for the loss of Beatrice, and he further draws a melancholy picture of what he supposes Dante's married life to have been.

"Dante," he says, "formerly had been used to spend his time over his precious studies whenever he was inclined, and would converse with kings and princes, dispute with philosophers, and frequent the company of poets, the burden of whose griefs he would share, and thus solace his own. Now, whenever it pleased his new mistress, he

---

[1] Some think that Gemma Donati is the "donna gentile" of the concluding chapters of the *Vita Nuova* (§§ 36-9). See, for instance, Fraticelli, *Vita di Dante*, cap. 5, where, in reference to the appearance of the lady at a window (*Vita Nuova*, § 36), he points out that the houses of the Donati and of the Alighieri were opposite to each other, back to back.

[2] See above, pp. 39, 51.   [3] See above, pp. 58-9.

must at her bidding quit this distinguished company, and
bear with the talk of women, and to avoid a worse vexation must not only assent to their opinions, but against
his inclination must even approve them. He who, whenever the presence of the vulgar herd annoyed him, had
been accustomed to retire to some solitary spot, and there
to speculate on the motions of the heavens, or the source
of animal life, or the beginnings of created things, or, may
be, to indulge some strange fancy, or to compose somewhat which after his death should make his name live into
future ages—he now, as often as the whim took his new
mistress, must abandon all such sweet contemplation, and
go in company with those who had little mind for such
things. He who had been used to laugh or to weep, to
sing or to sigh, according as pleasing or painful thoughts
prompted him, now must not dare, or, should he venture,
must account to his mistress for every emotion, nay, even
for every little sigh. Oh! what unspeakable weariness to
have to live day by day, and at last to grow old and die,
in the company of such a suspicious being!"[1]

In spite of Boccaccio's express avowal that he cannot
positively assert the truth of all this,[2] nevertheless his picture
has been accepted seriously by many writers as an accurate
representation of Dante's married life. As a matter of
fact there is very little real ground for supposing that
Dante lived unhappily with Gemma. The arguments adduced in support of the contention are as follows: that
men of genius are notoriously "gey ill to live with," and
consequently, even if Gemma was not the shrew painted
by Boccaccio, Dante no doubt was an unbearable companion, wherefore they must have been unhappy together;

[1] *Vita di Dante*, ed. Macrì-Leone, § 3, pp. 20-1.
[2] " Certo io non affermo queste cose a Dante essere avvenute; chè nol
so " (*ed. cit.* p. 23).

again, that Dante nowhere in his works makes any reference to his wife; and lastly, that when Dante was exiled
from Florence he left Gemma behind him, and, so far as is
known, never saw her again. Only one of these arguments
has any real weight. The first is based on a pure assump-
tion. If the absence of any reference to Gemma in
Dante's works necessarily implies that they lived on bad
terms, the same must be assumed in the case of Dante's
parents, to whom his references are of the vaguest,[1] and of
his children. On the other hand, the fact that Gemma
did not subsequently live with Dante, so far as our information goes, when he settled at Ravenna with two of
his children, lends some colour to the supposition that the
affection between them was not of the strongest. Boccaccio makes the most of this circumstance. He concludes
his account of this ill-assorted match, as at any rate he
supposed it to have been, with the following words:
"Certainly I do not affirm that these things happened in
Dante's case, for I do not know. But, at any rate, whether
that be the truth or not, once Dante was separated from
her who had been given to console him in his grief, he
never would come where she was, nor would he ever allow
her to come to him."[2]

This is an explicit statement, and it is probable that
Boccaccio, who was in communication with members of
Dante's family, did not make it without some authority.
At any rate, whatever the domestic relations between
Dante and Gemma may have been, it is certain that they
had a family of four children, all of whom were born in
Florence before the year 1302. These children were two

---

[1] His father and mother are referred to as "i miei generanti" in the
Convivio (i. 13, l. 31); and his mother is referred to in the *Inferno* (viii.
45).

[2] *Vita di Dante*, ed. Macrì-Leone, § 3, p. 23.

sons, Pietro and Jacopo, and two daughters, Antonia and Beatrice. Pietro, the eldest son, who was the author of a commentary on the *Divina Commedia*,[1] became a lawyer, and died in Treviso in 1364.[2] Jacopo, who also wrote a commentary on the *Commedia* (or at any rate on the *Inferno*),[3] and a didactic poem called *Il Dottrinale*, entered the Church, became a canon in the diocese of Verona, and died before 1349. Of Antonia it is only known that she was still alive in 1332. Beatrice became a nun in the Con-

---

[1] Pietro's commentary, which was published by Lord Vernon at Florence in 1845, was written (in Latin) between 1340 and 1341. (See L. Rocca, *Il Commento di Pietro Alighieri, in Di Alcuni Commenti della D.C. composti nei primi vent' anni dopo la morte di Dante*, 1891, pp. 343-425).

[2] Dante's biographer, Leonardo Bruni (1369-1444), says of Pietro: "Dante, among other children, had a son Pietro, who studied law, and became distinguished. By his own gifts, and as being his father's son, he attained a great position and considerable means, and settled at Verona in very good circumstances. This Messer Pietro had a son called Dante, and to this Dante was born a son Leonardo, who is still living and has several children. Not long ago this Leonardo came to Florence, with other young men of Verona, well-to-do and much respected, and came to visit me as a friend to the memory of his great-grandfather Dante. And I showed him the house of Dante and of his ancestors, and gave him information about many things of which he was ignorant, owing to the fact that he and his family had been estranged from the home of their fathers ". (*Vita di Dante*, ad fin.).

Dante, the father of this Leonardo, died in 1428. Leonardo had a son Pietro (d. 1476), who had a son Dante (d. 1515), who had three sons, the youngest of whom, Francesco, died 12 August, 1563, and was buried at Verona. With Francesco the male descendants of Dante Alighieri came to an end (see Genealogical Table, in G. L. Passerini, *La Famiglia Alighieri*).

[3] Jacopo's commentary (in Italian) on the *Inferno*, which was published by Lord Vernon at Florence in 1848, was written certainly before 1333, and probably before 1325 (see L. Rocca, *Chiose attribuite a Jacopo di Dante, in op. cit.* pp. 1-42). On the question as to whether Jacopo wrote a commentary on the whole poem, see F. P. Luiso, *Chiose di Dante le quali fece el figliuolo co le sue mani*, 1904; and *Tra Chiose e Commenti Antichi alla D.C.*, 1903. Jacopo also wrote (in 1322) a *Capitolo* (a summary) in *terza rima* on the *Commedia* (see Rocca, *op. cit.* p. 33 ff.).

vent of Santo Stefano dell' Uliva at Ravenna, where in
1350 she was presented by Boccaccio with the sum of ten
gold florins on behalf of the Capitani di Or San Michele
of Florence.[1] She died before 1370, in which year there
is a record of the payment of a bequest of hers of three
gold ducats to the convent where she had passed her days.[2]
Three of Dante's children, Pietro, Jacopo, and Beatrice,
lived with him during the last three or four years of his
life at Ravenna. Gemma, who, as we have seen, is supposed never to have rejoined Dante after his exile from
Florence, was still living in 1332, eleven years after Dante's
death.

At some period not long after the death of Beatrice
Portinari, Dante appears to have been entangled in an
amour of a more or less discreditable nature. It seems
clear from the language used to Dante by Beatrice in the
Divina Commedia that this must have been the case. She
says that as soon as she was dead and gone, Dante became
unfaithful to her, and " gave himself to another," whereby
" he fell so low " that she despaired of his salvation.[3] The
names of several ladies which occur in Dante's lyrical
poems have been connected with this charge ; and there
can be little doubt that some similar entanglement took
place at Lucca after his exile, as appears from the account
of Dante's meeting with the Lucchese poet, Bonagiunta,
in Purgatory.[4]

In 1295 or 1296, whether before or after his marriage
we have no means of ascertaining, Dante, in order to

[1] See Del Lungo, *Dell' Esilio di Dante*, pp. 18, 161-2.

[2] See *Giornale Dantesco*, vii. 339-40. It has been conjectured, with
not much plausibility, that Beatrice may have been identical with Antonia,
who may have taken the name of Beatrice on becoming a nun (see
Giornale Dantesco, viii. 470-1).

[3] *Purgatorio*, xxx. 127-38.

[4] *Purgatorio*, xxiv. 37-45 (see below, p. 97).

qualify himself for the higher offices in the government of Florence, enrolled himself in the Guild of Physicians and Apothecaries,[1] he having now reached the age at which, by the Florentine law, he was entitled to exercise the full rights of citizenship. This was Dante's first step in his political career, which was destined within a few years to lead him into lifelong exile from his native city. The Guild selected by Dante was one of the wealthiest and most important in Florence, concerned as it was with the costly products of the East, in which were included not only spices and drugs, but also pearls, precious stones, and other valuables. Dante's choice of this particular Guild, however, may perhaps be explained by the fact that in those days books also were included among the wares dealt in by apothecaries; and further, to this Guild were attached those who practised the art of painting, an art which, it may be gathered, had special attractions for Dante, and in which, as we have already seen,[2] he was to some extent a proficient.

A few details of Dante's public life in Florence have been preserved in various documents in the Florentine archives.[3] It is recorded [4] that on 6 July, 1295, he gave his opinion in favour of certain proposed modifications of the " Ordinamenti di Giustizia," ordinances against the power of the nobles in Florence, which had been enacted a couple of years before. On 14 December of the same year he took part in the bi-monthly election of Priors; and on 5 June, 1296, he spoke in the Council of the Hundred

[1] See Fraticelli, *Vita di Dante*, pp. 112-13.

[2] See above, p. 65.

[3] See D' Ancona e Bacci, *Manuale della Letteratura Italiana*, i. 185 ff.

[4] Or supposed to be recorded, for M. Barbi has shown that the . . . *herii* in the torn document, hitherto conjectured to represent *Dante Alagherii*, must almost certainly refer to some other Alighieri (see *Bullettino della Società Dantesca Italiana*, N.S. (1899), vi. 225 ff., 237).

SAN GEMIGNANO

("Consiglio dei Cento"). In the spring of 1300 he went as ambassador to San Gemignano, a town about ten miles from Siena, to announce that an assembly was to be held for the purpose of electing a new captain of the Guelf League of Tuscany, and to invite the citizens of San Gemignano to send representatives. The room in the Palazzo of San Gemignano, where Dante was received as ambassador to Florence, and where he spoke in discharge of his office six hundred years ago, is still preserved in much the same condition in which it was on that occasion.

The contemporary record[1] of the event, which, like all similar records of that time, is in Latin, tells how " on 8 May the General Council of the commonwealth and people of San Gemignano having been convoked and assembled in the palace of the said commonwealth by the sounding of a bell and by the voice of the crier, according to custom, at the summons of the noble and valiant knight, Messer Mino de' Tolomei of Siena, the honourable Podestà of the commonwealth and people of the said city of San Gemignano, . . . the noble Dante Alighieri, ambassador of the commonwealth of Florence, explained to the assembled Council on behalf of the said commonwealth how it was expedient at that time for all the cities of the Tuscan League to hold a parliament and discussion in a certain place for the election and confirmation of a new Captain, and how further it was expedient that the appointed syndics and ambassadors of the said cities should assemble themselves together for the despatch of the said business ". It appears that Dante's mission was successful, for the record goes on to state that the proposition of the Florentine ambassador, having been debated, was approved and ratified by the Council.

A few weeks after his return from San Gemignano

[1] The original is printed by Fraticelli, *Vita di Dante*, pp. 138-9.

Dante was elected to serve as one of the six Priors, for the two months from 15 June to 15 August, this being the highest office in the Republic of Florence.[1] " From this priorate," says Leonardi Bruni, " sprang Dante's exile from Florence, and all the adverse fortunes of his life as he himself writes in one of his letters, the words of which are as follows : ' All my woes and all my misfortunes had their origin and commencement with my unlucky election to the priorate ; of which priorate, although I was not worthy in respect of worldly wisdom, yet in respect of loyalty and of years I was not unworthy of it ; inasmuch as ten years had passed since the battle of Campaldino, where the Ghibelline party was almost entirely broken and brought to an end, on which occasion I was present, not inexperienced in arms, and was in great fear, and afterwards greatly exultant, by reason of the varying fortunes of that battle.'   These are his words." [2]

[1] The only extant document relating to Dante's priorate is the record of the confirmation on 15 June, 1300, of a sentence against three Florentines, who were the creatures of Boniface VIII. (see Del Lungo, *Dal Secolo e dal Poema di Dante*, pp. 371-3).

[2] *Vita di Dante*, ed. Brunone Bianchi, 1883, p. xvii.

CHAPTER IV

Blacks and Whites in Pistoja—In Florence—Cerchi and Donati—May Day, 1300—Dante in office—Embassy to Rome—Charles of Valois in Florence—Triumph of the Blacks—Condemnation and Exile of Dante—His Possessions and Debts.

FLORENCE at the time of Dante's election to the priorate was in a dangerous state of ferment owing to the recent introduction from Pistoja of the factions of the Blacks and the Whites, which divided the Guelf party in Florence into two opposite camps, and were the occasion of frequent brawls and bloodshed in the streets.

These factions, according to the old chroniclers, originated in Pistoja in a feud between two branches of the Cancellieri, a Guelf family of that city, who were descended from the same sire, one Ser Cancelliere, but by different mothers. These two branches adopted distinctive names, the one being known as the Cancellieri Bianchi, or White Cancellieri, as being descended from Cancelliere's wife Bianca, the other as the Cancellieri Neri, or Black Cancellieri. A strong feeling of rivalry existed between the two branches, which at last, as the story is told, on the occasion of a trifling quarrel, broke out into actual hostilities.

It appears that one day the father of a certain Focaccia, who belonged to the White Cancellieri, chastised one of his nephews for assaulting another boy with a snowball.

75

The nephew in revenge a few days after struck his uncle, for which he was sent by his father to receive such punishment as the uncle should see fit to administer. The latter, however, laughed the matter off, and sent the boy away with a kiss. But Focaccia, catching his cousin as he came out of the house, dragged him into the stable and cut off his hand on the manger, and then, not content with this, sought out the boy's father, his own uncle, and murdered him. This atrocious crime naturally led to reprisals, and in a short time the whole city was in an uproar. One half the citizens sided with the Whites, the other half with the Blacks, so that Pistoja was reduced to a state of civil war. To put an end to this state of things the Florentines intervened ; and in the hope of extinguishing the feud they secured the leaders of both factions, and imprisoned them in Florence. Unhappily this measure only led to the introduction of the feud among the Florentines themselves. In Florence also there happened to be two rival families— the Donati, who were of ancient lineage, but in reduced circumstances, and the Cerchi, who were wealthy upstarts. The former, headed by the brave Corso Donati, one of the Guelf leaders at the battle of Campaldino, took the part of the Black Cancellieri, while the Cerchi, headed by Vieri de' Cerchi, who had also distinguished himself on the Guelf side at Campaldino,[1] took the part of the White Cancellieri. Thus it came about that through the private enmities of two Pistojan and two Florentine houses, Florence, which was ostensibly Guelf at the time, became divided into Black Guelfs and White Guelfs. These two divisions, which had originally been wholly unpolitical, by degrees became respectively pure Guelfs and disaffected Guelfs, the latter, the White Guelfs, eventually throwing in their lot with the Ghibellines.

[1] See above, pp. 58, 61.

"When the city of Pistoja," says Leonardo Bruni, "was divided into factions by reason of this wicked quarrel, it seemed good to the Florentines, in order to put an end to the trouble, to summon the leaders of both factions to Florence, so that they might not create any further disturbance in Pistoja. But this remedy was of such sort that it did more harm to the Florentines by drawing the plague upon themselves, than good to the Pistojans by ridding them of the ringleaders in the mischief. For, inasmuch as the latter had many friends and relations in Florence, through their partisanship the conflagration immediately burst out with greater fury in this city than it had done in Pistoja before they quitted it. And as the matter came to be discussed everywhere, in public and in private, the ill seed wondrous quickly took root, and the whole city was divided, so that there was hardly a family, noble or plebeian, but was divided against itself; nor was there a private individual of any consequence who did not join one side or the other. And the division spread even between own brothers, one holding with one faction, and one with the other. And after the dispute had lasted for several months, and disagreements became more frequent, not only in words but also in angry and harsh deeds, at first between young men, and afterwards between their elders, the city of Florence at last was everywhere in a state of ferment and disturbance." [1]

The degree of jealousy and suspicion with which the Cerchi and Donati, the respective champions of the Whites and Blacks in Florence, regarded each other may be gathered from the following incident related by a contemporary chronicler : [2]—

" It happened that there was a family who called them-

---

[1] *Vita di Dante*, ed. cit. pp. xvii-xviii.
[2] Dino Compagni, bk. i. ch. 20.

selves Cerchi, men of low estate, but good merchants and
of great wealth ; and they dressed richly, and kept many
servants and horses, and made a fine show ; and some of
them bought the palace of the Conti Guidi, which was
close to the houses of the Donati, who were more ancient
of blood but not so rich ; wherefore seeing the Cerchi rise
to great position, and that they had walled and enlarged
the Palace, and kept great state, the Donati began to
have a great hatred against them. Wherefrom great
scandal and peril ensued to private persons and to the
city at large.

" Now it came to pass one day that many people of the
city were gathered together, for the burying of a dead lady,
on the Piazza de' Frescobaldi ; and it being the custom
of the city that at such gatherings the citizens should
sit below on rush-bottomed stools, and the knights and
doctors above upon benches, the Donati and the Cerchi,
such of them as were not knights, being seated on the
ground, opposite to each other, one of them, either for the
purpose of adjusting his dress, or for some other reason,
rose to his feet. Whereupon those of the opposite party
likewise rose up, suspecting somewhat, and laid their
hands on their swords ; and the others doing the same,
they began to make a brawl. But the rest of those who
were present interfered between them, and would not let
them come to blows. The disturbance, however, was not
so completely quelled but that a large crowd collected at
the residence of the Cerchi, and straightway at a word
would have made for the Donati, had not some of the
Cerchi forbidden it."

The commencement of actual hostilities in Florence between the Blacks and the Whites was due to a street
brawl on the evening of May Day in the year 1300—the
year of Dante's priorate—between some of these same

Cerchi and Donati on the occasion of a dance in the Piazza of Santa Trinita. Two parties of young men on horseback belonging to either side, while looking on, began hustling each other. This soon led to serious fighting, during which one of the Cerchi had his nose cut off.

"At this time (in the year of Christ 1300)," says Villani, "our city of Florence was in the greatest and happiest state it had ever been in since it was rebuilt, or even before, as well in size and power as in the number of her people, for there were more than thirty thousand citizens in the city, and more than seventy thousand fit to bear arms in the districts belonging to her territory; and by reason of the nobility of her brave knights and of her free people, as well of her great riches, she was mistress of almost the whole of Tuscany.

"But the sin of ingratitude, with the help of the enemy of the human race, out of this prosperity brought forth pride and corruption, whereby the feasting and rejoicings of the Florentines were brought to an end. For up to this time they had been living in peace, in great luxury and delicacy, and with continual banquets; and every year on May Day, through nearly the whole of the city, there were gatherings and companies of men and women, with entertainments and dancing. But now it came about that through envy there arose divisions among the citizens; and the chief and greatest of these began in that quarter of strife, the quarter of Porte San Piero, between those belonging to the house of the Cerchi and those of the Donati, on the one side through envy, on the other through rudeness and ungraciousness.

"The head of the house of the Cerchi was M. Vieri de' Cerchi, and he and his house were men of great consequence, and powerful, with great connections, and very

wealthy merchants, for their company was one of the
largest in the world; and they were touchy and uncouth,
rude in their manners and harsh, after the manner of
those who have risen in a short time to great power and
estate.   The head of the house of the Donati was M. Corso
Donati, and he and his house were of gentle birth, and
men of war, with no great wealth.

" And the Cerchi and Donati were neighbours in Florence and in the country, and what with the boorish temper
of the one house and the jealousy of the other, there
sprang up between them a bitter scorn, which was greatly
inflamed by the ill seed of the Black and White parties
introduced from Pistoja, for the Cerchi were the heads of
the Whites in Florence, and the Donati were the heads of
the Blacks.   And by the said two parties all the city of
Florence and her territory was divided and infected.   For
which cause the Guelf party, fearing lest these divisions
should turn to the advantage of the Ghibellines, sent to
Pope Boniface to ask him to heal them.   Wherefore the
Pope sent for M. Vieri de' Cerchi, and when he was come
into his presence, besought him to make peace with M.
Corso Donati and his party, and to submit their differences
to him, promising to advance him and his friends to a
great position, and offering him any spiritual favours he
might ask.   M. Vieri, although in other matters he was a
prudent knight, in this matter showed little wisdom, but
was obstinate and touchy, and would do nothing of what
the Pope asked, saying that he had no quarrel with any
man; and so he returned to Florence, and left the Pope
very wrathful against him and his party.

" Not long after this it happened that certain of each
party were riding on horseback through the city, armed
and on the alert, young men of the Cerchi, with some of
the Adimari, and others, to the number of more than

thirty horsemen, and young men of the Donati, with some
of the Pazzi, and others of their following; and it being
the evening of May Day in this year 1300, as they were
looking on at a dance of ladies which was being held in
the Piazza of Santa Trinita, one party began to provoke
the other, and to push their horses one against the other,
whence there arose a great scuffle and uproar, and several
were wounded, and by ill-luck Ricoverino, son of M. Ricovero de' Cerchi, had his nose cut from off his face; and
by reason of the scuffle that evening the whole city was
in alarm and under arms.

"And this was the beginning of the dissensions and
divisions in the city of Florence and in the Guelf party,
wherefrom ensued much evil and great danger to the
Guelf party and to the Ghibellines, and to all the city of
Florence, and to the whole of Italy also. And in like
manner as the death of M. Buondelmonte was the beginning of the Guelf and Ghibelline parties in Florence, so
was this the beginning of the great ruin of the Guelf party
and of our city." [1]

In consequence of the repeated disturbances caused by
the quarrels between the Blacks and the Whites, during
Dante's priorate it was decided to banish from Florence the
leaders of both parties, in the hope of restoring the city to
peace and quiet. Among the leaders of the Whites was
the poet, Guido Cavalcanti, Dante's earliest friend. It thus
came about that in the impartial exercise of his office Dante
was instrumental in sending his dearest friend into exile,
and, as it proved, to his death; for, though the exiles were
recalled after a few weeks, Guido never recovered from
the effects of the malarious climate of Sarzana in
Lunigiana, to which he had been banished, and died in

[1] Villani, bk. viii. ch. 39.

Florence at the end of August in the same year
(1300).[1]

The feuds between the two factions now reached such
a height that, as we have seen, the interference of Pope
Boniface was invoked, and at this time the Blacks were
clamouring for Charles of Valois, brother of the King of
France, to come to Florence as the Pope's representative.
The Whites, on the other hand, to which faction Dante
himself belonged, were bitterly opposed both to Boniface
and to Charles of Valois.

In April of the next year (1301), in the midst of these
troubles, Dante was entrusted with the charge of super-
intending the works on the street of San Procolo, which
were intended to facilitate the bringing of troops from
the outside districts into the city.[2] On 19 June in this
year Dante voted in the Council of the Hundred against
the proposal to supply a contingent of a hundred soldiers
to serve with the Papal forces, on the requisition of Pope
Boniface;—" Dante Alighieri," the record runs, " advised
that in the matter of furnishing assistance to the Pope,
nothing should be done ". He recorded his vote on various

[1] From Guido's last poem, written at Sarzana during his exile, it is evident that he never expected to return. If certain expressions in this poem
are to be taken literally, it would appear that Guido already felt the hand
of death upon him :—

> " Perch' i' no spero di tornar giammai,
> Ballatetta, in Toscana,
> Va tu, leggera e piana
> Dritt' a la Donna mia . . .
>
> *   *   *
>
> Tu senti, ballatetta, che la morte
> Mi stringe sì che vita m' abbandona."
>
> (*Rime*, ed. Ercole, pp. 406-8).

[2] The documents relating to this matter and to Dante's votes in the
" Consiglio dei Cento" are printed in *Annual Report of the Cambridge*
(U.S.A.) *Dante Society* for 1891 (pp. 36-47).

matters several times in one or other of the Councils during the month of September, the last of which mention is preserved being on 28 September. In the following October, in order to protest against the Papal policy, which aimed at the virtual subjection of Florence, and if possible to avert the coming of Charles of Valois, the Whites sent an embassy to Rome, of which Dante was a member. But while Dante was still absent at Rome, the Pope's "peacemaker" Charles arrived in Florence, which he entered on All Saints' Day (1 November, 1301), his entrance having been unopposed, on the faith of his promise to hold the balance between the two parties, and to maintain peace. No sooner, however, had he obtained command of the city, than he treacherously espoused the cause of the Blacks, armed his followers, and threw the whole of Florence into confusion. In the midst of the panic Corso Donati, one of the exiled leaders of the Blacks, made his way into the city, broke open the prisons and released the prisoners, who, together with his own adherents, attacked and pillaged the houses of the Whites during five days, Charles of Valois meanwhile, in spite of his promises, making no attempt to interfere.

The Blacks, having thus gained the upper hand in Florence, began without delay to strengthen themselves by getting rid of their opponents. On 27 January, 1302, the Podestà, Cante de' Gabrielli of Gubbio, pronounced a sentence against Dante and four other Whites, who had been summoned before the Podestà and had failed to appear. The charge against them was the infamous one of "barratry," that is, of fraud and corrupt practices in office, including the extortion of money and the making of illicit gains. They were further charged with having conspired against the Pope, against the admission into the city of his representative, Charles of Valois, and against the peace of the city of Florence and of the Guelf party. The penalty was a fine of five thousand florins, and the restitution of the sums illegally exacted; payment was to be made within three days of the promulgation of the sentence, in default of which all their goods were to be forfeited [1] and destroyed. In addition to the fine, the delinquents were sentenced to banishment from Tuscany for two years, and to perpetual deprivation from office in the commonwealth of Florence, their names to that end being recorded in the book of the Statutes of the People, as peculators and malversators in office.

This sentence having been disregarded, on 10 March in the same year a second severer sentence [2] was pronounced against Dante and the others (with whom ten more were now included), condemning them to be burned alive [3] should they ever be caught: "if any of the aforesaid at any time should come into the hands of the said Commonwealth, such an one shall be burned with fire so that he die".

That Dante was entirely innocent of the charge of corruption brought against him there can hardly be the

---

[1] That this was no empty threat is proved by the mention in a document (dated 14 August, 1305) of a levy in Florence " in bonis Dantis de Allaghieris et Francischi eius fratris rebellium et condempnatorum comunis Florentie " (see *Bullettino della Società Dantesca Italiana*, N.S. (1907), xiv. 125) ; and by the deed of restitution (dated 9 January, 1343) to Dante's son Jacopo of his father's confiscated property (see Del Lungo, *Dell' Esilio di Dante*, pp. 158-60).

[2] The text of both sentences is printed by Del Lungo in *Dell' Esilio di Dante*, pp. 97-106.

[3] That burning alive was no uncommon punishment in those days, as in later times, is evident from the fact that in an old Sienese inventory occurs the entry " due pezzi di catene da ardere huomini ". Maestro Adamo of Brescia was burned alive in 1281 for coining counterfeit gold florins (*Inf.* xxx. 109-10) ; and Dante himself refers in the *Purgatorio* (xxvii. 17-18) to his having seen men burned alive ; cf. also *Inferno*, xxix. 110.

smallest doubt. It was merely a base device on the part of his enemies within the city to disqualify him and the rest of the Whites from taking any further part in the government of Florence. None of his early biographers believes in his guilt, while his contemporary and fellow-citizen, the chronicler, Giovanni Villani, who belonged to the opposite party, states frankly that he was driven into exile for no other fault than that of being an adherent of the Whites. " The said Dante," he says, " was one of the chief magistrates of our city, and was of the White party, and a Guelf withal; and on that account, without any other fault, with the said White party he was driven out and banished from Florence."[1]

Dante's private property, which, as stated above, was condemned to be confiscated at the time of his exile, was, it may be gathered, not inconsiderable. Boccaccio states that his father's fortune at the time of his birth was abundant, abundant at any rate for those days;[2] and Leonardo Bruni tells us that before his exile, though not very wealthy, he was by no means a poor man, but had a sufficient patrimony to enable him to live comfortably.[3] Bruni adds that, besides house property in Florence, he owned land in the neighbourhood of the city, which is known from other sources to have consisted of farms, vineyards, oliveyards, and plantations.[4] He also says, on

[1] Villani, bk. ix. ch. 136.

[2] " Nacque questo singulare splendore italico nella nostra città . . . ricevuto nella paterna casa da assai lieta fortuna: lieta dico, secondo la qualità del mondo che allora correva ' (Vita di Dante, ed. Macrì-Leone, § 2, p. 11).

[3] " Dante innanzi la cacciata sua di Firenze, contuttochè di grandissima ricchezza non fusse, nientedimeno non fu povero, ma ebbe patrimonio mediocre e sufficiente al vivere onoratamente " (Vita di Dante, ed. Brunone Bianchi, 1883, p. xxii).

[4] See Zingarelli, Dante, p. 31. The information is derived from a document (dated 15 May, 1332) relating to the division of the family property

Dante's own authority, that he possessed a quantity of valuable furniture.[1] It might be supposed consequently that Dante was possessed of ample means ; but it appears, not only from certain allusions in a sonnet addressed to him by Forese Donati,[2] but also from documentary evidence, that even before his exile he was in embarrassed circumstances, and was obliged to borrow considerable sums of money. Thus, on 11 April, 1297, he and his half-brother, Francesco, borrowed $277\frac{1}{2}$ gold florins ("fiorini di buon peso d' oro di Firenze") from Andrea di Guido de' Ricci ;[3] on 23 December, of the same year they borrowed 480 florins from Jacopo di Lotto and Pannochia di Riccomanno ; Dante further borrowed ninety florins from Perso Ubaldino, and forty-six florins from Filippo di Lapo Bonaccolti ; these three last sums on the security of Manetto Donati, Dante's father-in-law, as we learn from the will of his widow, Maria, dated 17 February, 1315.[4] Again, on 14 March, 1299, Dante borrowed 125 florins from his halfbrother, Francesco ; and another ninety florins from the same on 11 June of the following year, four days before he entered on his office as Prior.[5]

between Dante's half-brother, Francesco, and Dante's two sons, Pietro and Jacopo, which is printed by Imbriani in his *Studi Danteschi*, pp. 86 ff.

[1] " Case in Firenze ebbe assai decenti, congiunte con le case di Gieri di messer Bello suo consorto; possessioni in Camerata e nella Piacentina e in piano di Ripoli ; suppellettile abbondante e preziosa, secondo egli scrive " (*op. cit.* p. xxii). It is supposed that the letter here referred to was the " epistola assai lunga," beginning " Popule mee, quid feci tibi," mentioned by Bruni elsewhere as having been written by Dante to the people of Florence after his exile (see below, p. 91).

[2] *Son.* liii*. in the Oxford Dante.

[3] This document is printed by M. Barbi, in *Bullettino della Società Dantesca Italiana*, No. 8 (1892), p 11.

[4] Printed by Imbriani, *Studi Danteschi*, pp. 406 ff.

[5] See *Bullettino della Società Dantesca Italiana*, No. 8 (1892), p. 9, where Barbi prints an extract from the document already mentioned relating to the division of the Alighieri family property in 1332 (printed in full by Imbriani, *Studi Danteschi*, pp. 86 ff.).

For what purpose these debts, amounting in all to more than 1000 florins, were contracted there is nothing to show. From the facts that in several of the loans Dante was associated with his half-brother, and that his father-in-law was security, it may be inferred that they were incurred in the family interest. At any rate, to whatever cause they may have been due, they were all punctiliously discharged after Dante's death by his half-brother, Francesco, and his sons, Pietro and Jacopo, who sold sundry parcels of land for the purpose, as is recorded in various documents still preserved in the Florentine archives.[1]

[1] The documents are printed by Barbi, *op. cit.* pp. 11 ff.

PART III

DANTE IN EXILE

CHAPTER I

1302–1321

Wanderings—Dante's fellow-exiles—Henry VII in Italy—His death—Fresh sentence against Dante—His retirement to Ravenna—Alleged visits to Mantua, Verona, and Piacenza—Reputed a Sorcerer—Death and burial—His tomb and epitaphs—Elegies.

NEVER again after the sentence of banishment pronounced against him by Cante de' Gabrielli did Dante set foot within the walls of his native city. The rest of his life, nearly twenty years, was spent in exile, and for the most part in poverty, such as is foretold to him by his ancestor Cacciaguida in the Heaven of Mars : " Thou shalt leave every thing beloved most dearly ; and this is the shaft which the bow of exile first lets fly. Thou shalt prove how salt the taste is of another's bread, and how hard a path it is to go up and down another's stairs." [1]

In a passage at the beginning of the *Convivio* Dante gives a pathetic account of the miseries and mortifications

[1] *Paradiso*, xvii. 55-60. It is most natural to suppose that among the " things beloved most dearly " left behind in Florence Dante intended to include his wife. But this is not admitted by those who hold that Dante's marriage was an unhappy one.

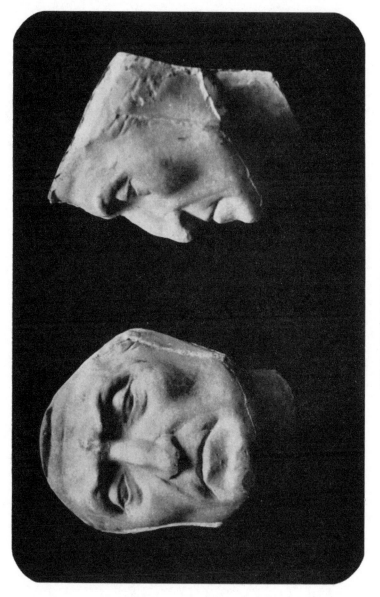

CAST OF DANTE'S FACE TAKEN AFTER DEATH

he endured during his wanderings as an exile. "Alas,"
he says, "would it had pleased the Dispenser of the Universe that I should never have had to make excuses for
myself; that neither others had sinned against me, nor I
had suffered this punishment unjustly, the punishment I
say of exile and of poverty! Since it was the pleasure of the
citizens of the fairest and most renowned daughter of
Rome, Florence, to cast me out from her most sweet bosom
(wherein I was born and brought up to the climax of my
life, and wherein I long with all my heart, with their good
leave, to repose my wearied spirit, and to end the days
allotted to me), wandering as a stranger through almost
every region to which our language reaches, I have gone
about as a beggar, showing against my will the wound of
fortune, which is often wont to be imputed unjustly to the
fault of him who is stricken. Verily I have been as a ship
without sails and without rudder, driven to various harbours
and shores by the parching wind which blows from pinching
poverty. And I have appeared vile in the eyes of many,
who, perhaps from some report of me, had imagined me
in a different guise." [1]

Elsewhere, in another of his works, he expresses his pity
for those who, like himself, languish in exile, and revisit
their home only in their dreams. [2]

Of Dante's movements from the time of his banishment
very little is known for certain. Leonardo Bruni says
that when the tidings of his ruin reached him at Rome,
he hastened back to Tuscany and went to Siena, where
he learned further particulars of his sentence, and consequently determined to make common cause with the other
exiles. He certainly appears at first to have thrown in his
lot with the rest, and to have looked, like them, to a return

[1] *Convivio*, i. 3, ll. 15-40.
[2] *De Vulgari Eloquentia*, ii. 6, ll. 36-9.

to Florence by forcible means. To this end they assembled at Gargonza, a castle of the Ubertini between Arezzo and Siena, and decided to enter into an alliance with the Ghibellines of Tuscany and Romagna, fixing their head-quarters at Arezzo, where they remained until 1304. Dante, at any rate, was present at a meeting of the exiles, held on 8 June, 1302, in the church of San Godenzo, in the Tuscan Apennines, about twenty miles from Florence, when a convention was entered into with the Ubaldini, the ancient enemies of Florence.

In the prophecy of Cacciaguida, already referred to, Dante is warned that what should gall him most would be the folly and wickedness of the company into which he should be thrown; and it is foretold to him that he should after a while dissociate himself from the rest of the exiles, and make a party for himself.[1] At what particular juncture Dante did dissociate himself from his fellow-exiles we cannot tell. It was probably before the summer of 1304, for in July of that year the exiles, dis-appointed in their expectations of a peaceable return to Florence through the mediation of Cardinal Niccolò da Prato, the legate of Benedict XI (who had recently suc-ceeded Boniface VIII), made an abortive attempt from Lastra, in concert with the Pistojans, to effect an entry into the city—an attempt from which Dante appears to have held aloof.

There is evidence of his having been at Forlì in 1303,[2] and it was doubtless about this time that he separated himself from "the worthless and vile company" of his fellow-exiles ; not long after which he took refuge with

---

[1] *Paradiso*, xvii. 61-9.

[2] This is supplied by Flavio Biondo in his *Historiae ab inclinato Romano Imperio* (see *Bullettino della Società Dantesca Italiana*, No. 8 (1892), pp. 21-8, where the evidence is discussed by M. Barbi).

one of the Scaliger family, most probably Bartolommeo della Scala, at Verona, which Cacciaguida foretells to him as his "first refuge".[1] "Here," writes Leonardo Bruni, "he was very courteously received, and remained some time, being now become very humble and seeking by good deeds and good behaviour to win back the favour of being allowed to return to Florence by a spontaneous recall from the Government of the city. To this end he laboured much, and wrote many times, not only to individual members of the Government, but also to the people; and amongst the rest was a long letter beginning, 'My people, what have I done to you?'"[2]

How long Dante remained at Verona is not known. It is impossible, for lack of information, to follow him with any certainty in his wanderings, which, as he records in the above-quoted passage of the *Convivio*, took him into nearly every part of Italy. It is presumed, from a legal document[3] still in existence, that he was at Padua on 27 August, 1306; and from others[4] it is known that he was shortly after (on 6 October in the same year) at Sarzana in Lunigiana as agent for the Malaspini, where he was the guest of Franceschino Malaspina. This visit to the Malaspini, "the honoured race which ceases not to be adorned with the glory of the purse and of the sword," is foretold to Dante by Currado Malaspina, Franceschino's first cousin,

---

[1] *Paradiso*, xvii. 70-2.

[2] *Vita di Dante*, ed. cit. pp. xx.-xxxi. No other trace of this letter has been preserved.

[3] See Imbriani, *Studi Danteschi*, pp. 385-8. There is, however, grave reason to doubt whether the "Dantinus quondam Alligerii de Florentia" mentioned in this document can be Dante, since a "Dantinus" (presumably the same) is mentioned again several times in Paduan documents many years after Dante's death, e.g. in 1339, 1345, 1348, and 1350 (see Zingarelli, *Dante*, p. 214).

[4] See *Annual Report of the Cambridge* (U.S.A.) *Dante Society* for 1892 (pp. 15-24).

whom he meets in Purgatory.[1]   Dante on this occasion
acted as procurator for the Malaspini family in their negotiations for peace with their neighbour, the Bishop of Luni,
which by Dante's means was successfully concluded.   The
duration of his stay in Lunigiana is uncertain, but it probably did not last beyond the summer of 1307.

His movements during the next few years are largely
a matter of conjecture.   Some of his biographers state
that he went from Lunigiana to the Casentino (the upper
valley of the Arno above Florence) and to Forlì [2] again,
and returned once more to Lunigiana [3] on his way to
Paris.   That Dante visited Paris during his exile is stated
both by Boccaccio and by Villani in his chronicle,[4] but at
what precise period this visit took place it is impossible to
say.   Some are inclined to believe, from a phrase in a Latin
poem addressed to Petrarch by Boccaccio, that Dante

---

[1] *Purgatorio*, viii. 118-34.

[2] See *Bullettino della Società Dantesca Italiana*, No. 8 (1892), p. 27.

[3] To this period (about 1308) is usually assigned Dante's supposed visit
to the Camaldolese Monastery of Santa Croce del Corvo in Lunigiana, an
account of which is given in a letter (of doubtful authenticity) from Frate
Ilario, one of the monks, to the Ghibelline leader, Uguccione della Faggiuola.   According to the writer, Dante presented himself at the monastery,
and, being asked what he sought, answered " Peace ".   The monk then
entered into conversation with Dante, who presently produced a book
(the *Inferno*) from his bosom, and gave it to him with a request that he
would forward it to Uguccione, adding that if Uguccione desired to see
the other two parts of the poem, he would find them in the hands of the
Marquis Moroello Malaspina and King Frederick of Sicily (to whom respectively the *Purgatorio* and *Paradiso* are said to have been dedicated).
This letter has long been regarded as a forgery, possibly from the hand
of Boccaccio.   But recent investigations have proved that at any rate
Boccaccio cannot have forged it, and there is now a tendency to accept it
as genuine (see Wicksteed and Gardner, *Dante and Giovanni del Virgilio*,
1902, pp. 326-34; and Rajna, *La Lettera di Frate Ilario*, Perugia, 1904).
A translation of this letter, which was written in Latin, is given in *Appendix B*.

[4] Bk. ix. ch. 136.

came to England;[1] and it is even stated by Giovanni da Serravalle, a fifteenth-century writer, that he studied in the University of Oxford,[2] but this is extremely doubtful.

There seems little doubt that Dante was in Italy between September, 1310, and January, 1311, when he addressed a letter to the Princes and Peoples of Italy on the advent of the Emperor Henry VII into Italy,—the Emperor through whose means Dante hoped to be restored to Florence. "Lo! now is the acceptable time," he writes, "wherein arise the signs of consolation and peace. For a new day is beginning to break, showing forth the dawn, which even now is dispersing the darkness of our long night of tribulation ; already the breezes from the East are springing up, the face of the heavens grows rosy, and confirms the hopes of the peoples with a peaceful calm. And we too, who have long kept vigil through the night in the desert, we too shall behold the looked-for joy."[3]

He was certainly in Tuscany (probably as the guest of Guido Novello of Battifolle at the castle of Poppi in the Casentino) when he wrote his terrible letter to the Florentines, dated "from the springs of the Arno," 31 March, 1311, after he learned that they were preparing to resist the Emperor by force. In this letter,[4] which is headed "Dante Alighieri, a Florentine and undeservedly an exile, to the most iniquitous Florentines within the city," he uses no measured terms, and does not hesitate to threaten

[1]   " Novisti forsan et ipse
Traxerit ut juvenem * Phœbus per celsa nivosi
Cyrrheos, mediosque sinus tacitosque recessus
Naturae, coelique vias terraeque marisque,
Aonios fontes, Parnasi culmen, et antra
Julia, Pariseos dudum serusque Britannos."

[2] "Dilexit theologiam sacram, in qua diu studuit tam in Oxoniis in regno Angliae, quam Parisius in regno Franciae."

[3] *Epistola* v. § 1.   [4] *Epistola* vi.

———————————————

* I.e. Dantem.

the Florentines with the direct vengeance of the Emperor. "You," he thunders, "you, who transgress every law of God and man, and whom the insatiable maw of avarice urges headlong into every crime, does not the dread of the second death haunt you, seeing that you first and you alone, refusing the yoke of liberty, have set yourselves against the glory of the Roman Emperor, the king of the earth, and the servant of God? The hope which you vainly cherish in your madness will not be furthered by this rebellion of yours, but by your resistance the just wrath of the king at his coming will be but the more inflamed against you. If my prophetic spirit be not deceived, your city, worn out with long sufferings, shall be delivered at the last into the hands of the stranger, after the greatest part of you has been destroyed in death or in captivity, and the few that shall be left to endure exile shall witness her downfall with weeping and lamentation." [1]

From the same place a few weeks later (on 16 April), Dante addressed a letter to the Emperor himself, who was at that time besieging Cremona, urging him to lay everything else aside, and to come and crush without further delay the viper Florence, as the most obstinate and dangerous rebel against the Imperial authority. From this letter it appears that Dante had been present at the coronation of Henry with the iron crown at Milan, on the day of Epiphany (6 January, 1311), when ambassadors were sent from nearly every city of Italy, except Florence and her allies. "I too, who write for myself as well as for others, have beheld thee most gracious, as beseems Imperial Majesty, and have heard thee most clement, when my hands touched thy feet, and my lips paid their tribute." [2]

On 2 September of this same year (1311) was issued at

---

[1] *Epistola* vi. §§ 2, 3, 4.　　　　[2] *Epistola* vii. § 2.

Florence a proclamation [1] (known as the "Riforma di Messer Baldo d' Aguglione," from the name of the Prior who was responsible for it), offering pardon to a portion of the Florentine exiles, but expressly excepting certain others by name. Among these names was that of Dante Alighieri, whose exclusion was no doubt largely due to the letters mentioned above, and to his active sympathy with the Imperial cause. To this proclamation the Emperor issued a counterblast in the following December from Genoa, in the shape of an edict declaring Florence to be outside the pale of the Empire, which was followed by another from Poggibonsi in February, 1313, containing the names of more than 600 Florentine citizens and subjects, who were branded as rebels.

Nothing is known of Dante's whereabouts during these years of deferred hopes and disappointments. Leonardo Bruni states,[2] apparently on the authority of a letter of Dante's which has not been preserved, that when the Emperor advanced against Florence and laid siege to the city (in the autumn of 1312), Dante out of reverence for his native place would not accompany him, although he had urged him to the attack. Dante had scoffed at the idea that the Florentines could stand up against the Imperial host. "Do you trust," he had written in the letter already quoted,[3] "do you trust in your defence, because you are girt by a contemptible rampart? What shall it avail you to have girt you with a rampart, and to have

---

[1] The text is printed by Del Lungo in *Dell' Esilio di Dante*, pp. 107 ff.

[2] *Vita di Dante*, ed. cit. p. xxi: "Il tenne tanto la riverenza della patria, che, venendo l' imperadore contro a Firenze e ponendosi a campo presso alla porta, non vi volle essere, secondo lui scrive, contuttochè confortatore fusse stato di sua venuta".

[3] *Epistola* vi. § 3.

fortified yourselves with bulwarks and with battlements,[1] when, terrible in gold, the eagle shall swoop down upon you, which, soaring now over the Pyrenees, now over Caucasus, now over Atlas, borne up by the breath of the soldiery of heaven, gazed down of old upon the vast expanse of ocean in its flight ? "

But the Imperial eagle was obliged to retire baffled, leaving the viper uncrushed; and in the following year, while the Emperor was marching southward against Naples, he was suddenly seized with sickness at Buonconvento near Siena, where he died on 24 August, 1313. The news of his death was received with savage exultation by the Florentines.[2] To Dante it meant the final aban-

---

[1] " The Florentines," says Villani, " fearing the coming of the Emperor, resolved to enclose the city with moats from the Porta San Gallo to the Porta Santo Ambrogio, and thence to the Arno; and then from the Porta San Gallo to the Porta dal Prato d' Ognissanti, where the walls were already begun, they had them raised eight cubits. And this work was done at once and very quickly; and it was without doubt the salvation of the city, for it had been all open, the old walls having been in great part pulled down, and the materials sold " (bk. ix. ch. 10).

[2] A few days after the event the following letter was addressed by the Signoria of Florence to their allies announcing the news : " To you our faithful brethren, with the greatest rejoicing in the world we announce by these presents the blessed news, which our Lord Jesus Christ, looking down from on high as well to the necessities of ourselves, and other true and faithful Christians, the devoted servants of Holy Mother Church, as to those of His own cause, has vouchsafed to us. To wit, that the most savage tyrant, Henry, late Count of Luxemburg, whom the rebellious persecutors from old time of said Mother Church, namely the Ghibellines, the treacherous foes of you and of ourselves, called King of the Romans, and Emperor of Germany, and who under cover of the Empire had already consumed and laid waste no small part of the Provinces of Lombardy and Tuscany, ended his life on Friday last, the twenty-fourth day of this month of August, in the territory of Buonconvento. Know further, that the Aretines and the Ghibelline Conti Guidi have retired themselves towards Arezzo, and the Pisans and Germans towards Pisa taking his body, and all the Ghibellines who were with him have taken refuge in the strongholds of their allies in the neighbourhood. . . . We beseech

donment of any hope of a return to Florence. "On the Emperor Henry's death," writes Bruni, "every hope of Dante's was utterly destroyed; for he had himself closed up the way to forgiveness by his abusive writings against the government of the commonwealth; and there was no longer any hope of return by force."

Where Dante was when the fatal news reached him, and what his movements were at this time, is not known. After the death of Clement V, on 20 April, 1314, Dante addressed a letter[1] to the Italian cardinals in conclave at Carpentras, rebuking them for their backslidings and corruption, and calling upon them to make amends by electing an Italian Pope, who should restore the Papal See to Rome. At some date subsequent to 14 June of that year, when Lucca fell into the hands of the Ghibelline captain, Uguccione della Faggiuola, Dante appears to have been in that city; and it has been conjectured that it may have been during this stay that he formed the attachment for a Lucchese lady named Gentucca, which is supposed to be alluded to by Bonagiunta in Purgatory.[2] What was the real nature of his relations with this lady, who has been identified with a certain Gentucca Morla,[3] wife of Cosciorino Fondora of Lucca, we have no means of ascertaining.

you, therefore, dear brethren, to rejoice with ourselves over so great and fortunate accidents."

(The original Latin text of this letter is printed by F. Bonaini, in *Acta Henrici VII Romanorum Imperatoris et Monumenta quædam alia suorum temporum historiam illustrantia*, 1877, vol. ii. p. ccclxv; an Italian translation is given by Del Lungo, in *Dino Compagni e la sua Cronica*, 1880, vol. i. pp. 637-8.

[1] *Epistola* viii.

[2] *Purgatorio*, xxiv. 37, 43-5.

[3] This Gentucca was the daughter of Ciucchino di Guglielmo di Morla of Lucca. Her husband, Buonaccorso di Lazzaro di Fondora (familiarly known as Coscio or Cosciorino Fondora) several times mentions her in his will (dated 15 December, 1317). Dante's Gentucca is identified with

In August, 1315, the Ghibellines under the leadership of Uguccione della Faggiuola, completely defeated the Florentines and Tuscan Guelfs at Monte Catini, between Lucca and Pistoja.   This event was followed by a fresh sentence from Florence against the exiled Whites.   In this sentence,[1] which is dated 6 November, 1315, Dante and those named with him, including Dante's sons this time, were branded as Ghibellines and rebels, and condemned, if captured, "to be taken to the place of justice (i.e. the place of public execution), and there to have their heads struck from their shoulders, so that they die outright." On 2 June in the next year, however, an amnesty was proclaimed by the Florentine chief magistrate, Lando of Gubbio,[2] and permission was granted to the majority of the exiles to return to Florence, under certain degrading conditions, including the payment of a fine and the performance of penance in the Baptistery.   From this amnesty all the exiles who had been originally condemned by the Podestà, Cante de' Gabrielli, among whom of course was Dante, were expressly excluded.   Many of the exiles appear to have accepted the terms ; but Dante, who seems at first to have been unaware of his exclusion, scornfully rejected them.

"Is this, then," he writes to a friend in Florence, "is this the generous recall of Dante Alighieri to his native

this lady on the strength of the statement of an early commentary on the *Divina Commedia* (as yet unpublished), confirmed by documentary evidence (see C. Minutoli, *Gentucca e gli altri Lucchesi nominati nella D. C.*, in *Dante e il suo Secolo*, pp. 221-31).

[1] The text is printed by Del Lungo in *Dell' Esilio di Dante*, pp. 148 ff.

[2] This man, who bore the title of "bargello" is described by Villani (bk. ix. ch. 76) as "uomo carnefice e crudele".   He was appointed chief magistrate in May, 1316, but was displaced in the following October by Count Guido of Battifolle, who was appointed Vicar in Florence by King Robert of Naples.

city, after the miseries of nearly fifteen years of exile? Is this the reward of innocence manifest to all the world, of unceasing sweat and toil in study? Far be it from the friend of philosophy, so senseless a degradation, befitting only a soul of clay, as to submit himself to be paraded like a prisoner, as some infamous wretches have done! Far be it from the advocate of justice, after being wronged, to pay tribute to them that wronged him, as though they had deserved well of him! No! this is not the way for me to return to my country. If another can be found which does not derogate from the fame and honour of Dante, that will I take with no lagging steps. But if by no such way Florence may be entered, then will ¡I re-enter Florence never. What! can I not everywhere gaze upon the sun and the stars? can I not under any sky meditate on the most precious truths, without first rendering myself inglorious, nay ignominious, in the eyes of the people and city of Florence? Nay, bread will not fail me!"[1]

After again seeking shelter with the Scaligers at Verona, this time as the guest of Can Grande della Scala, Dante, on the invitation of Guido Novello da Polenta, went to Ravenna (probably in 1317 or 1318), "where," says Boccaccio, "he was honourably received by the lord of that city, who revived his fallen hopes with kindly encouragement, and, giving him abundantly such things as he needed, kept him there at his court for many years, nay, even to the end of his days".[2] At Ravenna, his last refuge, where his sons Pietro and Jacopo and his daughter Beatrice resided with him, Dante appears to have lived in

---

[1] *Epistola* ix. §§ 3, 4. A critical text of this letter is printed in the *Bullettino della Società Dantesca Italiana*, N.S. (1905), xii. 122-3, by A. della Torre, who points out that the correct reading at the beginning of § 3 is not, as hitherto usually printed, *revocatio gloriosa*, but *revocatio generosa*.

[2] *Vita di Dante*, ed. Macrì-Leone, § 5, p. 30.

congenial company;[1] and here he put the finishing touches to his "sacred poem," the *Divina Commedia*, his work upon which he tells us "had made him lean for many years".[2]

Boccaccio states that at Ravenna many scholars came to Dante for instruction in the poetic art, especially in vernacular poetry, which he first brought into repute among Italians.[3] While he was here, after the *Inferno* and *Purgatorio* had been completed and made public, Dante was invited by a poet and professor of Bologna, Giovanni del Virgilio, in a Latin poem,[4] to come and receive the laurel crown at Bologna. To this suggestion Dante sent a reply in the form of a Latin eclogue[5] declining the invitation, the laurel having no attraction for him unless conferred by his own fellow-citizens in the same Baptistery where as a child he had received the name which he was to make so famous.

At the end of 1319 or beginning of 1320 Dante appears to have paid a visit to Mantua, on which occasion a dis-

---

[1] Among Dante's friends and acquaintances at Ravenna the names have been preserved of Dino Perini, a young notary of Florence (see Ricci, *L' Ultimo Rifugio di Dante*, pp. 99 ff.), and Fiduccio de' Milotti, a physician of Certaldo (see Ricci, *op. cit.* pp. 100 ff.), who figure respectively as Meliboeus and Alphesiboeus in Dante's Latin eclogues (see below, pp. 254-6). Another friend was Menghino Mezzano, a notary (and, apparently, later an ecclesiastic) of Ravenna, who wrote an epitaph on Dante, and whose intimacy with the poet is attested by Coluccio Salutati (see below, p. 105; and Ricci, *op. cit.* pp. 218 ff.). Yet another acquaintance is said to have been Bernardo Canaccio, of Bologna, the author of the epitaph inscribed on Dante's tomb (" Jura Monarchiae," etc.) (see below, p. 105; and Ricci, *op. cit.* pp. 237 ff.). Besides these, Boccaccio mentions Piero di Giardino (see below, pp. 103, 119; and Ricci, *op. cit.* pp. 209 ff.).

[2] *Paradiso*, xxv. 1-3.

[3] *Vita di Dante*, ed. cit. § 6, p. 31.

[4] Printed in the Oxford Dante, pp. 185-6.

[5] Printed in the Oxford Dante, pp. 186-7. As to the genuineness of this poetical correspondence between Giovanni del Virgilio and Dante, see below p. 252.

cussion was started as to the relative levels of land and
water on the surface of the globe. Dante subsequently
wrote a treatise on the subject (if we may trust the evidence of the treatise *De Aqua et Terra* [1] traditionally ascribed to him), which was delivered as a public dissertation
at Verona, on 20 January, 1320.

From the mention of Dante's name in a document
lately discovered in the Vatican [2] it has been inferred that
Dante was at Piacenza some time in 1319 or 1320. The
document in question, which is incomplete, contains the
account of a process instituted at the Papal Court at Avignon against Matteo Visconti of Milan, and his son Galeazzo,[3] for an attempt upon the life of Pope John XXII by
means of sorcery. The story of the episode, which is an
exceedingly curious one, as showing that in his own lifetime Dante had the reputation of a sorcerer, is briefly as
follows. In October, 1319, Matteo Visconti sent for a
certain Bartolommeo Canolati who was reputed to be an
adept in the black art, and showed him a small silver figure
of a man, on the forehead of which was written " Jacobus [4]
papa Johannes ". He then explained to Bartolommeo
that he wanted him to apply to this image [5] the requisite
" fumigations " and incantations to ensure the death of the

---

[1] See below, pp. 256 ff.

[2] See *Giornale Dantesco*, iv. 126-30.

[3] This is the Galeazzo who is referred to by Dante in *Purgatorio*, viii.
79-81, in connection with his marriage to Beatrice of Este, the widow of
Nino Visconti of Pisa.

[4] The Pope's name was Jacques D' Euse.

[5] Dante refers in the *Divina Commedia* to the practice of witchcraft
upon people by means of images made in their likeness. Speaking of the
witches in Malebolge, he says " Fecer malìe con erbe e con imago " (*Inf.*
xx. 123); upon which the *Anonimo Fiorentino* comments: " Puossi fare
malìe per virtù di certe erbe medianti alcune parole, o per imagini di cera
o d' altro fatte in certi punti et per certo modo che, tenendo queste imagini
al fuoco o ficcando loro spilletti nel capo, così pare che senta colui a cui
imagine elle son fatte, come la imagine che si strugga al fuoco."

Pope, who was his bitter enemy.[1]   Bartolommeo declared
that he did not know how to do anything of the sort, but
being taxed with having in his possession a powerful drug
adapted for the purpose, he admitted that he had once had
it, but protested that at the bidding of a friar he had
thrown it all away. Matteo thereupon dismissed him
with an injunction to hold his tongue, on pain of death.
Bartolommeo, however, divulged what he had seen, and
the matter came to the ears of the Pope, who summoned
him to Avignon, where he was examined before three
cardinals, one of whom was Bertrand du Pouget, the same
who subsequently condemned Dante's *De Monarchia* to the
flames.[2]   As the result of this inquisition, in the following
February proceedings were initiated against the Visconti
for conspiring against the life of the Pope.   Meanwhile
another sorcerer whom Matteo had employed having failed
to produce any effect by his incantations, Galeazzo sent
for Bartolommeo to Piacenza, and repeated the proposal
that he should practise on the image.   By way of putting
him on his mettle Galeazzo told him that he had sent for
Maestro Dante Alighieri of Florence to perform the task,
but that he had far rather that Bartolommeo should under-
take it, as he had no wish to let Dante have any hand in
the matter.[3]   The record states that Bartolommeo said

[1] " Vide Bartholomee, ecce istam ymaginem quam feci fieri ad de-
structionem istius pape qui me persequitur, et est necessarium quod sub-
fumigetur, et quia tu scis facere subfumigationem in talibus, volo quod
tu facias subfumigationes isti ymagini cum solemnitatibus convenientibus."

[2] See below, p. 232.

[3] " Galeas dixit eidem Bartholomeo : Scias quod ego feci venire ad
me magistrum Dante Alegriro (*sic*) de Florencia pro isto eodem negocio
pro quo rogo te. Cui Bartholomeus dixit : Sciatis quod multum placet
michi quod ille faciat ea que petitis. Cui Bartholomeo dictus Galeas dixit :
Scias Bartholomee quod pro aliqua re de mundo ego non sustinerem quod
dictus Dante Alegiro (*sic*) in predictas poneret manum suam vel aliquid
faceret nec revelarem sibi istud negocium qui daret michi mille floreni (*sic*)
auri, quia volo quod tu facias, quia de te multum confido."

he would think the matter over—but the sequel to the story is lost. If Galeazzo's statement about Dante is to be taken literally it would appear that Dante was in Piacenza somewhere about the date of this transaction, towards the end of 1319 or the beginning of 1320.

In the summer of 1321, a difference having arisen between Ravenna and Venice, on account of an affray in which several Venetian sailors were killed, Guido da Polenta sent an embassy to the Doge of Venice, of which Dante was a member. The ambassadors were ill received by the Venetians, who, it is said, refused them permission to return by sea, and obliged them to make the journey overland along the malarious seaboard. The consequences to Dante were fatal, for he contracted a fever (as is supposed) on the way, and, growing worse after his return to Ravenna, died in that city on 14 September, 1321, aged fifty-six years and four months.[1] At Ravenna Dante was buried, and there, "by the upbraiding shore," his remains still rest, in spite of repeated efforts on the part of Florence

[1] Boccaccio in his comment on the opening line of the *Commedia*, has an interesting note as to Dante's age at the time of his death, which proves incidentally how carefully Boccaccio made his inquiries with regard to the details of Dante's life. "That Dante was thirty-five," he says, "at the time when he first awakened to the error of his ways is confirmed by what was told me by a worthy man, named Ser Piero, son of M. Giardino of Ravenna, who was one of Dante's most intimate friends and servants at Ravenna. He affirmed that he had it from Dante, while he was lying sick of the illness of which he died, that he had passed his fifty-sixth year by as many months as from the previous May to that day. And it is well known that Dante died on the fourteenth day of September in the year 1321" (*Comento*, i. 104-5). Inasmuch as Giovanni del Virgilio and Menghino Mezzano in their epitaphs on Dante speak of his death as having taken place "septembris idibus," some suppose that he actually died on the evening of 13 September (see Corrado Ricci, *L' Ultimo Rifugio di Dante*, pp. 157-8). It is probable, however, that the exigencies of metre had more weight with these writers than considerations of scrupulous accuracy.

to secure possession of "the metaphorical ashes of the man of whom they had threatened to make literal cinders if they could catch him alive".[1]

"The noble knight, Guido da Polenta," writes Boccaccio, "placed the dead body of Dante, adorned with the insignia of a poet,[2] upon a funeral bier, and caused it to be borne upon the shoulders of his most reverend citizens to the place of the Minor Friars in Ravenna, with such honour as he deemed worthy of the illustrious dead. And having followed him to this place, in the midst of a public lamentation, Guido had the body laid in a sarcophagus of stone, wherein it reposes to this day. Afterwards returning to the house where Dante had formerly lived, according to the custom of Ravenna, Guido himself pronounced a long and ornate discourse, as well in commendation of the great learning and virtue of the dead man, as for the consolation of his friends whom he had left to mourn him in bitter sorrow. And Guido purposed, had his estate and life endured, to honour Dante with so splendid a tomb, that if no other merit of his had kept his name alive among future generations, this memorial alone would have preserved it. This laudable purpose was in a brief space made known to certain who at that time were the most renowned poets in Romagna; so that each, not only to exhibit his own powers, but also to testify to the love he bore toward the dead poet, and to win the grace and favour of the lord Guido, who they were aware had this at his heart—each, I say, composed an epitaph in verse for inscription on the tomb that was to be, which with fitting praise should make known to posterity what

[1] J. R. Lowell.

[2] The remains of laurel leaves, no doubt the relics of the poet's wreath, were found in the tomb when it was opened at the beginning of the sixteenth century, and again in 1865 (see below, pp. 113, 117).

manner of man he was who lay within. And these verses they sent to the illustrious lord, who through the evil stroke of Fortune not long after lost his estate and died at Bologna; on which account the making of the tomb and the inscription of the verses thereon was left undone." [1]

Boccaccio goes on to say that many years afterwards he was shown some of the verses which had been composed for Dante's epitaph, but that he did not consider any of them worthy of preservation, saving only fourteen lines by Giovanni del Virgilio of Bologna, which he transscribes.[2] The sarcophagus (no doubt an ancient one) in which Dante's remains were deposited by Guido da Polenta was apparently left without any inscription until late in the fourteenth century. It is known, from the record of an eye-witness, that in the year 1378 there were two epitaphs inscribed upon the tomb.[3] One of these, consisting of six hexameters,[4] was by Menghino Mezzano of Ravenna, a contemporary and friend of Dante;[5] the other, consisting of three rhyming hexameter couplets, was by a certain Bernardo Canaccio, who is conjectured also to have been personally acquainted with Dante. This second epitaph, which runs as follows:—

---

[1] *Vita di Dante*, ed. Macrì-Leone, § 6, pp. 32-3.

[2] It was long supposed that these lines (Latin elegiacs, beginning: " Theologus Dantes, nullius dogmatis expers ") were inscribed on Dante's tomb, but Corrado Ricci has shown that this was not the case (see *L' Ultimo Rifugio di Dante*, pp. 252 ff.).

[3] See Ricci, *op. cit.* p. 259.

[4] Beginning: " Inclita fama cuius universum penetrat orbem ".

[5] Coluccio Salutati, in a letter written from Florence on 2 October, 1399, speaks of him as " notus quondam familiaris et socius Dantis nostri," and says that he was a close student of the *Divina Commedia*, on which he believed him to have written a commentary (see F. Novati, *Epistolario di Coluccio Salutati*, vol. iii. p. 374).

Jura Monarchiae superos Phlegetonta lacusque
Lustrando cecini voluerunt fata quousque ;
Sed quia pars cessit melioribus hospita castris
Actoremque suum petiit felicior astris,
Hic claudor Dantes patriis extorris ab oris
Quem genuit parvi Florentia mater amoris.[1]—

was till comparatively recently supposed to have been written by Dante himself. The real author, however, was established to be Bernardo Canaccio by the discovery about fifty years ago of a passage in a fourteenth century manuscript of the *Commedia*, in the Bodleian Library at Oxford, in which the lines are ascribed to him by name.[2]

Dante's burial-place, left incomplete, as Boccaccio records, owing to the misfortunes which overtook Guido da Polenta, appears to have been neglected and to have gradually fallen into decay. The tomb was restored in 1483 by Bernardo Bembo (father of the celebrated cardinal, Pietro Bembo), who was at that time Prætor of the Venetian Republic in Ravenna. He entrusted the work to the Venetian sculptor and architect, Pietro Lombardi, who, among other things, recarved the face of the sarcophagus, and inscribed upon it the epitaph of Canaccio mentioned above, to which the letters S. V. F.[3] were prefixed, evidently under the impression that the author of

[1] Englished as follows by the English traveller, Fynes Moryson, when he was at Ravenna in 1594 :—

The Monarchies, Gods, Lakes, and Phlegeton,
I searcht and sung, while my Fates did permit ;
But since my better part to heaven is gone,
And with his Maker mongst the starres doth sit,
I *Dantes* a poore banished man lie here,
Whom *Florence* Mother of scant Love did beare.

For " scant " in the last line Moryson (or his printers) substituted " sweet " (see *Itinerary*, ed. 1617, part i. p. 95).

[2] See Ricci, *op. cit.* p. 264.

[3] That is, " Sibi Vivens Fecit ".

DANTE'S TOMB AT RAVENNA

the lines was Dante himself; while the epitaph of Menghino Mezzano was omitted.

Much of the work executed by Lombardi under Bembo's directions, including the inscribed epitaph, and the marble relief of Dante reading at a desk, remains to this day.[1]

The tomb was a second time restored, more than two hundred years later (in 1692) by Cardinal Domenico Maria Corsi, the Papal Legate[2]; and a third time, in 1780, by Cardinal Luigi Valenti Gonzaga, who erected the mausoleum, surmounted by a dome, as it now stands.

Not only was the death of Dante recorded as an event of importance by his fellow-citizen, Giovanni Villani, in his Florentine chronicle,[3] but numerous elegies were written on the occasion by friends and contemporaries of the poet in various parts of Italy. Among these were poems by Cino da Pistoja, and Giovanni Quirini of Venice, with both of whom Dante had exchanged sonnets in his lifetime.[4] Cino, who thirty years before had addressed a canzone to Dante on the death of Beatrice,[5] now wrote a canzone on Dante's own death, addressed to Love, whose

[1] See plate opposite. Bembo commemorated his restoration of the tomb in a Latin inscription (beginning : " Exigua tumuli Dantes hic sorte jacebas "), which was affixed to the wall at the left side of the tomb, and in which he states that before his restoration the tomb was almost un-recognisable. This inscription, which is still preserved, though in a different situation, was transcribed by Fynes Moryson in 1594.

[2] An interesting engraving of the tomb, as it appeared after this second restoration, is inserted in the first volume of the edition of Dante's works published by Antonio Zatta at Venice in 1757.

[3] " Nel anno 1321, del mese di Luglio,* morì Dante Alighieri di Firenze nella città di Ravenna in Romagna . . . e in Ravenna dinanzi alla porta della chiesa maggiore fu seppellito a grande onore, in abito di poeta e di grande filosafo " (bk. ix. ch. 136).

[4] See above, p. 50; see also Zingarelli's *Dante*, pp. 318-20. A sonnet of Dante to Quirini (*Son.* xxxvii.) is translated by Rossetti in *Dante and his Circle*, p. 240.

[5] See above, p. 49.

* Villani's mistake for September.

ardent and faithful votary Dante had ever been; after bewailing the bitter loss sustained by all lovers of the Italian tongue, of which Dante had been, as it were, the fount and source, he turns to Florence and points to the fulfilment of Dante's own prophecy in the *Inferno* (xv. 72) that however much his native city might desire to have him back her wish would be unavailing; he concludes with congratulations to Ravenna on being deservedly in possession of the great treasure which Florence had cast out.[1] Quirini, besides a lament on Dante's death, wrote a sonnet in defence of his friend's memory against the imputations of Cecco d' Ascoli, and he addressed another to Can Grande della Scala, urging him to give to the world without delay the cantos of the *Paradiso* which had not yet been made public.[2] Quirini's lament, which is an eloquent testimony to the estimation in which Dante was held by his contemporaries, is as follows :—

> If it hath happed for any mortal man
>   That sun or moon was darkened, or on high
>   Comet appeared, portending sudden change,
> Reverse of fortune, and disaster dire :
> A greater portent should we look for now,
>   And signs more strange than e'er were seen before,
>   Since death relentless, black and bitter death,
> Hath quenched the brilliant and resplendent rays
> That beamed from out the noble breast of him,
>   Our sacred bard, the father of our tongue,
>   Who glowed with radiance as of one divine.
> Alas! the Muses now are sunken low,
>   The poet's art hath fallen on evil days,
> Which erst was held in worship and renown.
> The whole world weeps the glorious Dante dead—
>   Him thou, Ravenna, heldest dear in life,
> And holdest now, and hence are held more dear.[3]

[1] The original is printed in *Rime di M. Cino da Pistoja, ordinate dà G. Carducci*, Firenze, 1862, pp. 136-7.

[2] See Zingarelli, *op. cit.* pp. 326, 330-1.

[3] The original is printed by Zingarelli, *op. cit.* p. 348.

CHAPTER II

THE history of Dante's remains from the time of their burial by Guido da Polenta in 1321 is a most curious one, and shows how jealously the people of Ravenna guarded the treasure which had been deposited in their keeping. Boccaccio, in a chapter of his *Life of Dante*, headed " A Rebuke to the Florentines," [1] reproaches them with their treatment of Dante, and urges them at least to recall his dead body from exile, adding, however, that he feels sure their request for his remains would be refused.

" Oh ! ungrateful country," he exclaims, " what madness, what blindness possessed you to drive out your most valued citizen, your chiefest benefactor, your one poet, with such unheard-of cruelty, and to keep him in exile ? If perchance you excuse yourself on the ground of the common fury of that time, why, when your anger was appeased and your passion abated, and you repented you of your act, why did you not recall him ? Alas ! your Dante Alighieri died in that exile to which you, envious of his merit, unjustly sent him. Oh ! unspeakable shame, that

[1] *Vita di Dante*, ed. Macrì-Leone, § 7, pp. 35-42.

109

a mother should regard with jealousy the virtues of her
own son ! Now you are freed from that disquietude, now
he is dead you live secure amid your own imperfections,
and can put an end to your long and unjust persecutions.
He cannot in death do to you what he never in life would
have done ; he lies beneath another sky than yours, nor
do you ever expect to behold him again, save on that day
when you shall see once more all your citizens, whose
iniquities by the just Judge shall be visited and rewarded.
If then, as we believe, all hatred, and anger, and enmity
cease at the death of whoso dies, do you now begin to
return to your old self, and to your right mind ; begin to
think with shame of how you acted contrary to your ancient
humanity ; prove yourself now a mother, and no longer
a foe, and grant to your son the tears that are his due,
and show to him the love of a mother ; seek at least to
regain him in death, whom when alive you rejected, nay
drove out as a malefactor, and restore to his memory the
citizenship, the welcome, the grace you denied to himself.
Of a truth, although you were wayward and ungrateful to
him, he always revered you as a mother, and, though you
deprived him of your citizenship, yet did he never seek
to deprive you of the glory which from his works must
ensue to you. A Florentine always, in spite of his long
exile, he called himself, and would be called, always preferring you and loving you. What then will you do?
Will you for ever remain stiff-necked in your injustice ?
Will you show less humanity than the pagans, who, we
read, not only begged back the bodies of their dead, but
were ever ready to meet death like heroes in order to get
them back? Who doubts that the Mantuans, who to this
day reverence the poor hut and the fields that once were
Virgil's, would have bestowed on him honourable burial
had not the Emperor Augustus transported his bones

from Brundusium to Naples, and ordained that city as
their last resting-place?

"Do you then seek to be the guardian of your Dante.
Ask for him back again, making a show of this humanity,
even if you do not desire to have him back; with this pretence at least you will rid yourself of a part of the reproach
you have so justly incurred.   Ask for him back again! I
am certain he will never be given back to you, and thus you
will at once have made a show of compassion, and, being
refused, may yet indulge your natural cruelty!

"But to what do I urge you?   Hardly do I believe, if
dead bodies have any feeling, that Dante's body would
remove from where it now lies, in order to return to you.
He lies in company more honourable than any you can
offer him.   He lies in Ravenna, a city by far more venerable
in years than yourself; and though in her old age she shows
somewhat of decay, yet in her youth she was by far more
flourishing than you are now.   She is, as it were, a vast
sepulchre of holy bodies, so that no foot can anywhere
press her soil, without treading above the most sacred
ashes.   Who then would wish to return to you and be laid
amongst your dead, who, one must believe, still retain the
evil passions they cherished in their lifetime, and fly one
from the other, carrying their enmities into the grave?

"Ravenna, bathed as she is in the most precious blood
of numberless martyrs, whose remains she to this day pre-
serves with the greatest reverence, as she does the bodies
of many high and mighty emperors and other men of high
renown, either for their long ancestry or for their noble
deeds, Ravenna, I say, rejoices not a little that it has been
granted to her of God, in addition to her other privileges,
to be the perpetual guardian of so great a treasure as the
body of him whose works are the admiration of the whole
world, him of whom you knew not how to be worthy.

But of a surety, her pride in possessing Dante is not so great as her envy of you by whose name he called himself; for she grieves that she will be remembered only on account of his last day, while you will be famous on account of his first. Persist then in your ingratitude, while Ravenna, decked with your honours, shall boast herself to the generations to come!"

Boccaccio was a true prophet. Five times the Florentines begged Ravenna to return to his native city the ashes of their great poet, each time in vain.

The first request was made in 1396, three-quarters of a century after Dante's death. On this occasion it was proposed to erect monuments in the Cathedral of Santa Maria del Fiore to five illustrious citizens of Florence, viz. Accursius the great legist, Dante, Petrarch, Zanobi da Strada, and Boccaccio (the names being mentioned in that order in the official document),[1] and it was resolved to secure if possible their mortal remains, doubtless for honourable interment at the same time. The petition for Dante's remains was refused by the Polenta family, the then lords of Ravenna; and a second request, preferred on similar grounds some thirty years later (1430), was likewise refused.[2]

A third attempt appears to have been made in 1476, when interest was made with the Venetian ambassador (presumably Bernardo Bembo) by Lorenzo de' Medici;[3] but, though the ambassador promised compliance, nothing was done, and the hopes of Florence were once more disappointed.

At the beginning of the sixteenth century a fourth and most determined attempt was made by the Florentines to

---

[1] The text is printed by Del Lungo in *Dell' Esilio di Dante*, pp. 170-5.
[2] See Del Lungo, *op. cit.* pp. 176-7.
[3] See Del Lungo, *op. cit.* pp. 178-9.

get possession of Dante's remains, an attempt which had very remarkable consequences.   From a letter written to Pietro Bembo, secretary to Leo X, in June, 1515, it appears that Leo, who belonged to the Medici family of Florence (he was the son of Lorenzo), and was also by virtue of the league of Cambrai (1509) lord of Ravenna, had granted or promised to the Florentines permission to remove the poet's remains from Ravenna.   Four years later (in 1519) a formal memorial[1] was presented to Leo by the Medicean Academy, urging that the removal should be carried out, among the signatories being one of the Portinari, a descendant of the family to which Beatrice belonged.   This memorial was endorsed by the great sculptor, Michel Angelo, who expressed his willingness to design and himself execute a fitting sepulchre.   Leo granted the request of the Academicians, and forthwith a mission was despatched to Ravenna to bring back Dante's bones to Florence.   But meanwhile the custodians of the poet's remains had taken the alarm, and when the tomb was opened by the Florentine envoys nothing was to be seen but some fragments of bone and a few withered laurel leaves, the relics no doubt of the poet's crown which was laid upon the bier at the time of burial.   In an account of the proceedings submitted to Leo the following " explanation " was offered of the disappearance of the remains : " The much wished-for translation of Dante's remains did not take place, inasmuch as the two delegates of the Academy who were sent for the purpose found Dante neither in soul nor in body ; and it is supposed that, as in his lifetime he journeyed in soul and in body through Hell, Purgatory, and Paradise, so in death he must have been received, body and soul, into one of those realms ".[2]

[1] The text is printed by Del Lungo, *op. cit.* pp. 183-8.
[2] See Corrado Ricci, *L' Ultimo Rifugio di Dante*, p. 339.

There is little doubt that Dante's bones, which were still intact in 1483 when Bernardo Bembo restored the tomb, were secretly removed by the Franciscans in charge, between 1515 and 1519, the period when the question of their translation to Florence was being agitated by the Medicean Academy, armed with the permission of Leo X.

The secret of their disappearance was well kept in Ravenna. Two hundred and sixty years later (in 1780) the tomb was once more restored, and, at the inauguration by Cardinal Valenti Gonzaga, it was opened for the purpose of verifying the remains. The official account of the proceeding was couched in vague terms, which were obviously intended to conceal the fact that the tomb was found to be empty. An unofficial account, however, in the shape of an entry by one of the Franciscan monks in his missal, which has been preserved at Ravenna, contains the bald statement that "Dante's sarcophagus was opened and nothing was found inside, whereupon it was sealed up again with the Cardinal's seal, and silence was observed as to the whole matter, thus leaving the old opinion (as to the presence of the remains) undisturbed".[1]

The secret of the removal of the remains was still preserved from the public, but that it was known to a select few is evident from the fact that sixty years after the above incident Filippo Mordani, in his memoir of Dionigi Strocchi, records that the latter said to him on 1 July, 1841: "I wish to tell you something, now that we are alone. The tomb of Dante is empty; the bones are no longer there. This was told me by your Archbishop, Mgr. Codronchi. But I pray you not to breathe a word of it, for it must remain a secret."[2]

At last, when preparations were being made throughout Italy for the celebration of the sixth centenary of Dante's

---

[1] See Ricci, *op. cit.* p. 346.   [2] See Ricci, *op. cit.* p. 347.

CHEST IN WHICH DANTE'S REMAINS WERE DISCOVERED AT RAVENNA IN 1 8 6 5

birth, in 1865, the Florentines once more petitioned for the return of Dante's remains to his native city. For the fifth and last time the request was refused, the Municipality of Ravenna claiming in their reply "that the deposit of the sacred bones of Dante Alighieri in Ravenna could no longer, in view of the happily changed conditions of Italy, be regarded as a perpetuation of his exile, inasmuch as all the cities of Italy were now united together by a lasting bond under one and the same government".[1]

Whether the Municipality, when they returned this answer, were aware that "the sacred bones" of Dante no longer reposed in the tomb which was supposed to contain them, does not appear. At any rate the secret of the empty tomb could not much longer be kept from the world at large, for the opening of the tomb and the identification of the poet's remains was part of the programme of the sexcentenary celebration. Preparations for this ceremony were already in progress when the startling announcement was made that a wooden coffin containing the actual bones of Dante had been accidentally discovered bricked up in a cavity in a neighbouring wall.

The story of this remarkable discovery is as follows. In the course of some operations in the Braccioforte Chapel, adjoining the tomb, in connection with the coming celebration, it became necessary to introduce a pump for the purpose of drawing off an accumulation of water. In order to give room for the pump-handle to work, it was decided to make a cavity in an old wall at the spot where the pump was to be fixed. While the mason was at work with his pick removing the stones, he suddenly struck upon something wooden, which gave back a hollow sound. Curious to find out what this might be, he carefully removed the remaining stones, and to his great surprise came upon a

[1] The correspondence is printed by Del Lungo, *op. cit.* pp. 195-200.

wooden chest or coffin. On lifting the chest one of the planks fell out and revealed a human skeleton, which on a closer inspection proved to be that of Dante, the identity of the remains being established beyond doubt by the discovery of two inscriptions on the chest. One of these, written in ink on the bottom plank, was: *Dantis ossa denuper revisa die* 3 *Junii* 1677.[1] The other, written on the lid of the chest, ran : *Dantis ossa a me Fre Antonio Santi hic posita Ano* 1677 *die* 18 *Octobris*.[2]

The precious relics were at once carefully removed and deposited in the adjoining mausoleum. The news of the discovery meanwhile spread rapidly through the city. The authorities, accompanied by notaries, arrived in haste, and in their presence an official account was drawn up, recording the facts of the discovery, and the result of a professional examination of the skeleton, which, with the exception of a few missing bones, was found to be intact.

The excitement amongst the populace was intense, and the crowd could with difficulty be prevented from breaking in. After this discovery the next step, in order to remove all possible doubt, was to open the sarcophagus in which Dante's remains had originally been deposited by Guido da Polenta in 1321, and in which they were supposed by all, except the few who had been in the secret, to have been left undisturbed ever since. It was an anxious moment for the authorities, who would have been terribly embarrassed if a second skeleton had been discovered— Dante could not have had two skeletons ! An account of the proceedings, furnished by an eye-witness, was given by Dr. Moore in the *English Historical Review* in October, 1888.

[1] " Dante's bones revisited anew on 3 June, 1677."
[2] " Dante's bones, placed here by me, Friar Antonio Santi, on 18 October 1677 " (see Ricci, *op. cit.* pp. 348-9).

" The writer," he says, " met, a few years ago, one who was present on this most interesting occasion, and who had carried away, and still preserved as a relic, a small portion of the precious dust which was found at the bottom of the tomb. This examination took place on 7 June, 1865, and the tomb was then *found to be empty*, with the exception of a little earthy or dusty substance, and a few bones corresponding with most of those missing in the chest recently discovered, and these were certified by the surgeon present to belong undoubtedly to the same skeleton. There were found in it, also, a few withered laurel leaves, which possess a special interest in reference to the description of Dante's burial.[1] . . . It contained, further, some broken fragments of Greek marble, of the same material as the sarcophagus itself. These were soon found to proceed from a rude hole which had been knocked through the sarcophagus itself at the back, precisely at the part accessible only from the inside of the monastery, through which, beyond all doubt, the removal of the bones had been effected. This hole had been stopped up with bricks and cement, and then plastered over outside so as to leave no mark."

The reason for the violation of Dante's tomb and for the secret removal of his remains by the Franciscans of the adjoining monastery was, it can hardly be doubted, the alarm created by the news that permission had been granted for the transference of the remains to Florence by Pope Leo X in 1515. The precious relics must have been secreted in the monastery for a hundred and fifty years and more before they were deposited in the cavity where they were found in 1865.

---

[1] It is evident from this account that the contents of the sarcophagus had not been disturbed since it was opened, three hundred and fifty years before, by the envoys of the Medicean Academy, who found that Dante's remains had been removed. See above, p. 113.

Having thus been satisfactorily verified, Dante's skeleton was put together and laid on white velvet under a glass case, which was exhibited during the three days of 24, 25, and 26 June, in the Braccioforte Chapel. Here the remains were reverently visited by thousands of visitors from every part of Italy. " The old and the infirm were supported through the crowd, and children, too young to be conscious of what they saw, were taken up to the crystal coffin, in order that in after years they might say that they also had gazed on Dante." [1]

On 26 June the bones were enclosed in a double coffin of walnut and lead, and then solemnly consigned once more to the original sarcophagus, in which they had first been laid at the time of the poet's death, and there they now rest, safe in the custody of the faithful citizens of Ravenna, who have been true to their charge for nearly 600 years. [2]

---

[1] *Dante at Ravenna*, by C. M. Phillimore, whose work is more or less of a compilation from *L' Ultimo Rifugio di Dante Alighieri* (Milano, 1891) by Corrado Ricci. From the latter is derived for the most part the information given above as to the fate of Dante's remains.

[2] A cast of the skeleton as it lay in state, and the wooden coffin in which the remains were placed in 1677, and in which they were discovered in 1865, are preserved in the Biblioteca Nazionale at Ravenna.

PORTRAIT OF DANTE
From Codex 1040 in the Riccardi Library at Florence

PART IV

CHARACTERISTICS OF DANTE

CHAPTER I

Boccaccio's account of Dante's person and character—His love of fame
—His failings—Account of him by his contemporary, Giovanni Villani.

IN his *Life of Dante* Boccaccio gives the following description of Dante's person and character, which was derived no doubt in part from the recollections of those who had been personally acquainted with the poet at Ravenna. Boccaccio paid several visits to Ravenna, the first of which took place in 1346, just five-and-twenty years after Dante's death, when there can have been little difficulty in collecting information from contemporaries of Dante who had frequented his society, chief among whom was Piero di Giardino, who, as we have already seen, conversed with Dante on his deathbed.[1]

"Our poet," says Boccaccio, "was of middle height, and after he had reached mature years he walked with somewhat of a stoop; his gait was grave and sedate; and he was ever clothed in most seemly garments, his dress being suited to the ripeness of his years. His face was long, his nose aquiline, his eyes rather large than small, his jaws heavy, with the under lip projecting beyond the upper. His complexion was dark, and his hair and beard

[1] See above, p. 103 note.

thick, black, and crisp ; and his countenance always sad
and thoughtful.   Whence it happened one day in Verona
(the fame of his writings having by that time been spread
abroad everywhere, and especially of that part of his
Commedia to which he gave the title of Hell, and he himself being known by sight to many men and women), that
as he passed before a doorway where several women were
sitting, one of them said to the others in a low voice, but
not so low but that she was plainly heard by him and by
those with him, 'Do you see the man who goes down to
Hell, and returns at his pleasure, and brings back news
of those who are below?'   To which one of the others
answered in all simplicity : 'Indeed, what you say must
be true ; don't you see how his beard is crisped and his
colour darkened by the heat and smoke down below?'
Dante, hearing these words behind him, and perceiving
that they were spoken by the women in perfect good
faith, was not ill pleased that they should have such an
opinion of him, and smiling a little passed on his way.

   " In his manners, whether in public or in private, he was
wonderfully composed and restrained, and in all his ways
he was more courteous and civil than any one else.   In
food and drink he was very moderate, both in partaking
of them at the regular hours, and in never indulging to
excess; nor did he ever particularly care for one thing
more than for another.   He commended delicate dishes,
but for the most part lived on plain fare ; condemning in
no measured terms those who study much to have choice
dainties, and to have them prepared with all possible care,
—declaring that such people do not eat in order to live,
but live in order to eat.

   "No man was more wakeful than he, whether in his
studies or in anything which gave him anxious thought,
to such an extent that many a time his household and his

wife used to be vexed at it, until, growing accustomed to his ways, they came to take no notice of it.   He rarely spoke, save when spoken to, and that with deliberation and in tones suited to the subject of his discourse.   Nevertheless, when occasion demanded, he was most eloquent and fluent, with an excellent and ready delivery.

"In his youth he took the greatest pleasure in music and singing, and was on friendly and familiar terms with all the best singers and musicians of the time.   And his love for music led him to compose many things, which he had set by them to pleasing and masterly accompaniments. How ardently he was devoted to love has already been shown; and it is firmly believed by all that it was this love which moved his genius to composition in the vulgar tongue, at first in the way of imitation; afterwards through his desire to express his emotions in more permanent shape, and for the sake of renown, he assiduously practised himself therein, and not only surpassed all his contemporaries, but also so illustrated and beautified the language that he made many then, and will make many others hereafter, eager to become skilled in their own tongue.

"He delighted also in solitude, holding himself aloof from other people, in order that his meditations might not be interrupted; and if while he was in company any thought occurred to him which pleased him well, however much he might be questioned about any other matter, he would make no reply to his questioner until he had either made sure of his idea or had rejected it—a thing which happened to him many a time when questions were put to him at table, or by his companions on a journey, or elsewhere.

"In his studies he was most diligent, and while he was occupied with them no news that he might chance to hear could take him away from them.   And it is related by

certain credible witnesses, with regard to his giving himself up wholly to what pleased him, that on one of the
occasions when he was in Siena, he chanced to be at an
apothecary's shop, where a book was brought to him which
had been previously promised him, this book being one
of much reputation among persons of worth, and having
never yet been seen by him. As he happened to be un-
able to take it elsewhere, he leant over on to the bench
in front of the apothecary's shop, and there, placing the
book before him, began most eagerly to examine it. Soon
afterwards, in that same quarter, close to where he was,
on the occasion of some general festival a great tourna-
ment took place among the noble youths of Siena, accompanied, as is usually the case on such occasions, with
a great deal of noise caused by the various instruments
and shouts of applause from the bystanders; yet, in spite
of all this, and of many other things likely to attract the
attention, such as fair ladies dancing, and youths' sports
of all kinds, he was never seen to stir from his place, nor
so much as to raise his eyes from his book. Indeed,
although it was about noon when he took his stand there,
it was not until past the hour of vespers when, having
examined the book thoroughly and taken a general
survey of its contents, he got up to leave it. He afterwards declared to several persons, who asked him how he
could refrain from looking on at such a splendid festival
as had taken place in his presence, that he had been
wholly unaware of it—an answer which made his
questioners wonder even more than they had done at
first.

"Dante, moreover, was of marvellous capacity, with a
most retentive memory, and keen intellect, insomuch that
when he was in Paris, and in a disputation held in the
theological schools, fourteen questions had been pro-

pounded by divers scholars on divers subjects, he without hesitation took them up and went over them in the order in which they had been given, together with the arguments for and against, adduced by the opponents ; and then, preserving the same order, he subtly replied to and refuted the arguments on the other side—which thing was regarded as little short of a miracle by those who were present.

" He was likewise of the most lofty genius and of subtle invention, as is made manifest by his works, to such as understand, far more clearly than my writing could express. He was very greedy of honour and glory, more so perhaps than beseemed his fame and virtue. Yet, what life is so humble as not to be touched by the sweetness of glory? And it was by reason of this desire, I think, that he loved poetry more than any other pursuit, perceiving that although philosophy surpasses all things else in nobility, yet her excellence can be communicated only to the few, and those who win fame thereby in the world are many ; whereas poetry is less abstruse and more pleasing to every one, and poets are exceeding few. Therefore, hoping by her means to attain to the unusual and glorious honour of the laurel crown, he devoted himself wholly to the study and composition of poetry. And of a surety his desire would have been fulfilled had Fortune favoured him so far as to allow him ever to return to Florence, where alone at the font of San Giovanni, he was willing to receive the crown ; to the end that in the same place where he had received his first name in baptism, there too he might receive the second by being crowned. But it so came about that although his sufficiency was great, and such that wherever he had chosen he might have received the laurel, yet, in expectation of that return which was destined never to take place, he would not consent to accept it anywhere else than in Florence; and so he died without the much coveted honour. . . .

"Our poet, further, was of a very lofty and scornful disposition, insomuch that when a certain friend of his, in answer to his entreaties to that effect, sought to bring about his return to Florence, which he most ardently longed for above all things else, and could find no other way with those who then had the government of the Republic in their hands, save this one only : that he should be kept in prison for a certain space, and afterwards on some solemn public occasion should be presented, as an act of mercy, in our principal church, being thereby restored to liberty and released from every sentence previously passed upon him—such a thing, in his opinion, being fitting to be practised only in the case of abject and infamous men and of no others, he, notwithstanding his great longing, chose rather to remain in exile than by such means to return to his home.

"Likewise Dante thought no little of himself, rating his own worth no less highly, according to the reports of his contemporaries, than was his actual due. Which thing was apparent on one occasion among others to a remarkable degree at the time when he and his party were at the head of affairs in the Republic; for, inasmuch as those who were out of power had, through the mediation of Pope Boniface VIII, invited a brother or relation of Philip, the then King of France, whose name was Charles, to come and set to rights the affairs of our city, all the chiefs of the party with which Dante was allied, met together in council to make provision concerning this matter ; and there among other things they resolved to send an embassy to the Pope, who was then at Rome, in order to induce the Pope to oppose the coming of the

said Charles, or to arrange for him to come in agreement
with the said party which was in power.   And when it
came to be debated who should be at the head of the proposed embassy, it was agreed by all that it should be
Dante.   To which request Dante, after a brief hesitation,
said: 'If I go, who remains?   If I remain, who goes?'[1]
As though he alone of them all was of any consequence,
or gave any consequence to the rest.   This saying was
understood and taken note of.

   "But, apart from all this, this worthy man in all his ad-
versities showed the greatest fortitude.   Only in one thing
he was, I know not whether I should say impatient or passionate, namely, he was more given to faction after his
exile than was becoming to a man of his parts, and more
than he would have had it believed of him by others.
And what I most blush for on account of his memory is
that in Romagna it is perfectly notorious to every one
that any feeble woman or little child who had spoken on
party matters, and found fault with the Ghibelline party
to which he belonged, would have stirred him to such a
pitch of madness that he would have thrown stones at
them if they had not held their peace; and this passion he
retained to the day of his death.   And assuredly I blush
to be obliged to blot the fame of so great a man with any
defect; but the manner in which I ordered my matter at
the outset in some sort demands it, for if I were to be

   [1] This anecdote was quoted in a letter written in 1624 by Lord Keeper
Williams to the Duke of Buckingham, in which he tried to persuade the
Duke to accept the office of Lord Steward.   "I will trouble your grace,"
he writes, "with a tale of *Dante*, the first *Italian* Poet of Note : who,
being a great and wealthy Man in Florence, and his Opinion demanded
who should be sent Embassador to the Pope ? made this Answer, that he
knew not who ; *Si jo vo, chi sta, si jo sto, chi va ;* If I go, I know not who
shall stay at Home ; If I stay, I know not who can perform this Employ-
ment " (see Paget Toynbee, *Dante in English Literature*, vol. i. p. 117).

silent regarding things not to his credit, I should shake the faith of my readers in the things already related which are to his credit. Therefore to him himself I make my excuse, who maybe from some lofty region of heaven looks down with scornful eye upon me as I write.

"Amid all the virtue and all the learning which has been shown above to have been possessed by this wondrous poet, the vice of lustfulness found no small place, and that not only in the years of his youth, but also in the years of his maturity;[1] the which vice, though it be natural and common, yet cannot be worthily excused. Nevertheless bearing in mind what is written of David, and Solomon, and of many others, our poet may be allowed to pass by, not excused, but accused with less severity than if he had been alone in this failing."[2]

With this account of Dante by Boccaccio it is interesting to compare the brief description of his personal characteristics furnished by his contemporary and neighbour in Florence, the chronicler Giovanni Villani, who, if his nephew Filippo is to be believed, was also a personal friend of Dante.[3]

"This Dante," he says, "was an honourable and ancient citizen of Florence, belonging to the Porta San Piero, and our neighbour. . . . This man was a great scholar in almost every branch of learning, although he was a layman : he was a great poet and philosopher, and a perfect rhetorician both in prose and verse, and in public debate he was a very noble speaker ; in rime he was supreme, with the most polished and beautiful style that ever had been in our language, up to his time and since. . . .

---

[1] There are several passages in the *Divina Commedia* which seem to hint at Dante's consciousness of this failing (see above, p. 71).

[2] *Vita di Dante*, ed. Macrì-Leone, §§ 8, 12, pp. 43-7, 59-62.

[3] See above, p. 37 note.

This Dante, on account of his great learning, was somewhat haughty and reserved and scornful, and after the
manner of a philosopher little gracious, not adapting himself to the conversation of the unlearned.   But on account
of his other virtues and knowledge and worth, it seems
right to perpetuate the memory of so great a citizen in
this our chronicle, albeit that his noble works left to us in
writing are the true testimony to his fame and a lasting
honour to our city." [1]

[1] Bk. ix. ch. 136.

CHAPTER II

FROM the written descriptions of Dante the transition is natural to the subject of the actual representation of the poet's face, depicted during his lifetime.

Of portraits from the life, so far as is known, there is one only, that most beautiful of all the portraits of Dante, painted by Giotto, the great Florentine artist, whose fame is inseparably connected with that of the great Florentine poet. An interesting account of this portrait, of its disappearance and rediscovery, together with a comparison of it with the mask supposed to have been modelled from Dante's face after death, is given by Professor Charles Eliot Norton, in his work *On the Original Portraits of Dante*, which was published in 1865 in honour of the six-hundredth anniversary of the poet's birth. After quoting Boccaccio's description of Dante's physiognomy, which has already been given above, Professor Norton writes :-

" Such was Dante as he appeared in his later years to those from whose recollections of him Boccaccio drew this description. But Boccaccio, had he chosen so to do, might have drawn another portrait of Dante, not the author of the *Divine Comedy*, but the author of the *New Life*. The likeness of the youthful Dante was familiar

PORTRAIT OF DANTE BY GIOTTO IN THE BARGELLO AT FLORENCE
From a drawing by Seymour Kirkup

to those Florentines who had never looked on the presence of their greatest citizen.

" On the altar-wall of the chapel of the Palace of the Podestà (now the Bargello) Giotto painted a grand religious composition, in which, after the fashion of the times, he exalted the glory of Florence by the introduction of some of her most famous citizens into the assembly of the blessed in Paradise. ' The head of Christ, full of dignity, appears above, and lower down, the escutcheon of Florence, supported by angels, with two rows of saints, male and female, attendant to the right and left, in front of whom stand a company of the magnates of the city, headed by two crowned personages, close to one of whom, to the right, stands Dante, a pomegranate in his hand, and wearing the graceful falling cap of the day.' [1]   The date when this picture was painted is uncertain, but Giotto represented his friend in it as a youth, such as he may have been in the first flush of early fame, at the season of the beginning of their memorable friendship.

" Of all the portraits of the revival of Art, there is none comparable in interest to this likeness of the supreme poet by the supreme artist of mediæval Europe.   It was due to no accident of fortune that these men were contemporaries and of the same country ; but it was a fortunate and delightful incident, that they were so brought together by sympathy of genius and by favouring circumstances as to become friends, to love and honour each other in life, and to celebrate each other through all time in their respective works.[2]   The story of their friendship is known only in its outline, but that it began when they were young

[1] Lord Lindsay's *History of Christian Art*, vol. ii. p. 174.

[2] Dante mentions Giotto in the *Commedia* : " Cimabue thought to hold the field in painting, and now Giotto has the cry, so that the fame of the other is obscured " (*Purg.* xi. 94-6).

is certain, and that it lasted till death divided them is a tradition which finds ready acceptance.

"It was probably between 1290 and 1300, when Giotto was just rising to unrivalled fame, that this painting was executed.[1]   There is no contemporary record of it, the earliest known reference to it being that by Filippo Villani,[2] who died about 1404.   Giannozzo Manetti, who

[1] Lord Lindsay says: "There can be little doubt, from the prominent position assigned Dante in this composition, as well as from his personal appearance, that this fresco was painted in, or immediately after, the year 1300, when he was one of the Priors of the Republic, and in the thirty-fifth year of his age". There is, however, a difficulty in accepting this early date for Giotto's portrait of Dante, in that in 1332 the Palazzo del Podestà was seriously damaged by fire, and had to be partially rebuilt, as is recorded by Villani: "a dì 28 di Febbraio s' apprese fuoco nel palagio del comune ove abita la podestà, e arse tutto il tetto del vecchio palazzo e le due parti del nuovo dalle prime volte in su.   Per la qual cosa s' ordinò per lo comune che si rifacesse tutto in volte infino a' tetti." (bk. x. ch. 182).   It is urged, therefore, that even if the fire did not destroy the fresco, it would almost certainly have left traces of damage.   Consequently some recent critics have argued that Giotto must have painted the fresco later than 1331, after the building had been repaired.   In this case the portraits of Dante and of those associated with him in the fresco must have been painted from memory.   But it is quite possible that the fresco may have been painted in 1300 and that any damage caused by the fire of 1332 may have been repaired either by Giotto himself or by one of his pupils.

[2] In the notice of Giotto in his *Liber de Civitatis Florentiae Famosis Civibus:* "Pinxit speculorum suffragio semetipsum, sibique contemporaneum Dantem, in tabula altaris Capellae Palatii Potestatis". A still earlier reference, however, occurs (as is supposed) in the following poem of Antonio Pucci, the author of the *Centiloquio,* who died c. 1390:—

> Questi che veste di color sanguigno,
>   Posto seguente alle merite sante,
>   Dipinse Giotto in figura di Dante,
> Che di parole fe' sì bell' ordigno.
> E come par nell' abito benigno,
>   Così nel mondo fu con tutte quante
>   Quelle virtù ch' onoran chi davante
> Le porta con effetto nello scrigno.
> Diritto paragon fu di sentenze:

died in 1459, also mentions it;[1] and Vasari, in his *Life of Giotto*, published in 1550, says that Giotto 'became so good an imitator of nature, that he altogether discarded the stiff Greek manner, and revived the modern and good art of painting, introducing exact drawing from nature of living persons, which for more than two hundred years had not been practised, or if indeed any one had tried it, he had not succeeded very happily, nor anything like so well as Giotto. And he portrayed among other persons, as may even now be seen, in the chapel of the Palace of the Podestà in Florence, Dante Alighieri, his contemporary and greatest friend, who was not less famous a poet than Giotto was painter in those days. . . . In the same chapel is the portrait by the same hand of Ser Brunetto Latini, the master of Dante, and of Messer Corso Donati, a great citizen of those times.'

"One might have supposed that such a picture as this would have been among the most carefully protected and jealously prized treasures of Florence. But such was not the case. The shameful neglect of many of the best and most interesting works of the earlier period of Art, which accompanied and was one of the symptoms of the moral

> Col braccio manco avvinchia la Scrittura,
> Perchè signoreggiò molte scienze.
> E 'l suo parlar fu con tanta misura,
> Chè 'ncoronò la città di Firenze
> Di pregio, ond' ancor fama le dura.
> Perfetto di fattezze è qui dipinto,
> Com' a sua vita fu di carne cinto.

(*Rime di Trecentisti Minori*, a cura di G. Volpi, 1907, pp. 105-6.)

[1] In his *Vita Dantis*: "Ejus effigies in Basilica Sanctae Crucis, et in Capella Praetoris Urbani utrobique in parietibus extat ea forma, qua revera in vita fuit a Giotto quodam optimo ejus temporis pictore egregie depicta". The portrait is mentioned also by Landino in the *Vita di Dante* prefixed to his commentary on the *Divina Commedia* (1481): "La sua effigie resta ancora di mano di Giotto in Santa Croce, e nella capella del Podestà".

and political decline of Italy during the sixteenth and seventeenth centuries, extended to this as to other of the noblest paintings of Giotto. Florence, in losing consciousness of present worth, lost care for the memorials of her past honour, dignity, and distinction. The Palace of the Podestà, no longer needed for the dwelling of the chief magistrate of a free city, was turned into a jail for common criminals, and what had once been its beautiful and sacred chapel was occupied as a larder or storeroom.[1] The walls, adorned with paintings more precious than gold, were covered with whitewash, and the fresco of Giotto was swept over by the brush of the plasterer. It was not only thus hidden from the sight of those unworthy indeed to behold it, but it almost disappeared from memory also; and from the time of Vasari down to that of Moreni, a Florentine antiquary, in the early part of the present century,[2] hardly a mention of it occurs. In a note found among his papers, Moreni laments that he had spent two years of his life in unavailing efforts to recover the portrait of Dante, and the other portions of the fresco of Giotto in the Bargello, mentioned by Vasari; that others before him had made a like effort, and had failed in like manner; and that he hoped that better times would come, in which this painting, of such historic and artistic interest, would again be sought for, and at length recovered. Stimulated by these words, three gentlemen, one an American, Mr. Richard Henry Wilde, one an Englishman, Mr. Seymour Kirkup, and one an Italian, Signor G. Aubrey Bezzi, all scholars devoted to the study of Dante,

[1] F. J. Bunbury, writing in 1852, says: "The Bargello of Florence, which at present contains the prisons, and some public offices of the Government, was once the Palace of the Podestà, . . . but for centuries the chamber [in which was the portrait of Dante] had been coated with white-wash, divided into two storeys, and partitioned for prisoners' cells." The whole Bargello building is now used as a museum.

[2] Norton was writing in 1865.

undertook new researches, in 1840, and, after many hindrances on the part of the Government,[1] which were at length successfully overcome, the work of removing the crust of plaster from the walls of the ancient chapel was entrusted to the Florentine painter, Marini.   This new and well-directed search did not fail.   After some months' labour the fresco was found,[2] almost uninjured, under the whitewash that had protected while concealing it, and at length the likeness of Dante was uncovered.[3]

"' But,' says Mr. Kirkup, in a letter [4] published in the *Spectator* (London), 11 May, 1850, 'the eye of the beautiful profile was wanting.   There was a hole an inch deep, or an inch and a half.   Marini said it was a nail.   It did seem precisely the damage of a nail drawn out.   Afterwards . . . Marini filled the hole and made a new eye, too little and ill designed, and then he retouched the whole face and clothes, to the great damage of the expression and character.[5]   The likeness of the face,[6] and the three colours in which Dante was dressed, the same with those of Beatrice, those of young Italy, white, green, and red, stand no more; the green is turned to chocolate colour; moreover, the form of the cap is lost and confounded.

[1] Of the Grand Duke.   [2] 21 July, 1840.

[3] " The enthusiasm of the Florentines," says Lord Lindsay, " on the announcement of the discovery, resembled that of their ancestors when Borgo Allegri received its name from their rejoicings in sympathy with Cimabue. ' L' abbiamo il nostro poeta ! ' was the universal cry, and for days afterwards the Bargello was thronged with a continuous succession of pilgrim visitors."

[4] This letter was written originally by Kirkup in Italian—it was a (not very accurate) translation which was published in the *Spectator*. G. B. Cavalcaselle printed a corrected translation in the same paper, on 13 July.

[5] In Cavalcaselle's version : " to the great damage of the expression as well as the character and costume".

[6] Cavalcaselle : " The likeness of the face *is changed ;* and the three colours . . . are no longer there ".

"'I desired to make a drawing. . . . It was denied to me. . . . But I obtained the means to be shut up in the prison for a morning; and not only did I make a drawing,[1] but a tracing also, and with the two I then made a fac-simile sufficiently careful. Luckily it was before the *rifacimento.*'

"This facsimile afterwards passed into the hands of Lord Vernon, well known for his interest in all Dantesque studies, and by his permission it has been admirably re-produced in chromo-lithography under the auspices of the Arundel Society.[2] The reproduction is entirely satisfactory

[1] The original drawing, made on the inside of the vellum cover of a copy of the 1531 edition of the *Convivio*, was acquired by Colonel W. J. Gillum, at the sale of Kirkup's library at Sotheby's in December, 1871, and was recently (April, 1908) presented by him to the Museo Nazionale (in the Bargello) at Florence. Kirkup gave the following interesting account to a friend (Mrs. Gillum, by whom it was kindly communicated to the writer), in Florence in 1873 of how he managed to get the drawing made. "I went to the Bargello Chapel, along with others of the public, and I had that book (the *Convivio*) and some colours in my pocket. For a while I man-aged to draw, holding the book within my wide felt hat, but by and by the man in charge of the room came up to me and said: 'You know, Signor Barone, the Grand Duke does not allow any copying'. I answered: 'I am making some notes,' and went on with the work. After a time the man came again, and said : ' It is late, Signor Barone, time for me to lock up and go to my dinner. Every one but yourself is gone.'—'You can go. You may lock me in to finish my notes.' As soon as I was alone, I wheeled up the stage which had been left by the workmen who removed the plaster, mounted it, and took a tracing on thin paper, so as to obtain the exact outline and precise size. I then replaced the stage, and took up my drawing again quite comfortably. So my 'notes' were finished before my gaoler returned from dinner." [Kirkup's description of himself as "Barone " in 1840 is an anachronism. He assumed the title (through a misunderstanding) after being created by King Victor Emmanuel, on the restoration of the Italian kingdom, a "Cavaliere di SS. Maurizio e Lazzaro".]

[2] The tracing which Kirkup made at the same time as the drawing was given by him to his friend Gabriele Rossetti, who handed it on to his son, Dante Gabriel Rossetti. It was sold after the death of the latter in 1882.

as a presentation of the authentic portrait of the youthful Dante, in the state in which it was when Mr. Kirkup was so fortunate as to gain admission to it.[1]

"This portrait by Giotto is the only likeness of Dante known to have been made of the poet during his life, and is of inestimable value on this account. But there exists also a mask, concerning which there is a tradition that it was taken from the face of the dead poet, and which, if its genuineness could be established, would not be of inferior interest to the early portrait. But there is no trustworthy historic testimony concerning it, and its authority as a likeness depends upon the evidence of truth which its own character affords. On the very threshold of the inquiry concerning it, we are met with the doubt whether the art of taking casts was practised at the time of Dante's death. In his *Life of Andrea del Verrocchio*, Vasari says that this art began to come into use in his time, that is, about the middle of the fifteenth century; and Bottari refers to the likeness of Brunelleschi, who died in 1446, which was taken in this manner, and was preserved in the Office of the Works of the Cathedral at Florence. It is not impossible that so simple an art may have been sometimes practised at an earlier period;[2] and if so, there is no inherent improbability in the supposition that Guido Novello,

---

[1] Interesting details of the discovery of the fresco and of the making of the drawing of the portrait of Dante are given in three letters from Kirkup to Gabriele Rossetti, which are printed in *Gabriele Rossetti: A Versified Autobiography*, edited by W. M. Rossetti, 1901. (See *Appendix C*.)

[2] As a matter of fact the art of taking casts from the human face was known to the ancients. It was at least 300 years old in the days of Pliny, by whom reference is made to it in his *Historia Naturalis*: "Hominis imaginem gypso e facie ipsa primus omnium expressit, ceraque in eam formam gypsi infusa emendare instituit Lysistratus Sicyonius"; i.e. Lysistratus of Sicyon (*c.* 320 B.C.) was the first who took a cast of the human face in plaster, and produced copies from this mould by pouring into it melted wax (xxxv. § 44).

the friend and protector of Dante at Ravenna, may, at the time of the poet's death, have had a mask taken to serve as a model for the head of a statue intended to form part of the monument which he proposed to erect in honour of Dante.   And it may further be supposed that, this design failing, owing to the fall of Guido from power before its accomplishment, the mask may have been preserved at Ravenna, till we first catch a trace of it nearly three centuries later.

"There is in the Magliabecchiana Library at Florence an autograph manuscript by Giovanni Cinelli, a Florentine antiquary who died in 1706, entitled *La Toscana letterata, ovvero Istoria degli Scrittori Fiorentini*, which contains a life of Dante.   In the course of the biography [1] Cinelli states that the Archbishop of Ravenna caused the head of the poet which had adorned his sepulchre to be taken therefrom, and that it came into the possession of the famous sculptor, Gian Bologna, who left it at his death, in 1608, to his pupil Pietro Tacca. 'One day Tacca showed it, with other curiosities, to the Duchess Sforza, who, having wrapped it in a scarf of green cloth, carried it away, and God knows into whose hands the precious object has fallen, or where it is to be found. . . . On account of its singular beauty, it had often been drawn by the scholars of Tacca.' It has been supposed that this head was the original mask from which the casts now existing are derived.   Mr. Seymour Kirkup, in a note on this passage from Cinelli, says that 'there are three masks of Dante at Florence, all of which have been judged by the first Roman and Florentine sculptors to have been taken from life [that is, from the face after death]—the

---

[1] An extract from this biography, along with some interesting remarks by Kirkup, is given in a letter from the latter to Charles Lyell from Florence, 27 February, 1842 (printed in *The Poems of the Vita Nuova and Convito of Dante*, translated by Charles Lyell, 1842, pp. xvii-xix).

MASK OF DANTE IN THE UFFIZI AT FLORENCE
Formerly in possession of the Marchese Torrigiani

slight differences noticeable between them being such as might occur in casts made from the original mask '.   One of these casts was given to Mr. Kirkup by the sculptor Bartolini, another belonged to the late sculptor, Professor Ricci,[1] and the third is in the possession of the Marchese Torrigiani.[2]

" In the absence of historical evidence in regard to this mask, some support is given to the belief in its genuineness by the fact that it appears to be the type of the greater number of the portraits of Dante executed from the fourteenth to the sixteenth century, and was adopted by Raffaelle as the original from which he drew the likeness which has done most to make the features of the poet familiar to the world.

" The character of the mask itself affords, however, the only really satisfactory ground for confidence in the truth of the tradition concerning it.   It was plainly taken as a cast from a face after death.[3]   It has none of the characteristics which a fictitious and imaginative representation of the sort would be likely to present.   It bears no trace of being a work of skilful and deceptive art.[4]   The difference between the sides of the face, the slight deflection in the line of the nose,[5] the droop of the corners of the

[1] The mask possessed by Ricci, who made use of it for the purposes of his statue of Dante in Santa Croce in Florence, eventually also passed into the hands of Kirkup, by whom it was presented to the Oxford Dante Society.

[2] This last is now in the Uffizi Gallery at Florence. (See plate opposite.)

[3] This was the opinion also of the eminent surgeon, the late Sir James Paget.

[4] Corrado Ricci, on the other hand, who persistently denies the genuineness of the death-mask, does not hesitate to declare that the trace of the sculptor's tool is everywhere evident ! (see L' *Ultimo Rifugio di Dante*, p. 279).

[5] Sir James Paget pointed out that this depression of the tip of the nose, which one is accustomed to regard as characteristic of Dante's face, was just such as would have been produced by the weight of the plaster in taking the cast.

mouth, and other delicate, but none the less convincing indications, combine to show that it was in all probability taken from nature.   The countenance, moreover, and expression, are worthy of Dante ; no ideal forms could so answer to the face of him who had led a life apart from the world in which he dwelt, and had been conducted by love and faith along hard, painful, and solitary ways, to behold

' L' alto trionfo del regno verace '.[1]

"The mask conforms entirely to the description by Boccaccio of the poet's countenance, save that it is beardless, and this difference is to be accounted for by the fact that to obtain the cast the beard must have been removed.[2]

"The face is one of the most pathetic upon which human eyes ever looked, for it exhibits in its expression the conflict between the strong nature of the man and the hard dealings of fortune,—between the idea of his life and its practical experience.   Strength is the most striking attribute of the countenance, displayed alike in the broad forehead, the masculine nose, the firm lips, the heavy jaw and wide chin ; and this strength, resulting from the main forms of the features, is enforced by the strength of the lines of expression.   The look is grave and stern almost to grimness ; there is a scornful lift to the eyebrow, and a contraction of the forehead as from painful thought ; but obscured under this look, yet not lost, are the marks of tenderness, refinement, and self-mastery, which, in combination with more obvious characteristics, give to the countenance of the dead poet an ineffable dignity and melancholy.   There is neither weakness nor failure here. It is the image of the strong fortress of a strong soul ' buttressed on conscience and impregnable will,' battered by

[1] " The high triumph of the true kingdom " (*Par.* xxx. 98).
[2] That Dante had a beard we know from himself (*Purg.* xxxi. 68).

the blows of enemies without and within, bearing upon its walls the dints of many a siege, but standing firm and un-shaken against all attacks until the warfare was at an end.

"The intrinsic evidence for the truth of this likeness, from its correspondence, not only with the description of the poet, but with the imagination that we form of him from his life and works, is strongly confirmed by a comparison of the mask with the portrait by Giotto. So far as I am aware, this comparison has not hitherto been made in a manner to exhibit effectively the resemblance between the two. A direct comparison between the painting and the mask, owing to the difficulty of reducing the forms of the latter to a plain surface of light and shade, is unsatis-factory. But by taking a photograph from the mask,[1] in the same position as that in which the face is painted by Giotto, and placing it alongside of the facsimile from the painting,[2] a very remarkable similarity becomes at once apparent. In the two accompanying photographs the striking resemblance between them is not to be mistaken. The differences are only such as must exist between the portrait of a man in the freshness of a happy youth, and the portrait of him in his age, after much experience and many trials. Dante was fifty-six years old at the time of his death, when the mask was taken; the portrait by Giotto represents him as not much past twenty. There is an interval of at least thirty years between the two. And what years they had been for him!

"The interest of this comparison lies not only in the mutual support which the portraits afford each other, in the assurance each gives that the other is genuine, but also in their joint illustration of the life and character

[1] A representation of the mask, in two positions, is given on plate op-posite p. 88.

[2] See plate, opposite p. 128.

of Dante.   As Giotto painted him, he is the lover of
Beatrice, the gay companion of princes,[1] the friend of
poets, and himself already the most famous writer of love
verses in Italy.   There is an almost feminine softness in
the lines of the face, with a sweet and serious tenderness
well befitting the lover, and the author of the sonnets and
canzoni which were in a few years to be gathered into the
incomparable record of his *New Life*.   It is the face of
Dante in the May-time of youthful hope, in that serene
season of promise and of joy, which was so soon to reach
its foreordained close in the death of her who had made
life new and beautiful for him, and to the love and honour
of whom he dedicated his soul and gave all his future
years.   It is the same face with that of the mask ; but the
one is the face of a youth, ‘ with all triumphant splendour
on his brow,’ the other of a man, burdened with ‘ the dust
and injury of age ’.   The forms and features are alike,
but as to the later face,

> ‘ That time of year thou mayst in it behold
> When yellow leaves, or none, or few, do hang
> Upon those boughs which shake against the cold,
> Bare ruined choirs, where late the sweet birds sang.’

The face of the youth is grave, as with the shadow of distant sorrow ; the face of the man is solemn, as of one who
had gone

> ‘ Per tutti i cerchi del dolente regno ’.[2]

The one is the young poet of Florence, the other the
supreme poet of the world—

> ‘ Che al divino dall’ umano,
> All’ eterno dal tempo era venuto ’.” [3]

[1] Compare the reference to Charles Martel of Hungary, *Paradiso*, viii.
55-7.

[2] “ Through all the circles of the woeful kingdom ” (*Purg.* vii. 22).

[3] “ Who was come from the human to the divine, from time to eternity ”
(*Par.* xxxi. 37-8).

BRONZE BUST OF DANTE AT NAPLES

From the death-mask described above appears to have been modelled the famous bronze bust of Dante, now in the National Museum at Naples.[1]

Another contemporary artist, besides Giotto, is known to have painted Dante's portrait, but this unfortunately has perished. In his *Life of Dante*, Leonardo Bruni says: "His exact likeness, most excellently drawn from the life, by an accomplished painter of those times, is to be seen in the Church of Santa Croce, about half way up the church on the left side as you go towards the high altar".[2] The painter of this portrait was Taddeo Gaddi,[3] as we learn from Vasari, who in his *Life of Taddeo Gaddi*, speaking of Santa Croce, says: "Below the partition which divides the church, on the left, above the crucifix of Donatello, Taddeo painted in fresco a miracle of St. Francis, how, appearing in the air, he restored to life a child who had been killed by falling from a loggia. In this fresco Taddeo introduced the portraits of his master Giotto, of the poet Dante, and of Guido Cavalcanti, or, as some assert, of himself."[4] This fresco was destroyed by Vasari himself when, in 1566, by order of Cosimo I, he removed the partition on which it was painted.[5]

[1] See plate opposite.

[2] "L' effige sua propria si vede nella chiesa di Santa Croce, quasi al mezzo chiesa dalla mano sinistra andando verso l' altare maggiore, e ritratta al naturale ottimamente per dipintore perfetto di quel tempo" (*Vita di Dante*, ed. Brunone Bianchi, 1883, p. xxii). This portrait cannot have been painted "from the life" in Florence, since Dante left Florence never to return within a year or two of Taddeo Gaddi's birth, who was little more than twenty when Dante died.

[3] c. 1300-1366.

[4] "Sotto il tramezzo che divide la chiesa, a man sinistra sopra il Crocifisso di Donato, dipinse a fresco una storia di San Francesco, d' un miracolo che fece nel risuscitar un putto che era morto cadendo da un verone coll' apparire in aria. Ed in questa storia ritrasse Giotto suo maestro, Dante poeta e Guido Cavalcanti: altri dicono sè stesso" (*Opere di Vasari*, ed. Milanesi, 1878, vol. i. pp. 573-4).

[5] See *Opere di Vasari*, ed. cit., vol. i. p. 574 *n.*, vol. vii. p. 711 *n.*

So-called portraits of Dante in various frescoes and illuminated manuscripts are numerous. The best known of the latter is the one prefixed to Codex 1040 in the Riccardi Library in Florence, which was pronounced by the commission appointed to examine into the question in 1864 to be the most authentic portrait of Dante in existence.[1] This opinion, however, which was disputed at the time, has not by any means met with general acceptance.[2]

[1] See plate, opposite p. 119.

[2] In 1864, in view of the approaching celebration in Florence of the sixth centenary of Dante's birth, the Minister of Public Instruction commissioned Gaetano Milanesi and Luigi Passerini to report upon the most authentic portrait of the poet, as it was proposed to have a medallion executed in commemoration of the centenary. Milanesi and Passerini communicated the results of their invistigations to the Minister in a letter which was published in the *Giornale del Centenario* for 20 July, 1864. After stating their doubts with regard to the Bargello portrait, and disposing of the claims of two other portraits contained in MSS. preserved in Florence, they go on to say: "Very precious on the other hand is the portrait prefixed to Codex 1040 in the Riccardi Library, which contains the minor poems of Dante, together with those of Messer Bindi Bonichi, and which appears from the arms and initials to have belonged to Paolo di Jacopo Giannotti, who was born in 1430. This portrait, which is about half the size of life, is in water-colour, and represents the poet with his characteristic features at the age of rather more than forty. It is free from the exaggeration of later artists, who, by giving undue prominence to the nose and under-lip and chin, make Dante's profile resemble that of a hideous old woman. In our opinion this portrait is to be preferred to any other, especially for the purposes of a medallion."

Cavalcaselle, among other authorities, declined to accept these conclusions.* Checcacci, on the contrary, who carefully compared the Riccardi portrait with a very exact copy of that in the Bargello, asserted that if the difference of age be taken into consideration, the two resemble each other "like two drops of water":—"The Bargello portrait lacks the wrinkles of the other, while the colouring is more fresh, and the prominence of the lower lip is less marked, but the nose, which does not change with advancing years, is identical, as are the shape and colour of the eyes, and the shape of the skull, which may be distinguished in both portraits". He added further that the sculptor Dupré was greatly struck

* See *Giornale del Centenario* for 20 August, 1864.

A very interesting representation of Dante, with his book (the *Divina Commedia*) in his hand, and in the background a view of Florence on one side, and of the three kingdoms of the other world on the other, is placed over the north door in the Cathedral of Florence. This picture was painted in 1466, about 150 years after Dante's death, by Domenico di Michelino, a pupil of Fra Angelico; and though it cannot in any sense claim to be a portrait of Dante it has great value as a characteristic representation of the poet, in the Florentine costume of the day, and crowned with the poet's crown of laurel.[1]

with the Riccardi portrait, which he considered might be the work of Giotto himself, and that he availed himself of it for the medallion which he was commissioned to execute in commemoration of the centenary. (See *Giornale del Centenario* for 10 Sept., 1864.)

[1] See plate, opposite p. 193. This picture was for a long time attributed to Orcagna, until the discovery of documentary evidence in Florence established the fact that it was the work of Domenico di Michelino (1417-1491) (see *Opere di Vasari*, ed. Milanesi, 1878, vol. i. p. 607 *n.*, vol. ii. p. 85 *n.*). The picture attracted the attention of most English travellers in Florence. The first notice of it by an Englishman occurs in the *Epitaphia et Inscriptiones Lugubres* (published in 1554), of William Barker, the translator of Gelli's *Capricci del Bottaio*, who transcribed the Latin inscription ('Qui caelum cecinit, mediumque imumque tribunal,' etc.), on the frame, which was Englished 200 years later (in 1730) by Edward Wright, another English traveller, as follows:—

> " Behold the poet, who in lofty verse
> Heav'n, hell, and purgatory did rehearse ;
> The learned Dante ! whose capacious soul
> Survey'd the universe, and knew the whole.
> To his own Florence he a father prov'd,
> Honour'd for counsel, for religion lov'd.
> Death will not hurt so great a bard as he,
> Who lives in virtue, verse, and effigy."

(See *Dante in English Literature*, vol. i. pp. 41, 216, and index). Another picture of Dante worthy of mention here is the painting by Andrea del Castagno (*c.* 1390-1457) of the poet in a red robe, and red hood bordered with fur, with his book in his right hand, which (now in the Museo Nazionale at Florence) originally formed one of a series of portraits (including Farinata degli Uberti, Petrarch, and Boccaccio) executed for the Villa di Legnaia dei Pandolfini (see *Opere di Vasari*, ed. cit., vol. ii. p. 670 *n.*; see also plate, opposite p. 231.

CHAPTER III

Anecdotes of Dante—Dante and Can Grande della Scala—Belacqua and Dante—Sacchetti's stories—Dante and the blacksmith—Dante and the donkey-driver—Dante's creed—Dante and King Robert of Naples—Dante's reply to the bore—Dante and the Doge of Venice—Dante a kleptomaniac—Dante and Cecco d' Ascoli.

MANY anecdotes and traditions concerning Dante have been preserved by various Italian writers, the majority of which are undoubtedly apocryphal. Some of them, however, are worth recording, as representing the popular conception of what Dante was like in ordinary life.

One of the earliest is that told by Petrarch[1] of Dante at the court of Can Grande della Scala at Verona, after he had been exiled from Florence :—

"Dante Alighieri, erewhile my fellow-citizen, was a man greatly accomplished in the vulgar tongue ; but on account of his pride he was somewhat more free in his manners and speech than was acceptable to the sensitive eyes and ears of the noble princes of our country. Thus, when he was exiled from his native city, and was a guest at the court of Can Grande, at that time the refuge and resort of all who were in misfortune, he was at first held in high honour; but afterwards by degrees he began to lose favour, and day by day became less pleasing to his host. Among the guests at the same time were, according to the custom of those days, mimics and buffoons of every

[1] In bk. ii. of the *Res Memorandae.*

144

description, one of whom, an impudent rascal, by means of his coarse remarks and broad jests made himself a universal favourite and a person of considerable influence. Can Grande, suspecting that this was a cause of vexation to Dante, sent for the buffoon, and, after lavishing praise upon him, turned to Dante and said: ' I wonder how it is that this man, fool though he be, understands how to please us all, and is petted by every one; while you, for all your reputed wisdom, can do nothing of the kind!' Dante replied: ' You would hardly wonder at that, if you remembered that like manners and like minds are the real causes of friendship '." [1]

A similar anecdote is told by Michele Savonarola, the grandfather of the famous Florentine preacher and reformer, Girolamo Savonarola: " I will tell you the answer made by Dante to a buffoon at the court of the Lord della Scala of Verona, who, having received from his master a fine coat as a reward for some piece of buffoonery, showed it to Dante, and said : ' You with all your letters, and sonnets, and books, have never received a present like this '. To which Dante answered: ' What you say is true; and this has fallen to you and not to me, because you have found your likes, and I have not yet found mine. There, you understand that!' " [2]

John Gower introduces a story of Dante and a flatterer into the *Confessio Amantis* (c. 1390):—

> " How Dante the poete answerde
> To a flatour, the tale I herde.
> Upon a strif bitwen hem tuo
> He seide him, ' Ther ben many mo
> Of thy servantes than of myne.

---

[1] Or, as we should say, " birds of a feather flock together ".

[2] Quoted by Papanti in *Dante secondo la tradizione e i novellatori*, p. 94.

For the poete of his covyne
Hath non that wol him clothe and fede,
But a flatour may reule and lede
A king with al his lond aboute ' ".
(Bk. vii. ll. 2329*-37*.) [1]

Another story of Dante and Can Grande turns on his host's name, Cane ("dog"):—"Once when Dante was at his table Cane della Scala, who was a very gracious lord, wishing to have a joke with the poet and to incite him to some smart saying, ordered his servants to collect all the bones from the repast and to put them privily at Dante's feet. When the tables were removed, and the company saw the pile of bones at Dante's feet, they all began to laugh, and asked him if he were a bone-merchant. Whereupon Dante quickly replied: ' It is no wonder if the dogs have eaten all their bones ; but I am not a dog, and so I could not eat mine'. And he said this because his host was called Cane (' dog')." [2]

The author of an old commentary on the *Divina Commedia*, written probably not many years after Dante's death, relates Dante's retort to the musical-instrument maker of Florence, whom the poet has placed among the negligent in his Ante-Purgatory: [3] " Belacqua was a citizen of Florence, who made the necks of lutes and guitars, and he was the laziest man that ever was known. It was said that he used to come in the morning to his shop and sit himself down, and never stir again except to go to dinner or to his siesta. Now Dante was a familiar acquaintance of his, and often rebuked him for his laziness ; whereupon one day when he was scolding him, Belacqua answered him with the words of Aristotle : ' By

---

[1] In the margin Gower has put " Nota exemplum cujusdam poete de Ytalia, qui Dantes vocabatur ". The above passage was omitted by Gower from the latest recension of his poem.

[2] Quoted by Papanti, *op. cit.*, pp. 90-1.

[3] *Purgatorio*, iv. 106-27.

repose and quiet the mind attains to wisdom'. To which Dante retorted : 'Certainly if repose will make a man wise, you ought to be the wisest man on earth'."[1]

Benvenuto da Imola, another commentator on the *Commedia*, says that besides being a maker of musical instruments, this Belacqua was also something of a musician, and he explains that it was on this account that Dante, who was a lover of music, became intimate with him.

The following two stories of Dante in Florence are told by Franco Sacchetti, the Florentine writer of tales, who was born within twenty years of Dante's death, and belonged to a family which had a long-standing blood-feud with Dante's family, Geri del Bello, the first cousin of the poet's father, having been killed by one of the Sacchetti.[2] The first story contains also a characteristic anecdote of Dante's uncompromising ways, which according to Sacchetti largely contributed to bring about his exile.

"That most excellent poet in the vulgar tongue, whose fame will never die, Dante Alighieri of Florence, lived in Florence not far from the Adimari family, one of whom, a young man, got into trouble through some misdoing or other, and was like to be sentenced to punishment by one of the magistrates. As the magistrate was a friend of Dante's, the young man begged the latter to intercede in his favour, which Dante readily consented to do. After dinner, Dante went out from his house, and started on his way to fulfil his promise. As he passed by the Porta San Piero, a blacksmith was hammering iron on his anvil, and at the same time bawling out some of Dante's verses, leaving out lines here and there, and putting in others of his own, which seemed to Dante a most monstrous outrage. Without saying a word he went up to the blacksmith's forge, where were kept all the tools he used to ply his

---

[1] *Anonimo Fiorentino.*   [2] See above, p. 42.

trade, and seizing the hammer flung it into the street; then he took the tongs and flung them after the hammer, and the scales after the tongs; and he did the same with a number of the other tools. The blacksmith, turning round to him with a coarse gesture, said: 'What the devil are you doing? are you mad?' Dante replied: 'What are you doing?' 'I am about my business,' said the smith, 'and you are spoiling my tools by throwing them into the street.' Dante retorted: 'If you do not want me to spoil your things, do not you spoil mine'. The smith replied: 'And what of yours am I spoiling?' Dante said: 'You sing out of my book, and do not give the words as I wrote them. That is my business, and you are spoiling it for me.' The blacksmith, bursting with rage, but not knowing what to answer, picked up his things and went back to his work. And the next time he wanted to sing, he sang of Tristram and Lancelot, and let Dante's book alone.

"Dante meanwhile pursued his way to the magistrate; and when he was come to his house, and bethought himself that this Adimari was a haughty young man, and behaved with scant courtesy when he went about in the city, especially when he was on horseback (for he used to ride with his legs so wide apart that if the street happened to be narrow he took up the whole of it, forcing every passer-by to brush against the points of his boots—a manner of behaviour which greatly displeased Dante, who was very observant), Dante said to the magistrate: 'You have before your court such a young man for such an offence; I recommend him to your favour, though his behaviour is such that he deserves to be the more severely punished, for to my mind usurping the property of the commonwealth is a very serious crime'. Dante did not speak to deaf ears. The magistrate asked what property of the commonwealth the young man had usurped. Dante answered: ' When he rides through the city he sits on his horse with his legs so wide apart that whoever meets him is obliged to turn back, and is prevented from going on his way '. The magistrate said : ' Do you regard this as a joke ? it is a more serious offence than the other ! ' Dante replied : ' Well, you see, I am his neighbour, and recommend him to you '. And he returned to his house, where the young man asked him how the matter stood. Dante said: ' He gave me a favourable answer '. A few days afterwards the young man was summoned before the court to answer the charge against him. After the first charge had been read, the judge had the second read also, as to his riding with his legs wide-spread. The young man, perceiving that his penalty would be doubled, said to himself: ' I have made a fine bargain ! instead of being let off through the intervention of Dante, I shall now be sentenced on two counts '. So returning home he went to Dante and said: ' Upon my word, you have served me well ! Before you went to the magistrate he had a mind to sentence me on one count ; since you went he is like to sentence me on two,'—and in a great fury he turned to Dante and said : ' If I am sentenced I shall be able to pay, and sooner or later I will pay out the person who got me sentenced '. Dante replied : ' I did my best for you, and could not have done more if you had been my own son. It is not my fault if the magistrate does not do as you wish.' The young man, shaking his head, returned home ; and a few days afterwards was fined a thousand lire for the first offence, and another thousand for riding with his legs wide-spread—a thing he never ceased to resent, both he and all the rest of the Adimari. And this was the principal reason why not long after Dante was expelled from Florence as a member of the White party, and eventually died in exile at Ravenna, to the lasting shame of his native city." [1]

This story, Sacchetti informs his readers, reminded him of another one about Dante, which he thought too good to be omitted from his collection. It runs as follows :—

"On another occasion as Dante was walking through the streets of Florence on no particular errand, and, according to the custom of the day, was wearing a gorget and arm-piece, he met a donkey-driver whose donkeys were loaded with refuse. As he walked behind the donkeys the driver sang some of Dante's verses, and after every two or three lines he would beat one of the donkeys, and cry out : *Arri !* [2] Dante going up to him gave him a great thump on the back with his arm-piece, and said : 'That *Arri !* was not put in by me'. The driver not knowing who Dante was, nor why he had struck him, only beat his donkeys the more, and again cried out : *Arri !* But when he had got a little way off, he turned round and put out his tongue at Dante, and made an indecent gesture, saying : 'Take that !' Dante, seeing this, said to him : 'I would not give one word of mine for a hundred of yours'. Oh ! gentle words, worthy of a philosopher ! Most people would have run after the donkey-driver with threats and abuse ; or would have thrown stones at him. But the wise poet confounded the donkey-driver, and at the same time won the commendation of every one who had witnessed what took place." [3]

The following story professes to account for the poetical version of the Creed in *terza rima*, which is often included among Dante's works, together with a similar version of the seven penitential Psalms. [4]

"At the time when Dante was writing his book (the

---

[1] *Novella*, cxiv.   [2] Equivalent to our " Gee up ! "
[3] *Novella* cxv.   [4] See pp. 193-202 of the Oxford Dante.

Divina Commedia) many people who could not understand it said that it was contrary to the Christian faith.   And it came about that Dante was exiled from Florence, and forbidden to come within a certain distance of the city, which prohibition being disregarded, he was proclaimed by the Florentines as a rebel.   After wandering about for some time in many countries he at last came to Ravenna, an ancient city of Romagna, and settled down at the court of Guido Novello, who was at that time lord of Ravenna ; and here he died, in the year 1321, on the fourteenth day of September, that is on the day of the Exaltation of the Holy Cross, and was buried with great honour by the lord of the city.   Now at Ravenna there was a learned Franciscan friar, who was an inquisitor. This man, having heard of Dante's fame, became desirous of making his acquaintance, with the intention of finding out whether he were a heretic or no.   And one morning, as Dante was in church, the inquisitor entered, and Dante being pointed out to him, he sent for him.   Dante reverentially went to him, and was asked by the inquisitor if he were the Dante who claimed to have visited Hell, Purgatory, and Paradise.   Dante replied: 'I am Dante Alighieri of Florence'.   Whereupon the inquisitor angrily said : 'You go writing canzoni, and sonnets, and idle tales, when you would have done much better to write a learned work, resting on the foundations of the Church of God, instead of giving your time to such like rubbish, which may one of these days serve you out as you deserve'. When Dante wished to reply to the inquisitor, the latter said : 'This is not the time ; but on such a day I will see you again, and I will inquire into this matter'.   Dante thereupon answered that he should be well pleased for this to be done; and taking leave of the inquisitor, he went home to his own room, and there and then wrote out the composition known as the 'Little Creed,' the which creed is an affirmation of the whole Christian faith. On the appointed day he went in quest of the inquisitor, and, having found him, put into his hands this composition, which the inquisitor read ; and having read it he thought it a remarkable work, insomuch that he was at a loss to know what to say to Dante.   And while the inquisitor was thus confounded, Dante took his leave, and so came off safe and sound.   And from that day forward Dante and the inquisitor became great friends.   And that is how it came about that Dante wrote his Creed." [1]

Giovanni Sercambi, the Lucchese novelist, tells several stories of Dante, in one of which he relates how Dante turned the tables on King Robert of Naples, the Guelf champion, who was the bitter opponent of Dante's ideal Emperor, Henry of Luxemburg.

" In the days when King Robert of Naples was still alive, Dante, the poet of Florence, having been forbidden to live in his native city or anywhere within the States of the Church, took refuge sometimes with the Della Scala family at Verona, and sometimes with the lord of Mantua, but oftenest with the Duke of Lucca, namely, Messer Castruccio Castracani.   And inasmuch as the fame of the said Dante's wisdom had been noised abroad, King Robert was desirous of having him at his court, in order that he might judge of his wisdom and virtue; wherefore he sent letters to the Duke, and likewise to Dante, begging him to consent to come.   And Dante having decided to go to King Robert's court, set out from Lucca and made his way to Naples, where he arrived, dressed, as poets mostly are, in somewhat shabby garments.   When his arrival was announced to King Robert, he was sent for to the King; and it was just the hour of dinner as Dante

[1] Quoted by Papanti, *op. cit.* pp. 47-9.

entered the room where the King was. After hands had
been washed and places taken at table, the King sitting
at his own table, and the barons at theirs, at the last
Dante was placed at the lowest seat of all. Dante, being
a wise man, saw at once how little sense the King showed.
Nevertheless, being hungry, he ate, and after he had eaten,
he, without waiting, took his departure, and set out towards Ancona on his way back to Tuscany. When King
Robert had dined, and rested somewhat, he inquired what
had become of Dante, and was informed that he had left
and was on his way towards Ancona. The King, knowing
that he had not paid Dante the honour which was his
due, supposed that he was indignant on that account, and
said to himself: 'I have done wrong; after sending for
him, I ought to have done him honour, and then I should
have learned from him what I wanted'. He therefore
without delay sent some of his own servants after him,
who caught him up before he reached Ancona. Having
received the King's letter Dante turned round and went
back to Naples; and dressing himself in a very handsome
garment presented himself before King Robert. At
dinner the King placed him at the head of the first table,
which was alongside of his own; and Dante finding himself at the head of the table, resolved to make the King
understand what he had done. Accordingly, when the
meat and wine were served, Dante took the meat and
smeared it over the breast of his dress, and the wine he
smeared over his clothes in like manner. King Robert
and the barons who were present, seeing this, said : 'This
man must be a good-for-nothing; what does he mean by
smearing the wine and gravy over his clothes?' Dante
heard how they were abusing him, but held his peace.
Then the King, who had observed all that passed, turned
to Dante and said: 'What is this that I have seen you

doing? How can you, who are reputed to be so wise, indulge in such nasty habits?' Dante, who had hoped for some remark of this kind, replied: 'Your majesty, I know that this great honour which you now show me, is paid not to me but to my clothes; consequently I thought that my clothes ought to partake of the good things you provided. You must see that what I say is the case; for I am just as wise now, I suppose, as when I was set at the bottom of the table, because of my shabby clothes; and now I have come back, neither more nor less wise than before, because I am well dressed, you place me at the head of the table.' King Robert, recognising that Dante had rebuked him justly, and had spoken the truth, ordered fresh clothes to be brought for him, and Dante after changing his dress ate his dinner, delighted at having made the King see his own folly. When dinner was over, the King took Dante aside, and, making proof of his wisdom, found him to be even wiser than he had been told; wherefore King Robert paid Dante great honour and kept him at his court, in order that he might have further experience of his wisdom and virtue."

The famous Florentine story-teller, Francesco Poggio Bracciolini, more commonly known as Poggio, besides the two anecdotes of Dante and Can Grande which have already been given, relates the following of how Dante disposed of a bore:—

" At the time when our poet Dante was in exile at Siena, as he was standing one day deep in thought, with his elbow on one of the altars in the Church of the Minor Friars, as though he were revolving in his mind some very abstruse matter, some busybody went up to him, and disturbed him by speaking to him. Dante turned to him and said: 'What is the biggest beast in the world?' 'The elephant,' was the reply. Then said Dante: 'Oh! elephant, leave

me alone in peace, for I am pondering weightier matters
than your silly chatter'." [1]

Another version of this story is included among *The
Most Elegant and Witty Epigrams* (first published in
1615) of Sir John Harington. It is entitled

> *A good answere of the Poet* Dant *to an Atheist.*
>
> The pleasant learn'd *Italian Poet Dant*,
> Hearing an Atheist at the Scriptures jest,
> Askt him in jest, which was the greatest beast ?
> He simply said ; he thought an Elephant.
> Then *Elephant* (quoth *Dant*) it were commodious,
> That thou wouldst hold thy peace, or get thee hence,
> Breeding our Conscience scandal and offence
> With thy prophan'd speech, most vile and odious.
>   Oh Italy, thou breedst but few such *Dants*,
>   I would our England bred no Elephants.[2]

The following anecdote of Dante and the Doge of
Venice belongs to quite the end of Dante's life, the occasion in question being when he was in Venice on his
embassy from Guido da Polenta in the summer of 1321,
a few months before his death :—

"Dante of Florence being once on a mission in Venice,
was invited to dinner by the Doge on a fast-day. In front
of the envoys of the other princes who were of greater
account than the Polenta lord of Ravenna, and were served
before Dante, were placed the largest fish ; while in front
of Dante were placed the smallest. This difference of
treatment nettled Dante, who took up one of the little fish
in his hand, and held it to his ear, as though expecting it
to say something. The Doge, observing this, asked him
what this strange behaviour meant. To which Dante
replied : 'As I knew that the father of this fish met his

---

[1] *Facezie di Poggio fiorentino*, No. lxvi.

[2] Book iv. No. 17 (see Paget Toynbee, *Dante in English Literature*,
vol. i. p. 84).

death in these waters, I was asking him news of his father'.
' Well,' said the Doge, ' and what did he answer ? ' Dante
replied : ' He told me that he and his companions were
too little to remember much about him ; but that I might
learn what I wanted from the older fish, who would be
able to give me the news I asked for '. Thereupon the
Doge at once ordered Dante to be served with a fine large
fish." [1]

An English traveller in Italy at the beginning of the
eighteenth century picked up in Florence the following
curious story about Dante :—

" This great man, we are told, had a most unhappy itch
of pilfering ; not for lucre (for it was generally of mere
trifles), but it was what he could not help ; so that the
friends whose houses he frequented, would put in his way
rags of cloth, bits of glass, and the like, to save things
of more value (for he could not go away without something) ; and of such as these, at his death, a whole room
full was found filled." [2]

Another anecdote is given by Isaac D'Israeli in his
Curiosities of Literature :—

" A story is recorded of Cecco d' Ascoli and of Dante,
on the subject of natural and acquired genius. Cecco
maintained that nature was more potent than art, while
Dante asserted the contrary. To prove his principle, the
great Italian bard referred to his cat, which, by repeated
practice, he had taught to hold a candle in its paw, while
he supped or read. Cecco desired to witness the experi-
ment, and came not unprepared for the purpose ; when
Dante's cat was performing its part, Cecco, lifting up the lid

[1] Quoted by Papanti, op. cit. p. 157.
[2] Edward Wright, Some Observations made in Travelling through
France, Italy, etc. in the Years MDCCXX, MDCCXXI, and MDCCXXII
(London, 1730), ed. 1764, p. 395 (see Dante in English Literature, vol i.
pp. 216-17).

of a pot which he had filled with mice, the creature of art instantly showed the weakness of a talent merely acquired, and dropping the candle flew on the mice with all its instinctive propensity. Dante was himself disconcerted, and it was adjudged that the advocate for the occult principle of native faculties had gained his cause." [1]

Many of these stories are obviously much older than the time of Dante, and have been told of various famous persons at different periods. Their association, however, with Dante's name is sufficient proof of the estimation in which he was held within a few years after his death, and of the way in which his fame as a poet impressed the popular imagination in Italy.

[1] Ed. 1866, vol. ii. (*Anecdotes of the Fairfax Family*), p. 464 (see *Dante in English Literature*, vol. i. p. 508, and Papanti, *op. cit.* p. 197).

PART V

DANTE'S WORKS

CHAPTER I

Italian Works—Lyrical Poems—The *Vita Nuova*—The *Convivio*.

DANTE'S earliest known composition is the sonnet beginning

"A ciascun' alma presa e gentil core,"[1]

which, as he tells us in the *Vita Nuova*, he wrote after seeing the marvellous vision which followed on the episode of his being publicly saluted by Beatrice for the first time in the streets of Florence, when they were both in their eighteenth year (i.e. in the year 1283). This sonnet, he further tells us, he sent to many famous poets of the day,

[1] "To every captive soul and gentle heart
  Unto whose ken these present words shall come,
  That they may write me back their thoughts thereon,
Be greeting in their Lord's name, that is Love.
A third part well-nigh of those hours had passed
  Wherein shines brightly every star on high,
  When on a sudden Love appeared to me;
And still I shudder when I think on him.
Methought Love stood all joyful as he held
  My heart within his hand, and in his arms
My Lady bore enshrouded and asleep.
  Whom then he waked, and of this flaming heart
Humbly did make her eat, she sore afraid—
  Then, as I looked, he wept and went his way."

from whom he received sonnets in reply. Among those
to whom he sent were his first friend, Guido Cavalcanti,
Cino da Pistoja, and Dante da Majano, whose replies have
been preserved.[1]

Canzoniere.—This sonnet and thirty other poems
(twenty-four sonnets, five canzoni, and one ballata) are
grouped together in a symmetrical arrangement in the
Vita Nuova (or *New Life*), the prose text of which is a
vehicle for the introduction and interpretation of the
poems. Others of Dante's lyrical poems are introduced
in his *Convivio* (or *Banquet*), which contains three canzoni,
and in his Latin work on the vulgar tongue (*De Vulgari
Eloquentia*), which contains quotations from nine poems,
canzoni and sestine. In addition to these there is a collection of between ninety and a hundred lyrical poems
attributed to Dante, some of which are almost certainly
not his.[2] Such of the poems of the *Canzoniere* as do not
belong to the *Vita Nuova* and *Convivio* appear to have
been composed at various times as independent pieces,
though attempts have been made to distinguish one or
more definite groups. Both Villani and Boccaccio make
mention of Dante's lyrical poems. The former says:[3]
"When he was in exile he wrote about twenty very excellent canzoni, both moral and on the subject of love".
Boccaccio says:[4] "He composed numerous lengthy canzoni, and sonnets, and sundry ballate, both amorous and
moral, besides those which are included in the *Vita*

---

[1] Translations of these three sonnets in reply (which are in the same
rimes as Dante's sonnet) are given by D. G. Rossetti in *Dante and his
Circle* (ed. 1874), pp. 131, 183, 198.

[2] See *Dante Dictionary*, s.v. *Canzoniere*; and *The Vita Nuova and
Canzoniere of Dante*, by T. Okey and P. H. Wicksteed (1906), pp. 155-
357.

[3] Bk. ix. ch. 136.

[4] *Vita di Dante*, ed. Macrì-Leone, § 16, p. 74.

Nuova".[1]   The earliest printed collection of Dante's lyrical poems is that included in *Sonetti e Canzoni di diversi antichi Autori Toscani in dieci libri raccolte* (Florence, 1527), the first four books of which contain forty-five sonnets, nineteen canzoni, eleven ballate, and one sestina, attributed to Dante.   A few, however, of the canzoni and madrigali (as they are described) had been printed at Venice in 1518, and reprinted at Milan in the same year, in a collection entitled *Canzoni di Dante. Madrigali del detto. Madrigali di M. Cino et di M. Girardo Novello.*   Fifteen canzoni of Dante are printed at the end of the *editio princeps* of the *Vita Nuova* (Florence, 1576).

Vita Nuova.—Dante's *Vita Nuova* or *New Life* (i.e. according to some, his "young life," but more probably his "life made new" by his love for Beatrice), the first autobiographical work in modern literature, as it has been described, was written probably between 1292 and 1295, when Dante was under thirty, and some seven or eight years before his exile from Florence.   The poems were obviously written before the prose text, which was necessarily composed later than the death of Beatrice in 1290.

The following positive dates are supplied by Dante in the course of the narrative of the *Vita Nuova*, viz. that he first saw Beatrice in the spring of 1274, when he had nearly completed his ninth year (§ 2, ll. 1-5, 15), and she

---

[1] There are three English translations of the *Canzoniere*, viz. by Charles Lyell (in unrimed verse, in the metres of the original) in *The Canzoniere of Dante, including the poems of the Vita Nuova and Convito* (1835, 1840, 1845; a revised version of *The Poems of the Vita Nuova and Convito* was issued, with other matter, in 1842); by Dean Plumptre (in rimed verse) in *The Commedia and Canzoniere of Dante*, vol. ii. pp. 199-317 (1887); by P. H. Wicksteed (in prose) in *The Convivio of Dante* (1903), and in *The Vita Nuova and Canzoniere of Dante*, pp. 156-357 (1906).

was at the beginning of her ninth year (§ 2, ll. 9-15); that Beatrice saluted him for the first time nine years later, in the spring of 1283 (§ 3, ll. 1-15), when he wrote the sonnet, "A ciascun' alma presa e gentil core' (*Son.* i.), his earliest known composition; that Beatrice died on the evening of 8 June, 1290[1] (§ 30, ll. 1-13); that on the first anniversary of her death (8 June, 1291) he wrote the sonnet, "Era venuta nella mente mia" (*Son.* xviii.), in commemoration of her (§ 35, ll. 1-20); that not long after (i.e. probably as appears from *Convivio*, ii. 2, ll. 1-10, in September, 1291),[2] he saw for the first time the "donna gentile" (whom some have identified with Gemma Donati)[3] (§ 36, ll. 1-13). To these, if the identity of Beatrice with Beatrice Portinari be accepted, may be added the date of the death of Folco Portinari,[4] viz. 31 December, 1289 (§ 22, ll. 1-7).

Boccaccio, who asserts that in later life Dante was ashamed of this work of his youth,[5] gives the following account of the *Vita Nuova* :—

" This glorious poet composed several works in his time, of which I think it fitting to make mention in order, lest any work of his be claimed by another, or the works of others be perchance attributed to him.

" He, first of all, while his tears for the death of Beatrice were yet fresh, when he was nigh upon his twenty-

[1] See note on p. 47.

[2] See G. R. Carpenter, *The Episode of the Donna Pietosa*, in *Annual Report of the Cambridge* (U.S.A.) *Dante Society* for 1889, p. 60.

[3] See note on p. 67.　　　　[4] See above pp. 46-7.

[5] This is not borne out by what Dante himself says of it at the beginning of the *Convivio*: " E se nella presente opera, la quale è *Convivio* nominata e vo' che sia, più virilmente si trattasse che nella *Vita Nuova*, non intendo però a quella in parte alcuna derogare, ma maggiormente giovare per questa quella; veggendo siccome ragionevolmente quella fervida e passionata, questa temperata e virile essere conviene. Chè altro si conviene e dire e operare a una etade, che ad altra" (i. 1, ll. 111-20).

sixth year, collected together in a little volume, to which
he gave the title of *Vita Nuova*, certain small works, such
as sonnets and canzoni, composed by him in rime at
divers times before, and of marvellous beauty. Above
each of these, severally and in order, he wrote the occasions which had moved him to compose them; and below he added the divisions of each poem. And although
in his riper years he was much ashamed of having written
this little book, yet, if his age be considered, it is very
beautiful and delightful, especially to unlearned folk." [1]

"The *New Life*," writes Professor Norton,[2] "is the
proper introduction to the *Divine Comedy*. It is the story
of the beginning of the love through which, even in Dante's
youth, heavenly things were revealed to him, and which
in the bitterest trials of life—in disappointment, poverty,
and exile—kept his heart fresh with springs of perpetual
solace. It was this love which led him through the hard
paths of Philosophy and up the steep ascents of Faith,
out of Hell and through Purgatory, to the glories of Paradise and the fulfilment of Hope.

"The narrative of the *New Life* is quaint, embroidered
with conceits, deficient in artistic completeness, but it has
the simplicity of youth, the charm of sincerity, the freedom
of personal confidence; and so long as there are lovers in
the world, and so long as lovers are poets, this first and
tenderest love-story of modern literature will be read with
appreciation and responsive sympathy.

"It is the earliest of Dante's writings, and the most
autobiographic of them in form and intention. In it we
are brought into intimate personal relations with the poet.
He trusts himself to us with full and free confidence; but
there is no derogation from becoming manliness in his

---

[1] *Vita di Dante*, ed. cit., § 13, p. 63.
[2] *The New Life of Dante Alighieri*, pp. 93 ff.

confessions. He draws the picture of a portion of his youth, and displays its secret emotions; but he does so with no morbid self-consciousness and with no affectation. Part of this simplicity is due, undoubtedly, to the character of the times, part to his own youthfulness, part to downright faith in his own genius. It was the fashion for poets to tell of their loves; in following this fashion, he not only gave utterance to genuine feeling, and claimed his rank among the poets, but also fixed a standard by which the ideal expression of love was thereafter to be measured.

" This first essay of his poetic powers rests on the foundation upon which his later life was built. The figure of Beatrice, which appears veiled under the symbolism, and indistinct in the bright halo of the allegory of the *Divine Comedy*, takes its place in life and on the earth through the *New Life* as definitely as that of Dante himself. She is no allegorized piece of humanity, no impersonation of attributes, but an actual woman,—beautiful, modest, gentle, with companions only less beautiful than herself,—the most delightful personage in the daily picturesque life of Florence. She is seen smiling and weeping, walking with other fair maidens in the street, praying at the church, merry at festivals, mourning at funerals; and her smiles and tears, her gentleness, her reserve, all the sweet qualities of her life, and the peace of her death, are told of with such tenderness, and purity, and passion, as well as with such truth of poetic imagination, that she remains, and will always remain, the loveliest and most womanly woman of the Middle Ages,—at once absolutely real and truly ideal.

" The meaning of the name *La Vita Nuova* has been the subject of animated discussion. Literally *The New Life*, it has been questioned whether this phrase meant simply early life, or life made new by the first experience and lasting influence of love. The latter interpretation seems the most appropriate to Dante's turn of mind and to his condition of feeling at the time when the little book appeared. To him it was the record of that life which the presence of Beatrice had made new."

The *Vita Nuova*, which was dedicated to Dante's earliest friend Guido Cavalcanti (§ 31, ll. 22-3), consists of three distinct elements, viz. the poems, the narrative of the events which gave rise to the poems, and the expositions of the structural divisions of the poems. Two distinctive features of the work are the frequency with which Dante, in accordance with the literary traditions of the day,[1] introduces the expedient of visions, of which there are no less than seven in the book (§§ 3, 9, 12, 23, 24, 40, 43); and the important part played by the number *nine*, in connection with the hour, day, month, and year of the various events related concerning Beatrice. Thus Dante first sees Beatrice when they were both in their *ninth* year ("quasi dal principio del suo *nono* anno apparve a me, ed io la vidi quasi alla fine del mio *nono*," § 2, ll. 13-15; cf. § 2, ll. 1-8: "*Nove* fiate già," etc.); he sees her again *nine* years later ("appunto erano compiuti li *nove* anni appresso l'apparimento soprascritto," § 3, ll. 2-3); and receives her first greeting at the *ninth* hour of the day ("l'ora, che lo suo dolcissimo salutare mi giunse, era fermamente *nona* di quel giorno," § 3, ll. 16-18); his subsequent vision takes place during the first of the last *nine* hours of the night ("fu la prima ora delle *nove* ultime ore della notte," § 3, ll. 63-5). When he was minded to write a poem containing the names of the sixty fairest ladies of Florence, the name of Beatrice would stand nowhere save in the *ninth* place ("in alcuno altro numero non sofferse il nome della

---

[1] See A. Bartoli, *Storia della Letteratura Italiana*, vol. iv. p. 173.

mia donna stare, se non in sul *nove*, tra' nomi di queste
donne," § 6, ll. 14-17). The third vision takes place at
the *ninth* hour of the day ("trovai che questa visione
m' era apparita nella *nona* ora del dì," § 12, ll. 74-5). The
vision in which he has a presentiment of the approaching
death of Beatrice, when he is laid low with sickness, occurs
on the *ninth* day of his illness (" nel *nono* giorno sentendomi
dolore quasi intollerabile, giunsemi un pensiero, il quale
era della mia donna . . . ," § 23, ll. 8-10). In the sonnet,
" Io mi sentii svegliar dentro allo core " (*Son.* xiv.), in which
Beatrice is mentioned, her name occurs in the *ninth* line [1]
(§ 24, l. 58). In the date of her death the number *nine*
comes in with special significance, in connection with the
day, the month, and the year, which are computed for the
purpose according to the Arabian, Syrian, and Roman
calendars respectively [2] ("secondo l' usanza d' Arabia,
l' anima sua nobilissima si partì nella prima ora del *nono*
giorno del mese ; e secondo l' usanza di Siria, ella si partì
nel *nono* mese dell' anno ; . . . e secondo l' usanza nostra,
ella si partì in quello anno della nostra indizione, cioè degli
anni Domini, in cui il perfetto numero *nove* volte era com-
piuto in quel centinaio nel quale in questo mondo ella fu
posta," § 30, ll. 1-12). Finally, his last vision of Beatrice,
when she appeared to him as she was when he first saw
her, took place just on the hour of *nones* ("si levò un dì,
quasi nell' ora di *nona*, una forte immaginazione in me," etc.,
§ 40, ll. 1-3). Dante himself draws particular attention to
the fact of this connection of the number *nine* with Beatrice,
and promises to explain the reason of it (§ 29, ll. 29-38),
which he subsequently does in detail (§ 30, ll. 13-32), his

[1] This might be used as an argument in favour of the reading " Bice "
instead of " Lagia " in the sonnet, " Guido, vorrei che tu e Lapo ed io "
(*Son.* xxxii.), where the name occurs in the *ninth* line.
[2] On this point see above, p. 47, note.

conclusion being that she was "a nine, that is to say a miracle, whose root is no other than the marvellous Trinity" ("questa donna fu accompagnata dal numero del *nove* a dare ad intendere, che ella era un *nove*, cioè un miracolo, la cui radice è solamente la mirabile Trinitade," § 30, ll. 37-41).

The form of the composition of the *Vita Nuova*, partly in prose, partly in verse (as in the famous *De Consolatione Philosophiae* of Boëthius, with which Dante was intimately acquainted, and the early French "chantefable," *Aucassin et Nicolete*), was no doubt borrowed from a Provençal model, the prose text being a vehicle for the introduction and interpretation of the poems. The latter, which are thirty-one in number, consisting of twenty-five sonnets (including two which are irregular), five canzoni(two of which are imperfect), and one ballata, are symmetrically arranged in groups around the three principal canzoni, the central poem of all being the canzone, " Donna pietosa e di novella etate " (*Canz.* ii.).[1]

The work falls naturally into two main divisions, viz. the period before the death of Beatrice (1274-1290), and the period after her death (1290-*c.*1295). Taken in more detail it may conveniently be divided into five parts,[2] viz. (§§ 1-17) Dante's youthful love for Beatrice, and his poems in praise of her physical beauty ; (§§ 18-28) his praises of the spiritual beauty of Beatrice ; (§§ 29-35) the death of Beatrice and the poems of lamentation ; (§§ 36-39) Dante's love for the "donna gentile," and the poems about her ; (§§ 40-43) Dante's return to his love for Beatrice, and reverence for her memory.

The division into numbered chapters was not made by Dante himself, and does not appear in any of the MSS.,

[1] See C. E. Norton, *The New Life of Dante* (1892), pp. 129-34. Norton's views, however, are contested by M. Scherillo, in *La Forma Architettonica della Vita Nuova,* in *Giornale Dantesco,* ix. (1901).

[2] See T. Casini, *La Vita Nuova* (1891), p. xxiii.

nor even in the printed editions before the middle of the nineteenth century.[1] It is, however, convenient for reference, and is now generally adopted in modern editions.[2]

Analysis of the *Vita Nuova* :—

Part I. §§ 1-17.—§ 1. (" Proemio ") Introductory, explaining the title of the book (" Incipit Vita Nova "), and the author's purpose.—§ 2. First meeting of Dante with Beatrice (in the spring of 1274), he being nearly nine years old, and she not yet nine.—§ 3. Nine years later (in the spring of 1283), at the ninth hour of the day, Dante for the first time receives a greeting from Beatrice ; his first vision (Love appears to him holding a lady asleep in his arms, and in his hand Dante's heart in flames, of which he gives the lady to eat, and then disappears, bearing her away with him) ; he describes the vision in the sonnet : " A ciascun' alma presa, e gentil core " (*Son.* i.), which he sends to the most famous poets of the day for interpretation ; he receives a reply among others from Guido Cavalcanti.—§ 4. Dante falls ill through the intensity of his passion for Beatrice ; questioned as to the object of his passion he refuses to reply.—§ 5. He dissembles his love for Beatrice under pretence of devotion to another lady.—§ 6. He composes a *serventese* containing the names of the sixty fairest ladies in Florence, among

[1] It was first introduced in the edition of A. Torri, Livorno, 1843.

[2] Unfortunately all editors have not adopted the same numeration. Witte (Leipzig, 1876) and Casini, for example, do not number the opening paragraph, which Dante himself refers to as " il proemio che precede questo libello " (§ 29, ll. 17-18) ; while Torri, the Oxford Dante, and others count it as § 1. Again, Torri's § 3 is divided by Witte and Casini into two (§§ 2, 3) ; while, on the other hand, Torri's and Witte's §§ 26, 27, are run by Casini into one (§ 26). In the critical edition recently published by M. Barbi (Florence, 1907) for the *Società Dantesca Italiana* the chapter divisions differ from those of all previous editions ; and in the Oxford Dante, the arrangement of which is followed in this book, yet another system is adopted.

which that of Beatrice will stand in no other than the ninth place.—§ 7. The lady of his pretended devotion leaves Florence; he laments her departure in a sonnet: "O voi, che per la via d' Amor passate" (*Son.* ii.).—§ 8. He writes two sonnets on the death of a beautiful damsel, a friend of Beatrice: "Piangete, amanti, poichè piange Amore" (*Son.* iii.); "Morte villana, di pietà nemica" (*Son.* iv.).—§ 9. He is obliged to take a journey out of Florence in the direction taken by the lady of his pretended devotion; his second vision (Love appears to him in the guise of a pilgrim of sorrowful aspect, who calls to him and tells him that he brings back his heart from the keeping of the lady who had possessed it awhile, in order that it may be at the service of another lady; whereafter he vanishes); which he describes in the sonnet: "Cavalcando l' altr' ier per un cammino" (*Son.* v.).—§ 10. Dante's devotion to the second lady occasions remark, and causes Beatrice to deny him her salutation.—§ 11. He describes the marvellous effects on himself of the salutation of Beatrice.—§ 12. Dante's distress at Beatrice's denial to him of her salutation; his third vision, which takes place at the ninth hour of the day (Love appears to him in his sleep, sitting at his bedside, and weeping piteously; Dante questions him as to why Beatrice had denied him her salutation; Love explains and bids him write a poem which shall make manifest to Beatrice his faithful and unaltered devotion to her; he then disappears and Dante awakes); he composes the ballata: "Ballata io vo' che tu ritrovi Amore" (*Ball.* i.).—§ 13. Dante is assailed by doubts as to whether the lordship of Love is a good thing or the reverse; he describes his doubts in the sonnet: "Tutti li miei pensier parlan d' Amore" (*Son.* vi.).—§ 14. He is conducted by a friend to a marriage-feast where he finds himself in the presence of Beatrice; he is so overcome by emotion that his confusion is remarked, and the ladies, including Beatrice herself, whisper and mock at him, whereupon his friend, perceiving his distress, leads him away; on his return home he addresses to Beatrice the sonnet: "Coll' altre donne mia vista gabbate" (*Son.* vii.).—§ 15. He is torn between his longing to be in the presence of Beatrice, and his dread of appearing contemptible in her eyes; he addresses to her the sonnet: "Ciò che m' incontra, nella mente mora" (*Son.* viii.).—§ 16. He speaks of the pitiable condition to which he is reduced by the thought of his love; and describes how, though he longs for the sight of Beatrice, he is utterly overcome in her presence; he addresses to her the sonnet: "Spesse fiate vengonmi alla mente" (*Son.* ix.).—§ 17. Having disburdened his heart in the three preceding sonnets, Dante determines to speak of a new matter.

Part II. §§ 18-28.—§ 18. He discourses with certain ladies of his love for Beatrice, and resolves henceforth to devote himself to the theme of her praises.—§ 19. After a period of hesitation, at last one day, while walking beside a stream, his thoughts take shape, and on his return home he composes the canzone: "Donne, ch' avete l' intelletto d' amore" (*Canz.* i.).—§ 20. One of his friends, having become acquainted with the canzone, desires him to expound the nature of love, whereon he composes the sonnet: "Amore e 'l cor gentil sono una cosa" (*Son.* x.).—§ 21. He describes in the sonnet, "Negli occhi porta la mia donna Amore" (*Son.* xi.), the effect produced on others by Beatrice.—§ 22. Folco Portinari, the father of Beatrice, dies (31 December, 1289); Dante composes two sonnets: "Voi, che portate la sembianza umile" (*Son.* xii.), and, "Se' tu colui, c' hai trattato sovente" (*Son.* xiii.), treating of the discourse of certain ladies on the subject of Beatrice's grief, and of his grief for her.—§ 23. Dante falls ill; he has presentiments of the death of Beatrice, and on the ninth day of his illness he has a fourth vision (he dreams that Beatrice is dead, and that he is taken to see her as she lies on her death-bed)[1]; on coming to himself again he relates his vision to certain ladies who were at his bedside, and afterwards writes a description of it in the canzone: "Donna pietosa e di novella etate" (*Canz.* ii.).—§ 24. He has a fifth vision (Love comes to him from the dwelling-place of his lady, and bids him bless the day whereon he was possessed by Love; shortly after Beatrice herself appears to him, preceded by Giovanna, the lady of his friend Guido Cavalcanti), which he describes in the sonnet: "Io mi sentii svegliar dentro allo core" (*Son.* xiv.).—§ 25. Dante explains his use of figurative language, which is conceded to poets.—§ 26. Beatrice considered a marvel by all who beheld her; Dante's sonnet on the subject: "Tanto gentile e tanto onesta pare" (*Son.* xv.).— § 27. The praise and honour of Beatrice is reflected on the ladies about her; as is set forth by Dante in the sonnet: "Vede perfettamente ogni salute" (*Son.* xvi.).—§ 28. The effects upon him of his devotion to Beatrice intended to be described in a canzone: "Sì lungamente m' ha tenuto Amore" (*Canz.* iii.), which was left unfinished.

Part III. §§ 29-35.—§ 29. The composition of Dante's projected canzone (*Canz.* iii.) interrupted by the death of Beatrice; of the part played by the number nine in connection with her death.—§ 30. Of the date of the death of Beatrice, which befell on the ninth day, of the ninth month, of the year in which the perfect number (ten) was completed for the ninth time in the century in which she lived, (i.e. 8 June, 1290), according to the Arabian, Syrian and Italian reckonings respectively; of the significance of

---

[1] This is the subject of D. G. Rossetti's famous picture "Dante's Dream," now in the Walker Art Gallery at Liverpool.

the number nine, and of its intimate association with Beatrice.—§ 31. Dante in his desolation addresses a letter, beginning "Quomodo sedet sola civitas," to the chief personages of the city; his reasons for not transcribing the letter.—§ 32. He vents his grief in a canzone: "Gli occhi dolenti per pietà del core" (*Canz.* iv.).—§ 33. At the request of a brother of Beatrice, Dante writes the sonnet: "Venite a intender li sospiri miei" (*Son.* xvii.) on her death.—§ 34. Dissatisfied with the sonnet, he composes two stanzas of a canzone: "Quantunque volte lasso! mi rimembra" (*Canz.* v.), on the same subject, which he gives with the sonnet to Beatrice's brother.—§ 35. On the first anniversary of Beatrice's death, while drawing an angel, he is interrupted by visitors, to whom he addresses a sonnet, to which he made two beginnings: "Era venuta nella mente mia" (*Son.* xviii.).

Part IV. §§ 36-39.—§ 36. Dante in deep distress at the thought of the past, beholds a beautiful young lady ("una gentil donna giovane e bella") regarding him with compassion from a window; he addresses her in a sonnet: "Videro gli occhi miei quanta pietate" (*Son.* xix.).—§ 37. The "donna gentile" continues to show compassion for him; he addresses a second sonnet to her: "Color d' amore, e di pietà sembianti" (*Son.* xx.).—§ 38. He begins to take delight in the sight of the "donna gentile," and reproaches himself for his inconstancy; he composes a sonnet on the state of his feelings: "L' amaro lagrimar che voi faceste" (*Son.* xxi.).—§ 39. In another sonnet he describes the struggle between his heart and his soul as to this new love: "Gentil pensiero, che parla di vui" (*Son.* xxii.).

Part V. §§ 40-43.—§ 40. While engaged in this struggle Dante has a vision (the sixth) of Beatrice, youthful and clothed in crimson, as when he first saw her, whereon he

repents of his inconstancy and devotes himself solely to
the thought of her; he records the reconquest of himself,
and the effects of the violence of his weeping at the
recollection of his past unworthy passion, in a sonnet:
"Lasso! per forza de' molti sospiri" (*Son.* xxiii.).—§ 41.
He addresses a sonnet to certain pilgrims on their way
through Florence to visit the Veronica at Rome, whom
he assumes to be from a far country, as they show no sign
of grief in passing through the grieving city: "Deh peregrini, che pensosi andate" (*Son.* xxiv.).—§ 42. In response to a request from two ladies for verses of his, he
composes a sonnet describing his condition: "Oltre la
spera, che più larga gira" (*Son.* xxv.), which he sends to
them, together with the preceding: "Deh peregrini" (*Son.*
xxiv.), and another: "Venite a intender" (*Son.* xvii.).—
§ 43. After composing this sonnet he has a last vision
(the seventh), which makes him resolve to speak no more
of Beatrice until he shall be able to say of her what was
never said of any woman; he concludes with the prayer
that his soul may then be permitted to behold the glory
of Beatrice in the presence of the Everlasting God.

With the exception of the *Latin Eclogues* and *Letters*,
the *Vita Nuova* was the last of Dante's works to be
printed. The *editio princeps*, which was printed at
Florence, together with fifteen of Dante's *canzoni*, and
Boccaccio's *Vita di Dante*, did not appear until 1576, more
than a hundred years later than the first edition of the
Divina Commedia. It was not reprinted for a hundred
and fifty years, when it was included by Anton Maria
Biscioni, together with the *Convivio*, in his *Prose di Dante
Alighieri e di Messer Gio. Boccacci*, published at Florence
in 1723. Since that date there have been some five-and-
twenty other editions, exclusive of mere reprints. The

editio princeps, which was issued with the *imprimatur* of the Inquisition, contains a mutilated text, many passages or phrases, which were considered offensive to the Church or to religion, having been altered or suppressed.[1] A critical edition was published at Florence by Michele Barbi, under the auspices of the *Società Dantesca Italiana*, in 1907.

Forty manuscripts of the *Vita Nuova* are known to exist, including three which are incomplete. Of these, eight belong to the fourteenth century, sixteen to the fifteenth, and sixteen to the sixteenth. None of these was executed in Dante's lifetime, the earliest being assigned to about the year 1350, that is about thirty years after Dante's death.[2]

Convivio.—Besides the *Vita Nuova* Dante wrote in Italian prose the philosophical treatise to which he gave the name of *Convivio*[3] or Banquet. This work consists of a philosophical commentary, which Dante left incomplete, on three of his canzoni. According to the original scheme it was to have been a commentary on fourteen canzoni,[4] and would have consisted of fifteen books, the first being introductory.

[1] See Paget Toynbee, *The Inquisition and the Editio Princeps of the Vita Nuova*, in *Modern Language Review*, April, 1908, vol. iii. pp. 228-31.

[2] See the introduction (pp. xvii. ff.) to Barbi's critical edition. There are eight English translations of the *Vita Nuova*, of which the first, by Joseph Garrow, was published at Florence in 1846. Of the others the best known are those by D. G. Rossetti (1862), Theodore Martin (1862), and C. E. Norton (1867). The latest is that by Thomas Okey (1906).

[3] This is the form of the title in the MSS., almost without exception, and in the *editio princeps* (1490); in the three sixteenth-century editions (1521, 1529, 1531) the title is *L' amoroso Convivio*. The title *Convito* appears for the first time in the edition published by Biscioni (in *Prose di Dante Alighieri e di Messer Gio. Boccacci*) at Florence in 1723. The correct title *Convivio* was restored by Witte in 1879, and is now almost universally adopted (see Witte, *Dante-Forschungen*, vol. ii. pp. 574-80).

[4] See *Convivio*, i. 1, ll. 102-5.

Three of these projected books are specifically referred to by Dante, viz. the seventh, in which he was to have treated of temperance [1]; the fourteenth, in which he proposed to treat of justice [2] and allegory [3]; and the fifteenth, in which liberality was to have been treated of. [4]

Various attempts have been made to identify the remaining eleven canzoni, which were to have been the subject of commentary in the unwritten books, but none of these is wholly satisfactory. [5]

In its unfinished state the *Convivio* consists of four books, which show a tendency to become more and more prolix as the work proceeds, the fourth book containing thirty chapters, while the first, second, and third contain respectively thirteen, sixteen, and fifteen. The division of the books into chapters was made by Dante himself. [6]

Giovanni Villani in his Florentine chronicle says of this book :—

"Dante commenced a commentary on fourteen of his moral canzoni in the vulgar tongue, which is incomplete, save as regards three of them, in consequence of his death. This commentary, to judge by what we have of it, would have been a lofty, beautiful, subtle, and very great work, inasmuch as it is adorned by lofty style, and fine philosophical and astrological discussions." [7]

Boccaccio says :—

"Dante also composed a commentary in prose in the Florentine vulgar tongue on three of his canzoni at full length ; he appears to have intended, when he began, to

---

[1] *Conv.* iv. 26, ll. 66-7.   [2] *Conv.* i. 12, ll. 86-8 ; iv. 27, ll. 100-2.

[3] *Conv.* ii. 1, ll. 34-6.   [4] *Conv.* i. 8, ll. 130-2 ; iii. 15, l. 144.

[5] See Antonio Santi, *Il Canzoniere di Dante Alighieri*, vol. ii. pp. 13 ff. (Roma, 1907).

[6] See *Conv.* i. 4, l. 4 ; ii. 7, l. 1 ; iii. 6, l. 1 ; iv. 2, l. 77 ; etc. etc.

[7] Bk. ix. ch. 136. This passage is omitted from some MSS. of the *Cronica.*

write a commentary upon all of them, but whether he afterwards changed his mind, or never had time to carry out his intention, at any rate he did not write the commentary on more than these three. This book, which he entitled *Convivio*, is a very beautiful and praiseworthy little work." [1]

The *Convivio* was written some time after the *Vita Nuova*, but before the *Divina Commedia*, in which Dante sometimes corrects opinions he had expressed in the *Convivio*, such as his theories as to the spots on the moon,[2] and the arrangement of the celestial hierarchies.[3] From the references to the Emperor Albert I (iv. 3, l. 42) and to Gherardo da Cammino (iv. 14, ll. 114 ff.) it would appear to have been composed (perhaps at Bologna) between April, 1306 (Gherardo having died on 26 March, 1306) and 1 May, 1308 (the date of Albert's death).[4] It was certainly written after Dante's exile from Florence, as at the beginning of the work there is a most pathetic reference to the miseries he endured during his wanderings as an outcast from his native city.[5]

Dante explains in the first book, which is introductory, the meaning of the title, the aim of the work, and the difference between it and the *Vita Nuova ;* he himself, he says, as the author, represents the servants at an actual banquet (*convivio*) ; he then points out that the book is of the nature of a commentary, and is written in a lofty style in order to give it an air of gravity and authority, and to counterbalance the objection of its being in Italian ; he next gives his reasons for writing it in the vulgar tongue instead of in Latin, in which respect it differs from other commentaries ; he

---

[1] *Vita di Dante*, ed. cit. § 16, p. 74.
[2] *Conv.* ii. 14, ll. 69 ff. ; *Par.* ii. 49-148 ; xxii. 139-41.
[3] *Conv.* ii. 6, ll. 39 ff. ; *Par.* xxviii. 40-139.
[4] See Zingarelli, *Vita di Dante* (1905), pp. 45, 52.
[5] *Conv.* i. 3, ll. 20 ff. ; see the passage quoted above, pp. 88-9.

further explains that the commentary stands in the same relation to the canzoni as a servant does to his master; and he concludes by declaring that in this work is made manifest the great excellence of the Italian language— that language which he was destined to bring to the highest degree of perfection in the *Divina Commedia*.

Analysis of the *Convivio*[1] :—

Book I.—*Chap*. 1. Introductory. The work undertaken in order to justify the universal desire for knowledge spoken of by Aristotle. Causes whereby men may be prevented from acquiring the highest knowledge. Happy those who sit at the table where the bread of angels is eaten. Dante himself sits not at the table, but gathers up the fragments which fall from it. Moved with pity for his kind, he reserves a part of his store, both bread and meat, to make a feast (*convivio*) for them. The meat will be served in fourteen canzoni, the bread will be served in the commentary which will give first the literal, then the allegorical interpretation of the canzoni. The author explains the reason for the difference in style between the present work and the *Vita Nuova*.— *Chap*. 2. As bread served at a banquet is freed from impurity by the servants, so must the commentary be freed from objection. Two objections may be urged, viz. that the author has to speak of himself, and that the commentary is difficult to understand. Teachers of rhetoric forbid a man to speak of himself, but it is allowable in exceptional cases, as in self-defence, and for the edification of others. Dante pleads both these reasons in the present instance: he wishes to defend himself from the charge of having yielded to passion in his canzoni, and to instruct

[1] Adapted, by kind permission of the author, from the "Summary of Contents" prefixed to each book in the translation of the *Convivio* by the Rector of Exeter College, Dr. W. W. Jackson (Oxford, 1909).

others in the writing and understanding of allegory.—
Chap. 3. As to the difficulty of the commentary, this is
intentional, in order to counteract certain disadvantages
under which the author labours. He has been exiled
from his beloved Florence, and has wandered in poverty
all over Italy, thus becoming known and despised in
every quarter. Report magnifies, and personal knowledge
diminishes, a man's good and evil qualities. Good report is magnified as it passes from one to another ; so too is
evil report.—*Chap*. 4. On the other hand a man's presence
diminishes his apparent worth for three reasons: viz. the
proneness of men, like children, to judge by the outside ;
their envy, which makes them blind to the truth ; and
the natural imperfection of the person judged. Wherefore
a prophet is without honour in his own country. As
Dante's presence has become familiar throughout Italy
during his wanderings as an exile, he wishes to counteract the effect of this familiarity by the adoption of a
somewhat lofty style for his commentary ; hence its difficulty.—*Chap*. 5. The commentary has been freed from
accidental flaws, but one defect is inherent in it, viz. that
it is written in Italian, not in Latin. Three reasons for
the choice of the vernacular, viz. to avoid disorder, for the
sake of liberality, and from natural affection for the
mother-tongue. As to the first reason : the best results
are obtained when the qualities of the agent are adapted
for the end in view. The qualities of a good servant are
subjection, intimate acquaintance with his master, and
obedience. Latin is devoid of all these qualities. Firstly,
it is not subject, but by nature sovereign.—*Chap*. 6.
Secondly, Latin has not the intimate acquaintance with
Italian which is needed for a commentary on the canzoni ;
it has only a general knowledge of Italian, and has no intimacy with its friends ; whereas a good servant should

have an intimate knowledge both of his master and of his master's friends.—*Chap*. 7. Thirdly, Latin could not be obedient. Perfect obedience should be free from bitterness; it should result from a command, not from choice; and it should be duly measured. Latin could not fulfil these conditions. Remarks on the inadequacy of translation.— *Chap*. 8. The second reason for choosing Italian is its liberality. Perfect liberality gives to many; its gifts are useful; and it gives without being asked. Explanation of these characteristics, which are shown to be essential.— *Chap*. 9. In the case of Latin, the liberality would not have been perfect, for it does not possess these characteristics. It would not have served many, for it would not have been understood, inasmuch as nobody learns Latin except for gain. It would not have been useful, for few would have used it. It would not have given itself unasked, for every one demands that commentaries should be in Latin.—*Chap*. 10. The third reason for choosing Italian is the natural affection which a man feels for his mother-tongue. Natural affection prompts a man to magnify its object, to be jealous for it, and to defend it. Dante displays his love for Italian in all these three ways. He magnifies it by displaying it in act, not merely in potentiality. His jealousy for it moved him to write his commentary in Italian, lest if he wrote it in Latin some bungler hereafter should translate it into Italian. He is anxious to defend his mother-tongue against those who disparage it, in favour of Provençal, for instance, and to exhibit it in its native beauty. This is best displayed in prose, as a woman's beauty is seen best when unadorned.— *Chap*. 11. Five detestable causes move men to disparage their mother-tongue, viz. lack of discernment, deceitful excuses, love of vainglory, the prompting of envy, and faint-heartedness. As to the first, those who lack discernment are like blind men, or senseless sheep. As to the second, the bad workman blames his tools or his materials, not himself. Those who are unskilled in the use of Italian lay the blame on it, and exalt another tongue at its expense. As to the third, vainglory impels a man to seek praise for mastering a tongue other than his own. As to the fourth, those who cannot use Italian envy those who can, and therefore decry it. As to the fifth, a faint-hearted man always thinks meanly of himself and his belongings, and therefore despises his mother-tongue.—*Chap.* 12. Dante's affection for his mother-tongue incontestable. Affection is inspired by propinquity and goodness, and increased by benefits conferred, and by common aims and intercourse. A man's mother-tongue is nearest to him. Also, it displays the characteristic excellence of language, in that it best enables a man to express his meaning.—*Chap.* 13. The conditions which increase affection are also present. If existence is the greatest boon, then a man's mother-tongue is to be loved as having given him existence, by bringing his parents together. Further, it led Dante into the way of knowledge by enabling him to learn Latin. The vernacular, moreover, if it could have a conscious aim, would seek to preserve itself by assuming the most durable shape, namely the poetic. It has been Dante's aim to give it this shape. All his life he has also had the most familiar intercourse with his mother-tongue. Dante may thus claim to have purged his Italian commentary from all stain, so that the meat may now be served up with this bread, and may be partaken of by the multitude.

Book II.—*Canzone:* "Voi ch' intendendo il terzo ciel movete".—*Chap.* I. The commentary on the canzoni will explain both the literal and allegorical sense. Four senses of writings to be distinguished, viz. the literal,

which lies on the surface; the allegorical, which is the truth
underlying the literal; the moral, which conveys a lesson
of life and conduct; and the anagogical, or spiritual,
which refers to heavenly things. Reasons why the literal
sense must first be determined.—*Chap.* 2. The first canzone says, literally, that Venus had completed two revolu-
tions when a gentle lady appeared to the poet in company
with Love. The victory of the new thought, concerning
this lady, over the former thought, concerning Beatrice,
impels him to address the heavenly powers whence the
new thought derived its strength. Division of the canzone
into three principal parts.—*Chap.* 3. To make the literal
sense of the first part clear, Dante explains who they are
whom he addresses, and what is the third heaven which
they move. Discussion of the number of the heavens;
eight enumerated by Aristotle; a ninth recognized by
Ptolemy.—*Chap.* 4. The order of the first eight heavens,
which are those of the Moon, Mercury, Venus, the Sun,
Mars, Jupiter, Saturn, and the Fixed Stars. Beyond
these is the Crystalline Heaven or *Primum Mobile.* Outside of this again is situated, according to the teaching of
the Church, the Empyrean, which is the abode of the
Deity and of Blessed Spirits, and which exists not in space
but only in the Primal Mind. Description of the construction of the heavens, each of which has two poles and
an equator. Of the epicycle of Venus.—*Chap.* 5. The
beings who move the heavens explained to be angelic
Intelligences. Opinions of Aristotle, Plato, and others on
the subject. Of the active, and contemplative, life. The
latter the most appropriate to Angels, as being the highest.
The motion of the heavens due to the thought of certain
of these Angels. These beings created by the Deity in
infinite numbers, as even the intellect of man, who sees
but darkly, can conceive.—*Chap.* 6. Of Angels according

to the Scriptures. Their division into three hierarchies, each consisting of three orders. Distribution of the nine orders among the various heavens. The manner of their contemplation determined by the nature of the Trinity. The Thrones assigned to the third heaven, that of Venus. Virgil, Ovid, and Alfraganus, cited as to the function, and threefold motion, of this heaven, the movers of which are those to whom Dante addresses himself.—*Chap.* 7. The meaning of his prayer for audience, his reasons for addressing the movers of the third heaven, and the inducement offered to them. Explanation of certain terms used in the canzone.—*Chap.* 8. Literal sense of the second part of the canzone, which has two subdivisions. Of the two contending thoughts mentioned above. Further explanations of terms employed. — *Chap.* 9. Solution of difficulty as to the inspiration of Dante's new thought by the same Intelligences which inspired the old. Digression on the immortality of the soul. Agreement of pagan and Christian teaching on the subject.—*Chap.* 10. Further explanation of expressions used in the canzone. Incidental statement as to how impressions enter the eye, and become stamped on the imagination. — *Chap.* 11. Consideration of the reasons alleged by the Spirit of Love in favour of the second lady, especially the qualities of pity and courtesy. Of the relation between "piety" and "pity". Definition of "courtesy," which if named from the courts of that day, especially in Italy, would mean baseness.—*Chap.* 12. Having dealt with the literal meaning of the part of the canzone addressed to the Intelligences of the third heaven, Dante now deals with the last part, the *tornata*, which is addressed to the canzone itself. Explanation of the term. Of the beauty and goodness of the canzone.—*Chap.* 13. The literal sense being disposed of, Dante now passes to the allegorical meaning. How, in his desire to find consolation for the loss of his soul's first delight, he turned to the study of Boëthius' *De Consolatione Philosophiae*, and to Cicero's *De Amicitia*, and was thereby led on to the study of philosophy, which in time banished all other thoughts. His canzone in praise of philosophy written in the vulgar tongue ostensibly about a lady, since philosophy *per se* was too exalted to be praised in the vernacular, and further, men would more readily credit him with love for a lady than for philosophy. The canzone thus being an allegory of philosophy, the third heaven and its movers must also receive an allegorical interpretation.—*Chap.* 14. Heaven allegorically interpreted signifies scientific knowledge, and the heavens signify the sciences.   Three points of resemblance between the heavens and the sciences.   Correspondence of the first seven heavens with the seven sciences of the *Trivium* and *Quadrivium*, of the eighth with physics and metaphysics, of the ninth with moral science, and of the tenth with divine science, or theology.   Detailed statement of points of comparison between the seven sciences and the first seven heavens.—*Chap.* 15. Points of comparison between physics and metaphysics and the eighth heaven, between moral philosophy and the ninth heaven, between theology and the tenth heaven.   Incidental discussion of the various opinions as to the nature of the Galaxy.   The third heaven shown to represent rhetoric.—*Chap.* 16. The movers of the third heaven represent rhetoricians, such as Boëthius and Cicero above mentioned.   The lady of the canzone thus shown to be philosophy, and her eyes the demonstrations of philosophy.

Book III.—*Canzone:* "Amor, che nella mente mi ragiona".—*Chap.* 1. Three reasons which impelled Dante to give expression to his passion for the gentle lady, viz. the desire of gaining honour for himself through his friendship with her, the desire that this friendship should be lasting, and the desire to avoid reproach by stating who the lady was. Division of the canzone into three principal parts.—*Chap.* 2. Explanation of the first part. Love defined as the spiritual union of the soul with the object loved. Of all things the human soul has most affinity with God, and consequently is most closely united with whatever most nearly resembles God. The love of which Dante speaks is the union of his soul with the gentle lady. The place where love discourses is the mind, or thinking faculty, which is the highest of the three faculties of the soul, and which belongs only to man and to divine substances.—*Chap.* 3. Man, though his essence be one, is capable of feeling every sort of love, such as is felt by simple and composite bodies, by plants, and by animals. The love which is the poet's theme is the highest of all ; he can neither fully apprehend it nor express it.—*Chap.* 4. Explanation of this incapacity of mind and speech, for which Dante is not to be blamed, since blame attaches to want of will, not to want of power.—*Chap.* 5. Discussion of the second stanza of the canzone, in which the lady is praised as a whole, both in soul and body. Long digression explaining and illustrating the revolution of the Sun round the Earth.—*Chap.* 6. Explanation of the meaning of "temporal" and "equal" hours. The Intelligences on high gaze on his lady, as a thought existing in the divine mind. She is beloved by God as being endowed with a special portion of the divine nature, and admired by man inasmuch as her soul dignifies the body, which is the actuality of the soul.—*Chap.* 7. Praise of the lady as regards her soul. The goodness of God is diffused over all things, but enters into various substances, as light does, in proportion to their receptivity. In the intellectual order are infinite gradations, hence it may be assumed that some human being is little lower than the angels. Such is this lady. Her speech and acts afford an example to others, and are an aid to the faith of all mankind, whereby they gain everlasting life.—*Chap*. 8. Praise of the lady in respect of her body, especially of those parts in which the soul chiefly operates, viz. the eyes and mouth. Explanation of sundry expressions in the fourth stanza of the canzone. Distinction between innate and habitual vices. Definition of the end and source of this lady's beauty.—*Chap*. 9. Discussion of third division of the canzone. Explanation why the lady, who was formerly called proud and disdainful, is now called humble. Illustration drawn from the sky, which always has the quality of brightness, but does not always appear bright. Statement of the theory of vision. Reference to Dante's own weakness of sight.—*Chap*. 10. Of judgment by outward appearance at the prompting of desire; and of the rhetorical figure known as dissimulation.—*Chap*. 11. Allegorical meaning of the canzone discussed. Origin of the terms " philosophy" and " philosopher," i.e. lover of wisdom. Of the nature of friendship. The name of philosophy given to the sciences, natural, moral, and metaphysical, above all to the last, which is called philosophy *par excellence*.— *Chap*. 12. Of two kinds of devotion (*studio*). Reasons why the Sun is worthy to be a type of God. As the Sun illumines first itself, and then all other sensible objects, so God illumines first Himself, and then all other intellectual beings. As injury done by the Sun is not intentional but accidental, so badness in things which partake of intellectual light, as in bad angels, is not designed but accidental. Philosophy part of the divine essence, and as it were the bride, the sister, and daughter of the Emperor of heaven. —*Chap*. 13. Philosophy resides also in the celestial Intelligences. Her highest gifts enjoyable only in use,

not merely in possession, though he who only possesses
her is still a philosopher, for philosophy is always transcendent.—*Chap.* 14. The allegorical interpretation, following the literal, passes from general commendation of the
lady to particular. Discussion and explanation of various
expressions in the third stanza of the canzone. Of the
distinction between "light" and "splendour". The
ancient philosophers indifferent to all things save wisdom.
Of the effect of philosophy on the soul, especially in aiding
faith.—*Chap.* 15. Discussion of the fourth stanza. The
eyes of philosophy explained to be her demonstrations,
and her smiles her persuasions. The difficulty of understanding her obliges man sometimes to be content with
negations; but the desire of wisdom is not futile in man
or angels, because it is always proportionate to their nature.
The beauty of wisdom signifies the moral virtues, which
are impaired by vanity and pride; hence she teaches
humility. Her highest praise is that she is mother of
first principles, hence she was the partner of God in the
creation of the world. Passing to the *tornata*, Dante
explains why at first he called philosophy fierce and
disdainful.

Book IV.—*Canzone*: "Le dolci rime d' amor, ch' io
solìa".—*Chap.* 1. Dante's love for philosophy makes him
love truth and hate falsehood. Hence his desire to lead
men to entertain true and reject false opinions with regard
to human goodness, or nobility. Nobility the theme of
the third canzone; consequently the exposition will not
be concerned with allegory, but will give a fuller treatment of the literal meaning.—*Chap.* 2. Division of the
canzone into two principal parts, the preface, and the main
argument. The preface subdivided into three parts. Importance of choosing the right time, as well for the speaker
as for the hearer. Dante's object both to refute what is

false, and, more especially, to emphasise the truth.—*Chap.*
3. Subdivision of the main argument (*trattato*) of the
canzone into three parts, the first of which is again subdivided into two. Nobility defined by the Emperor
Frederick II as ancestral wealth and fine manners.—
Chap. 4. Mention of the Emperor leads Dante to consider
at length the nature of the Imperial authority, its origin,
and necessity. The Roman Empire shown to be the seat
of this authority.—*Chap.* 5. The working of divine Pro-
vidence demonstrated in the rise and progress of the
Roman Empire, and in the noble deeds of her sons.—
Chap. 6. Discussion of the derivation and meaning of the
word "authority". Aristotle, the master and leader of
human reason, declared to be the highest authority. His
opinion, and that of other philosophers as to the "end of
human life" examined. Aristotle's opinion shown not to
conflict with the Imperial authority; both philosopher and
emperor needed to constitute the highest authority.—
Chap. 7. Of the danger of allowing a wrong opinion to
prevail unchecked. The defects of popular opinion due
to disregard of proper guidance. Those who go astray
for this reason the vilest of all, just as he is least excusable
who strays from the path with the footprints of others to
guide him. Such an one, in the words of the canzone,
"is dead while he liveth".—*Chap.* 8. Of discernment, and
of reverence, one of its fairest fruits. In rejecting common
opinion Dante appeals from the judgment of sense to that
of reason; and in rejecting the opinion of the Emperor, he
is not irreverent, since Imperial authority does not extend
to the domain of reason.—*Chap.* 9. Imperial authority has
jurisdiction over all human activities, but these are limited,
some being purely natural, while others are subject to reason
and will. Activities with which reason is concerned are
of four kinds. That activity which derives its character

solely from the act of the will is most completely under our control; and, generally speaking, responsibility is proportionate to the power exercised by the will. Law intended to be a guide to the will. Action may be compared with art, that is, production. Many processes of production are purely technical, and here art is supreme; but in others art is limited by the laws of its subject-matter. Similarly the Emperor's authority is limited by the law of reason and of nature. The definition of nobility therefore does not come within his scope.—*Chap.* 10. Criticism of previous opinions. In so far as definitions of nobility make fine manners essential to it they are right, though defective. But in introducing the notion of time, or of wealth, they are erroneous. Philosophical arguments against making nobility dependent on wealth.—*Chap.* 11. The inferiority of wealth attributable to three special imperfections, viz. lack of discrimination in its advent, dangers attendant upon its increase, and disasters consequent on its possession. Consideration of the first of these imperfections. Of that most noble exchange, made, alas! by so few, of riches for the hearts of men. Instances of munificence.—*Chap.* 12. Increase of wealth shown to be evil, inasmuch as it brings the torment of boundless and therefore futile desire. Those who would apply this same argument in the case of knowledge, ignore the essential difference between the two kinds of desire.—*Chap.* 13. The desire of riches is uniform and keeps growing, and is therefore never consummated; while the desire of knowledge is a succession of desires, each of which is consummated in turn. Consideration of the disasters consequent on the possession of wealth, which not only inflicts positive evil on its possessor, but also deprives him of good.—*Chap.* 14. Refutation of the error which makes nobility depend on time, by defining it as

consisting in ancestral wealth. The opinion that no one
who begins by being a clown can ever become a gentleman, and *vice versa*, antagonistic to the claim that time is
requisite for nobility. The contention that nobility begins
when low birth is forgotten, shown to be absurd on four
grounds. Firstly, a feeble memory, which is a bad thing,
would be the cause of nobility, which is a good thing, and
the shorter men's memories the quicker would nobility be
engendered. Secondly, the distinction between mean
and noble would not be applicable to anything but man,
whereas we often speak of a noble or mean horse, falcon,
pearl, etc. Thirdly, the thing engendered (nobility)
would often be in existence before its cause (oblivion)
came into operation. Fourthly, some would be considered
noble after death who were not noble during life.—
Chap. 15. Again, if a man cannot change from simple to
gentle, and *vice versa*, one of two absurdities must follow:
either nobility does not exist at all, or the world must
always have had more than one man in it, which is contrary
to both Christian and pagan belief. The error in question
is manifest to sound minds. Minds are sound when not
hampered by evil dispositions, three kinds of which are
specified, viz. boastfulness, dejection of mind, and levity
of nature.—*Chap*. 16. Dante now passes to the examination of the true definition of nobility. "Nobility" signifies
in each thing the perfection of the nature peculiar to it.
The word derived not from *nosco*, as some suppose, but
from *non vile*. The quality will be defined by its fruits,
viz. the moral and intellectual virtues.—*Chap*. 17. The
moral virtues peculiarly our own fruits, as being wholly in
our own power. Aristotle's classification of these virtues.
His definition of happiness. We have two kinds of happiness, according as we follow the active or the contemplative life, of which the latter is the higher, as Christ

teaches with reference to Martha in the Gospel of Luke.— *Chap.* 18. Every moral virtue springs from right choice. Right choice is also characteristic of nobility. One of these (virtue or nobility) therefore must come from the other, or both from a third. The more comprehensive of the two terms (nobility) must be taken as the original source of the characteristic.—*Chap.* 19. Nobility shown to be a wider term than virtue, as including divers other kinds of excellence, as well bodily as mental ; it even extends to regions where virtue is not found, as in the qualities of woman and of the young.—*Chap.* 20. Thus nobility enters into the conception of virtue, and is something divine. But the gift is bestowed only on the soul adapted for its reception. Hence nobility is a seed of blessedness placed by God in the soul fitted to receive it.—*Chap.* 21. Of the agencies, natural and spiritual, by which nobility descends into men. Theories of the ancients as to the nature and origin of the soul. Natural agencies, including the influences of the generating soul, of the heaven, and of the "complexion" of the material, prepare the material to receive the formative virtue which proceeds from the generating soul; the formative virtue in turn prepares it for the heavenly virtue from which life comes. The potential intellect, in which exist potentially the universal forms derived from the primal Intelligence, is imparted by the mover of the heaven. The purity of the soul is in proportion to the goodness of the various agencies ; and in proportion to its purity the divine excellence multiplies in the intellectual virtue, and becomes the seed of happiness. Divine agencies impart the sevenfold gift of the Spirit, but man is responsible for the cultivation of the seed.—*Chap.* 22. Of natural appetite, which at first is without discrimination, but afterwards becomes discriminated. Rational desire belonging to the

mind, i.e. the will and intellect, is the highest and brings
the highest happiness. Such as have not this desire im-
planted in them by nature, may get it ingrafted in them.
Of the higher blessedness of the contemplative over the
active life.—*Chap*. 23. Discussion of the seventh stanza
of the canzone. Dante shows how nobility is displayed
in the different stages of life. The life of man likened to
an arch rising to its highest point (at the thirty-fifth year)
and declining. Illustration from the life of the Saviour.
Correspondence between the four ages in man (adolescence,
youth, old age, decline) and the four divisions of the
year (the seasons) and of the day (the canonical tierce,
none, sext, and vespers, of which an explanation is
given).—*Chap*. 24. Of the duration of the four ages of
human life. Adolescence lasts till the twenty-fifth year;
youth to the forty-fifth; old age to the seventieth; after
which begins decline. Adolescence naturally endowed
with four things, obedience, suavity, sense of shame, and
comeliness. Of obedience.—*Chap*. 25. Of suavity in adolescence. Of the sense of shame, which consists in awe,
modesty, shamefacedness. These three qualities illustrated from the history of Adrastus in the *Thebaid* of
Statius. Of bodily comeliness.—*Chap*. 26. Five characteristics of youth, to be temperate, brave, full of love,
courteous, and loyal. Temperance and courage respectively the bridle and spur of desire, as exemplified by
Virgil in the history of Aeneas in the *Aeneid*, whence also
illustrations of the other three qualities are drawn.—
Chap. 27. Of the four virtues most suitable to old age, viz.
to be prudent, just, bountiful, and fairspoken (*affabile*).
Illustrations of these qualities drawn from the history of
Cephalus and Aeacus in the *Metamorphoses* of Ovid.—
Chap. 28. Of the two qualities most proper to the fourth
stage of life (decline), resignation of the soul to God, and

thankfulness for the journey ended. Illustrations from
the history of Marcia and Cato in Lucan's *Pharsalia.*—
Chap. 29. Of those who believe themselves noble because
they are of noble lineage. A family may be called noble
if the majority of its members are truly noble, but a
worthless member of it is not entitled to claim nobility on
that score. Illustration from a heap of grain.—*Chap.* 30.
Discussion of the *tornata* of the canzone. Its title (*Contra
gli erranti*) imitated from that of Aquinas' book *Contra
Gentiles.* The canzone bidden to address herself only to
such as have some love for the gentle lady, philosophy.
The friend of philosophy, mentioned in the last line, explained to be nobility, there being ever the deepest love
and admiration between these two.

The first printed edition of the *Convivio* was issued at
Florence in 1490, eighteen years later than the *editio
princeps* of the *Divina Commedia.* The treatise was three
times reprinted at Venice in the sixteenth century (1521,
1529, 1531). No edition of it was published in the seventeenth century. The fifth edition did not appear until
1723, when the work was printed by Anton Maria Biscioni (under the title of *Convito*),[1] together with the *Vita
Nuova*, in his *Prose di Dante Alighieri e di Messer Gio.
Boccacci*, published at Florence in that year. Critical editions, with a more or less improved text, were published
at Milan in 1826 (reprinted at Padua in the following year),
and at Modena in 1831 ; but the first really critical text,
based on the authority of all the available manuscripts,
was that of Dr. Moore, which was first printed in the Oxford Dante in 1894, and was reprinted in an amended
form in the third edition of that work in 1904.

Thirty-three manuscripts of the *Convivio* are known, of

[1] As to this form of the title of the treatise, see above, p. 173, note 3.

which three are in England.[1]   No critical account nor
classification of these manuscripts has yet been published,
but at least six of them belong to the fourteenth century.[2]

[1] One in the Canonici collection in the Bodleian Library at Oxford;
one in the Earl of Leicester's collection at Holkham; and one in the
possession of Dr. Edward Moore at Canterbury.   There are four English
translations of the *Convivio*, viz. by Elizabeth Sayer (1887), Katharine
Hillard (1889), P. H. Wicksteed (1903), and W. W. Jackson (1909).

[2] See Zingarelli, *Dante*, p. 389.

DANTE AND HIS BOOK
From the picture by Domenico di Michelino, in the Duomo at Florence

CHAPTER II

DIVINA COMMEDIA.—At the close of the *Vita Nuova* Dante says that "a wonderful vision appeared to me, in which I saw things which made me resolve to speak no more of this blessed one,[1] until I could more worthily treat of her. And to attain to this, I study to the utmost of my power, as she truly knows. So that, if it shall please Him through whom all things live, that my life be prolonged for some years, I hope to say of her what was never said of any woman." This promise to say of Beatrice what had been said of no other woman Dante fulfilled in the *Divina Commedia*, the central figure of which is Beatrice glorified.

"Several years after the composition of the *Vita Nuova*," says Boccaccio, "Dante, as he looked down from the high places of the government of the commonwealth of Florence wherein he was stationed, and observed over a wide prospect, such as is visible from such elevated places, what was the life of men, and what the errors of the common herd, and how few, and how greatly worthy of honour, were those who departed therefrom, and how greatly deserving of confusion those who sided with it, he, condemning the pursuits of such as these and commending

---

[1] i.e. Beatrice.

his own far above theirs, conceived in his mind a lofty
thought, whereby at one and the same time, that is in one
and the same work, he purposed, while giving proof of his
own powers, to pursue with the heaviest penalties the
wicked and vicious, and to honour with the highest rewards
the virtuous and worthy, and to lay up eternal glory for
himself. And inasmuch as he had preferred poetry to
every other pursuit, he resolved to compose a poetical
work; and after long meditation beforehand upon what
he should write, in his thirty-fifth year he began to devote
himself to carrying into effect that upon which he had
been meditating, namely, to rebuke and to glorify the lives
of men according to their different deserts. And inasmuch as he perceived that the lives of men were of three
kinds—namely, the vicious life, the life abandoning vices
and making for virtue, and the virtuous life—he divided
his work in wonderful wise into three books comprised in
one volume, beginning with the punishment of wickedness
and ending with the reward of virtue; and he gave to it
the title of *Commedia*. Each of these three books he
divided into cantos, and the cantos into stanzas. And he
composed this work in rime in the vulgar tongue with so
great art, and with such wondrous and beautiful ordering,
that never yet has any one been able with justice to find
fault with it in any respect. How subtly he exercised the
poet's art in this work may be perceived by all such as
have been endowed with sufficient understanding for the
comprehension of it. But inasmuch as we know that great
things cannot be accomplished in a brief space of time, so
must we understand that so lofty, so great, and so deeply
thought out an undertaking as was this of describing
in verses in the vulgar tongue all the various actions of
mankind and their deserts, could not possibly have been
brought to completion in a short time, especially by a man

who was the sport of so many and various chances of
fortune, all of them full of anguish and envenomed with
bitterness, as we have seen Dante was; he, therefore, from
the hour when he first set himself to this lofty enterprise
down to the last day of his life (notwithstanding that
meanwhile he composed several other works) continually
laboured upon it." [1]

Villani, whose chronicle repeatedly echoes the *Commedia*, gives the following account of the poem :—

" Dante also wrote the *Commedia*, in which in polished
rime, treating of grave and subtle questions of moral and
natural philosophy, astrology, and theology, with beautiful and wonderful figures, similes, and poetical devices, he
discoursed in a hundred *capitoli* or cantos of the nature
and condition of Hell, Purgatory, and Paradise, in as lofty
a style as language will allow, as may be gathered from
the poem itself by any one who has sufficient understanding.   Albeit in the *Commedia* he took delight in scolding
and crying out, after the fashion of poets, perhaps somewhat more than is altogether seemly; but maybe his
exile was the cause of this." [2]

In his letter to Can Grande, in which he dedicates to
him the *Paradiso*, Dante gives his own explanation of
the subject and aim of the poem, and of the reasons why
he called it a comedy.

" The subject of this work," he writes, "must be understood as taken according to the letter, and then as interpreted according to the allegorical meaning.   The subject,
then, of the whole work, taken according to the letter
alone, is simply a consideration of the state of souls after
death ; for from and around this the action of the whole
work turns.   But if the work is considered according

[1] *Vita di Dante*, ed. Macrì-Leone, § 13, pp. 63-4.
[2] Bk. ix. ch. 136.

to its allegorical meaning, the subject is man, liable to
the reward or punishment of justice, according as through
the freedom of the will he is deserving or undeserv-
ing. . . . The aim of the work is to remove those living
in this life from a state of misery and to guide them to a
state of happiness. . . . The title of the book is 'Here
beginneth the Comedy[1] of Dante Alighieri, a Florentine
by birth, but not by character'. And for the comprehension of this it must be understood that . . . comedy is a
certain kind of poetical narrative which differs from all
others. It differs from tragedy in its subject matter,—in
this way, that tragedy in its beginning is admirable and
quiet, in its ending or catastrophe foul and horrible. . . .
Comedy, on the other hand, begins with adverse circumstances, but its theme has a happy termination. . . . Likewise they differ in their style of language, for tragedy is
lofty and sublime, comedy lowly and humble. . . . From
this it is evident why the present work is called a comedy.
For if we consider the theme, in its beginning it is horrible
and foul, because it is Hell; in its ending fortunate, de-
sirable, and joyful, because it is Paradise; and if we consider the style of language, the style is lowly and humble,
because it is the vulgar tongue, in which even housewives
hold converse."[2]

---

[1] The title *Divina Commedia*, as appears from this statement, was not
Dante's own. It probably had its origin in Dante's own description of the
poem as "lo sacrato poema" (*Par.* xxiii. 62) and "il poema sacro" (*Par.*
xxv. 1). It occurs in some of the oldest manuscripts of the poem, and in
Boccaccio's *Life of Dante* (§ 14). The first printed edition bearing this title
is the Venice one of 1555; in a previous edition, with the commentary of
Landino (Florence, 1481), the epithet "divine" is applied to Dante himself, but not to the poem; which, however, had been styled "opus divinissimum" by the Florentine Coluccio Salutati eighty years before (see F.
Novati, *Epistolario di Coluccio Salutati*, vol. iii. p. 371). In the earliest
printed editions the title is simply "La Commedia di Dante Alighieri".

[2] Trans. by Latham (with modifications).

The form of Dante's poem (or vision, as he claims it to have been) is triple, the three divisions corresponding with the three kingdoms of the next world, Hell, Purgatory, and Paradise. Each division or cantica contains thirty-three cantos (with an introductory one to the first cantica). The opening canto of the *Inferno* forms an introduction to the whole poem, which thus contains a hundred cantos, the square of the perfect number ten.[1] These contain in all, 14,233 lines, namely, 4,720 in the *Inferno*, 4,755 in the *Purgatorio*, and 4,758 in the *Paradiso*.

Dante places the date of the action of the poem in the Jubilee year 1300.[2] Thus he describes his vision as having taken place "midway upon the pathway of our life" (*Inferno*, i. 1), that is, in his thirty-fifth year, the days of our life, according to the Psalmist, being "three-score years and ten," and Dante having been born in 1265.

As regards the duration of the action of the poem there is considerable difference of opinion. The most probable estimate, on the whole, seems to be that which puts it at seven days. Of these, twenty-four hours would be occupied in traversing Hell (i.e. from nightfall on the evening of Good Friday, 8 April, 1300, until shortly after sunset on Easter-eve); four days in traversing Purgatory (i.e. one day in Ante-Purgatory, two days in Purgatory proper, and one day in the Earthly Paradise at the summit of the mountain of Purgatory); and one day in traversing

[1] Cf. *Vita Nuova*, § 30, ll. 9-10 ; *Convivio*, ii. 15, ll. 30-6.

[2] This date has been disputed by some authorities in favour of the year 1301, on the ground that Dante in *Purg*. i. 19-21 makes Venus a morning star at Easter, which she was in 1301, whereas actually at Easter in 1300 she was an evening star. This argument, however, has now been disposed of, for it has recently been discovered that in the almanack which there is every reason to believe Dante made use of, by a curious mistake, Venus is shown as a morning star at Easter in 1300 (see Boffito e Melzi d' Eril, *Almanach Dantis Aligherii*, Florence, 1908, pp. xiv-xv; and E. Moore, *Studies in Dante*, iii. 172-5).

Paradise; the remaining time being occupied by the passage from Hell to Purgatory, and from Purgatory to Paradise.[1]

The dates of the completion of the several parts of the poem have not been fixed with any certainty, but the following limitations may be accepted:—The *Inferno* must have been completed after 20 April, 1314, the date of the death of Pope Clement V, because of the allusion to that event in the nineteenth canto (ll. 76-87); and not later than 1319, since it is referred to as finished in a Latin poem addressed to Dante in that year by a Bolognese professor, Giovanni del Virgilio, as well as in Dante's poem in reply.[2] The *Purgatorio* must have been completed not later than 1319, since it is alluded to as finished in the same poems. The *Paradiso* must have been completed after 7 August, 1316, the date of the accession of Pope John XXII, since that Pope is alluded to in the twenty-seventh canto (ll. 58-59); its latest limit is fixed by the date of Dante's death, 14 September, 1321.

The scheme of the *Commedia* is briefly as follows:—

Inferno. The Hell of Dante consists of nine concentric circles, of which the first and uppermost is co-extensive with the hemisphere of the Earth, which forms, as it were, a cover to it. The remaining circles successively diminish in circumference, forming roughly a sort of immense inverted cone or funnel, the lowest point of which is the centre of the Earth and of the Universe (*Inf.* xxxii. 73-4; xxxiv. 110-11). Each of the nine circles is presided over by one or more demons or evil spirits, and in each a distinct class of sinners is punished. Hell, as a whole, may

---

[1] For details of the chronology of the poem, see E. Moore, *Time-References in the Divina Commedia* (though the conclusions there arrived at are not by any means universally accepted).

[2] See below, p. 253.

be divided into two principal parts, which comprise four regions. Of these two parts, the first, in which sins of incontinence are punished, forming what may be described as Upper Hell, lies outside the City of Dis, which begins at the sixth circle; the other, or Lower Hell, in which sins of malice are punished, is situated within the City of Dis.

Upper Hell consists of the first five circles, which are contiguous. These are arranged as follows:—On the upper confines of the abyss, above the first circle, is a region which forms, as it were, an Ante-hell, where are placed those who did neither good nor evil, the neutrals, who were not "worthy" to enter Hell proper (iii. 16-69). In the first circle, or Limbo (under the guardianship of Charon, the ferryman, who conveys the souls of the damned across the river Acheron), are placed unbaptized infants, and the good men and women of antiquity; these are free from torture (iii. 70-iv. 151). At the entrance to the second circle (where the lustful are punished) is stationed Minos, the judge, who assigns to each soul its station and punishment; here begin the torments of Hell (v. 1-142). Circles two to five are appropriated to sins of incontinence; viz. gluttony in circle three (presided over by Cerberus) (vi. 1-111); avarice and prodigality in circle four (presided over by Pluto or Plutus) (vii. 1-66); wrath in circle five (under the guardianship of Phlegyas, ferryman of Styx) (vii. 100-63). Then come the walls of the City of Dis, which form the division between Upper and Lower Hell (viii. 67-ix. 105). Within these walls (guarded by the Furies) lies the sixth circle, where heretics are punished (ix. 106-xi. 9). After this circle comes a deep descent (xii. 10), and the second region is reached, which contains the three rounds of the seventh circle (under the guardianship of the Minotaur), appropriated to three classes of violence, viz. against God, Nature, or art, (e.g. blasphemers, sodomites, usurers), against self or one's possessions (e.g. suicides, spendthrifts), against one's neighbour or his possessions (e.g. tyrants, murderers, robbers) (xii. 11-xvii. 78). After a still more precipitous descent (xvi. 114), comes the third region, comprising the ten pits of the eighth circle, called *Malebolge* (under the guardianship of Geryon), appropriated to ten classes of fraud, viz. seducers and panders, flatterers, simoniacs, soothsayers, barrators, hypocrites, thieves and robbers, evil counsellors, schismatics, and, lastly, falsifiers (comprising alchemists, personators, coiners, liars) (xviii. 1-xxx. 148) ; these pits lie concentrically one below another on a slope, like the rows of an amphitheatre, and are divided from each other by banks, crossed at right-angles by radial bridges of rock, resembling the transverse gangways of a theatre. Below *Malebolge* is a third abyss (xxxi. 32), at the bottom of which lies the fourth or frozen region, consisting of an immense lake of ice formed by the frozen waters of the river Cocytus, and comprising the four divisions of the ninth circle (under the guardianship of the Giants), appropriated to four classes of traitors, and named respectively *Caina* (after Cain), where are those who have betrayed their kindred ; *Antenora* (after Antenor of Troy), where are those who have betrayed their country ; *Tolomea* (after Ptolemy of Jericho), where are those who have betrayed their guests and companions ; and *Giudecca* (after Judas Iscariot), where are those who have betrayed their benefactors (xxxi. 11-xxxiv. 69). In the last of these, in the nethermost pit of Hell, is fixed Lucifer (xxxiv. 20-67). Down through Hell, from end to end, flows the infernal stream, under the various names of Acheron, Styx, Phlegethon, and Cocytus.

Purgatorio. Purgatory, the place of purgation and

of preparation for the life of eternal blessedness (*Purg.* i. 4-6), according to Dante's conception, consists of an island-mountain, formed by the earth which retreated before Lucifer as he fell from Heaven into the abyss of Hell (*Inf.* xxxiv. 122-6). This mountain, which has the form of an immense truncated cone, rises out of the ocean in the centre of the southern hemisphere, where, according to the Ptolemaic system of cosmography followed by Dante, there was nothing (except of course, in Dante's view, the mountain of Purgatory) save a vast expanse of water. The mountain is the exact antipodes of Jerusalem (*Purg.* ii. 3 ; iv. 68 ; xxvii. 2), the central point of the northern hemisphere (*Inf.* xxxiv. 114) where Christ suffered for the sin of Adam (*Purg.* xxvii. 2), committed in the Garden of Eden (i.e. the Terrestrial Paradise at the summit of the mountain). The lower part of the mountain is not a department of Purgatory proper, but forms an Ante-purgatory, where are located the spirits of those who died without having availed themselves of the means of penitence offered by the Church. These are divided into four classes, viz. those who died in contumacy of the Church, and only repented at the last moment ; those who in indolence and indifference put off their repentance until just before their death ; those who died a violent death, without absolution, but repented at the last moment ; and, lastly, kings and princes who deferred their repentance owing to the pressure of temporal interests, these last being placed in a valley full of flowers (*Purg.* ii. 1-viii. 139). Purgatory proper, which is entered by a gate guarded by an angel, consists of seven concentric terraces, each about seventeen feet wide (x. 22-4 ; xiii. 4-5), which rise in succession with diminished circuit (xiii. 4-6) as they approach the summit, where is situated the Terrestrial Paradise. The ascent to the gate of Purgatory is by three steps of diverse colours,

the first being of polished white marble ; the second of
rock, almost black, rough and burnt as with fire, and
marked across its length and breadth, in the shape of a
cross ; the third and topmost of porphyry of a bright
blood-red colour.[1]   The threshold of the gate, whereon is
seated the guardian angel, is of adamantine rock (ix. 76-
105).   The terraces within the gate are connected by
steep and narrow stairways, the steps of which become
successively less steep as each terrace is surmounted.
Each of the seven terraces or circles corresponds to one of
the seven deadly sins, from the traces of which the soul
is there purged.   The seven terraces, together with Ante-
purgatory and the Terrestrial Paradise, form nine divisions,
thus corresponding to the nine circles of Hell, and the nine
spheres of Paradise.

At the foot of the mountain is stationed Cato of Utica
as guardian (i. 31); at the entrance to Purgatory proper,
and at the approach to each of the terraces, stands an
angel, who chants one of the Beatitudes to comfort those
who are purging them of their sins.   In the first circle,
where the sin of pride is purged, the angel of humility sings *Beati pauperes spiritu* (xii. 110).   In the second
circle, where the sin of envy is purged, the angel of
charity sings *Beati misericordes* (xv. 38).   In the third
circle, where the sin of wrath is purged, the angel of peace
sings *Beati pacifici* (xvii. 68).   In the fourth circle, where
the sin of sloth is purged, the angel of the love of God
sings *Beati qui lugent* (xix. 50).   In the fifth circle, where
the sin of avarice is purged, the angel of justice sings

---

[1] These three steps are symbolical of the state of mind with which penance is to be approached, and denote respectively, according to the interpretation of Maria Rossetti, " candid confession, mirroring the whole man ;
mournful contrition, breaking the hard heart of the gazer on the Cross;
love, all aflame, offering up in satisfaction the life-blood of body, soul, and
spirit " (*Shadow of Dante*, p. 112).

Beati qui sitiunt justitiam (xxii. 5). In the sixth circle, where the sin of gluttony is purged, the angel of abstinence sings *Beati qui esuriunt justitiam* (xxiv. 151). In the seventh circle, where the sin of lust is purged, the angel of purity sings *Beati mundo corde* (xxvii. 8). The system of purgation is explained by Dante as follows:— Love exists in every creature, and as, if rightly directed, it is the spring of every good action, so, if ill directed, it is the spring of every evil action; love may err through a bad object (thus giving birth to pride, envy, anger), through defect of vigour in pursuit of good (thus giving birth to sloth), through excess of vigour in the same (thus giving birth to avarice, gluttony, lust). The manner of purgation is threefold, consisting in, firstly, a material punishment intended to mortify the evil passions and incite to virtue; secondly, a subject for meditation, bearing on the sin purged, and its opposite virtue, with examples of persons conspicuous for the one or the other drawn from sacred and profane history; thirdly, a prayer, whereby the soul is purified and strengthened in the grace of God.[1]

In the Terrestrial Paradise are two streams, which both issue from one source, Lethe and Eunoë, the former of which washes away the remembrance of sin, while the latter strengthens the remembrance of good deeds (xxviii. 121-9).

Paradiso. According to Dante's conception, which is based upon the Ptolemaic system, the Universe consists of nine spheres or Heavens, concentric with the Earth, round which they revolve, it being fixed at the centre (*Convivio*, iii. 5, ll. 57-8). The Earth is surrounded by the spheres of air and fire, the latter being in immediate contact with that of the Moon (*Purg.* xviii. 28; *Par.* i.

---

[1] For an excellent account of Dante's Purgatory, see P. Perez, *I setti cerchi del Purgatorio* (Verona, 1867).

115 ; *Conv.* iii. 3, ll. 11-13), which is the lowest of the nine Heavens. Beyond the Heaven of the Moon come in order those of Mercury, Venus, the Sun, Mars, Jupiter, Saturn, the Fixed Stars, and last of all that of the *Primum Mobile* or First Movement. Each of these Heavens revolves with a velocity which increases in proportion to its distance from the Earth. Each of the planets revolves in the epicycle[1] of its own Heaven, except the Sun, which revolves round the Earth. The *Primum Mobile* (or Crystalline Heaven) governs the general motion of the Heavens from East to West, and by it all place and time are ultimately measured (*Par.* xxvii. 115-20; xxviii. 70-1; *Conv.* ii. 6, ll. 145-7; ii. 15, ll. 12-13).

Each of the Heavens is presided over by one of the Angelic Orders, and exercises its special influence on earthly affairs (*Par.* ii. 127-9; *Conv.* ii. 2, ll. 62-3; ii. 5, ll. 21-4; ii. 6, ll. 105-16.) The three lowest Heavens are allotted to the souls of those whose life on Earth was rendered imperfect through their having yielded to the temptations of the world. The next four are allotted to the souls of those whose actions were wholly directed by virtuous motives. The last two Heavens have no special occupants assigned to them, but serve apparently as common places of meeting, the one to the blessed spirits, the other to Angels. Finally, beyond and outside of all the other Heavens lies the Empyrean, an incorporeal and motionless Heaven, where is neither time nor place, but light only (*Par.* xxvii. 106-20; xxx. 39); this is the special abode of the Deity and resting-place of the Saints (*Conv.* ii. 4, ll. 28-30). The latter, arranged in the form of the

---

[1] An epicycle is a small circle whose centre is on the circumference of a larger circle, along which it travels. In the solar system the path of the Moon about the Earth forms an epicycle in respect of the orbit of the Earth around the Sun.

petals of a white Rose, gaze upon the beatific vision of the Deity, who is surrounded by the nine orders of the three Angelic Hierarchies.

Each of the first seven spheres or Heavens is representative of, and corresponds to, one of the seven Liberal Arts, the other three corresponding to Natural, Moral and Divine Science (or Theology) respectively (*Conv.* ii. 14, ll. 48-64). The general scheme of Dante's Paradise is as follows :—The first Heaven, that of the Moon, which is presided over by Angels, and is representative of Grammar, is tenanted by the spirits of those who failed to keep their holy vows (*Par.* ii. 34-v. 84). The second Heaven, that of Mercury, which is presided over by Archangels, and is representative of Logic, is tenanted by the spirits of those who for the love of fame wrought great deeds upon Earth (v. 85-vii.). The third Heaven, that of Venus, which is presided over by Principalities, and is representative of Rhetoric, is tenanted by the spirits of those who upon Earth were lovers (viii-ix.). The fourth Heaven, that of the Sun, which is presided over by Powers, and is representative of Arithmetic, is tenanted by the spirits of those who loved wisdom (x.-xiv. 78). The fifth Heaven, that of Mars, which is presided over by Virtues, and is representative of Music, is tenanted by the spirits of those who fought for the faith (xiv. 79-xviii. 51). The sixth Heaven, that of Jupiter, which is presided over by Dominions, and is representative of Geometry, is tenanted by the spirits of those who loved justice (xviii. 52-xx.). The seventh Heaven, that of Saturn, which is presided over by Thrones, and is representative of Astrology, is tenanted by the spirits of those who lived in contemplation of holy things (xxi.-xxii. 99). The eighth Heaven, that of the Fixed Stars, is presided over by Cherubim, and is representative of Natural Science (xxii. 100-xxvii. 87). The

ninth Heaven, that of the *Primum Mobile*, or the Crystalline Heaven, is presided over by Seraphim, and is
representative of Moral Science (xxvii. 88-xxix.).   The
tenth Heaven, that of the Empyrean, is representative of
Divine Science, and is the abode of the Deity and of the
Spirits of the Blessed.   The latter, as already mentioned,
are arranged in the petals of a vast white Rose, which, according to Dante's description, resembles a kind of
amphitheatre, the centre being formed of a sea of light.
On the highest tier, at the point where the light is most
dazzling, is seated the Virgin Mary.   Next below Mary
sits Eve, and below Eve, on the third tier, sits Rachel,
with Beatrice at her side; and on successive tiers below
them are Sarah, Rebekah, Judith, Ruth, and other Hebrew
women.   On the opposite side, facing Mary, on the same
tier, is seated St. John the Baptist, below whom on successive tiers are St. Francis, St. Benedict, St. Augustine,
and others.   These two lines (from Mary downwards on
one side, and from the Baptist downwards on the other)
form, as it were, a wall, which divides the Rose into two
parts.   In one part are the seats (all filled) of those who
believed in Christ to come (i.e. those who lived under the
Old Testament dispensation); in the other are the seats
(only partially filled) of those who believed in Christ
already come (i.e. those who lived under the New Testament dispensation), and who, when all the seats are filled,
will be equal in number to those on the opposite side.
The lowest tiers are filled by infants, who were saved, not
by their own merits, but through baptism by the merit of
Christ (xxx.-xxxiii.).

Boccaccio tells a story of how at Dante's death the
last thirteen cantos of the *Paradiso* were not to be
found, so that it was supposed that he had left his great
work unfinished, until the whereabouts of the missing

cantos was miraculously revealed to his son, Jacopo, in a
vision :—

"The friends Dante left behind him, his sons and his
disciples, having searched at many times and for several
months everything of his writing, to see whether he had
left any conclusion to his work, could in nowise find any
of the remaining cantos; his friends generally being much
mortified that God had not at least lent him so long to
the world, that he might have been able to complete the
small remaining part of his work; and having sought so
long and never found it, they remained in despair.
Jacopo and Piero were sons of Dante, and each of them
being a rhymer, they were induced by the persuasions of
their friends to endeavour to complete, as far as they were
able, their father's work, in order that it should not remain
imperfect; when to Jacopo, who was more eager about it
than his brother, there appeared a wonderful vision, which
not only induced him to abandon such presumptuous
folly, but showed him where the thirteen cantos were
which were wanting to the *Divina Commedia*, and which
they had not been able to find.

"A worthy man of Ravenna, whose name was Pier
Giardino, and who had long been Dante's disciple, grave
in his manner and worthy of credit, relates that after the
eighth month from the day of his master's death, there
came to his house before dawn Jacopo di Dante, who told
him that that night, while he was asleep, his father Dante
had appeared to him, clothed in the purest white, and his
face resplendent with an extraordinary light; that he,
Jacopo, asked him if he lived, and that Dante replied:
'Yes, but in the true life, not our life'. Then he, Jacopo,
asked him if he had completed his work before passing
into the true life, and, if he had done so, what had become
of that part of it which was missing, which they none of

them had been able to find. To this Dante seemed to answer: 'Yes, I finished it'; and then took him, Jacopo, by the hand, and led him into that chamber in which he, Dante, had been accustomed to sleep when he lived in this life, and, touching one of the walls, he said: 'What you have sought for so much is here'; and at these words both Dante and sleep fled from Jacopo at once. For which reason Jacopo said he could not rest without coming to explain what he had seen to Pier Giardino, in order that they should go together and search out the place thus pointed out to him, which he retained excellently in his memory, and to see whether this had been pointed out by a true spirit, or a false delusion. For which purpose, though it was still far in the night, they set off together, and went to the house in which Dante resided at the time of his death. Having called up its present owner, he admitted them, and they went to the place thus pointed out; there they found a mat fixed to the wall, as they had always been used to see it in past days; they lifted it gently up, when they found a little window in the wall, never before seen by any of them, nor did they even know that it was there. In it they found several writings, all mouldy from the dampness of the walls, and had they remained there longer, in a little while they would have crumbled away. Having thoroughly cleared away the mould, they found them to be the thirteen cantos that had been wanting to complete the *Commedia*."[1]

The missing cantos, adds Boccaccio, were at once sent to Can Grande della Scala, to whom Dante had been in the habit of sending every few cantos of his poem, as he finished them, in order that Can Grande might see them before they were submitted to any one else.

[1] *Vita di Dante*, ed. Macrì-Leone, § 14, pp. 68-70 (trans. by Bunbury).

Boccaccio is responsible for another interesting anecdote [1] about the *Commedia*, which, if we are to accept it as authentic, shows how the Florentines, by exiling Dante, were very near depriving the world of one of its most precious treasures.

"It should be known," he says, "that Dante had a sister, who was married to one of our citizens, called Leon Poggi, by whom she had several children. Among these was one called Andrea, who wonderfully resembled Dante in the outline of his features, and in his height and figure; and he also walked rather stooping, as Dante is said to have done. He was a weak man, but with naturally good feelings, and his language and conduct were regular and praiseworthy. And I having become intimate with him, he often spoke to me of Dante's habits and ways; but among those things which I delight most in recollecting, is what he told me relating to that of which we are now speaking. He said then, that Dante belonged to the party of Messer Vieri de' Cerchi, and was one of its great leaders; and when Messer Vieri and many of his followers left Florence, Dante left that city also and went to Verona. And on account of this departure, through the solicitation of the opposite party, Messer Vieri and all who had left Florence, especially the principal persons, were considered as rebels, and had their persons condemned, and their property confiscated. When the people heard this, they ran to the houses of those proscribed, and plundered all that was within them. It is true that Dante's wife, Madonna Gemma, fearing this, by the advice of some of her friends

---

[1] This story is given both in the *Vita di Dante* and in the *Comento*; in the latter (*Lezione* 33) the name of Boccaccio's informant is given, not as Pier Giardino, but as Ser Dino Perini of Florence, who is supposed to be the individual who figures in Dante's Latin Eclogues under the name of Meliboeus (see below, p. 254).

and relations, had withdrawn from his house some chests containing certain precious things, and Dante's writings along with them, and had put them in a place of safety. And not satisfied with having plundered the houses of the proscribed, the most powerful partisans of the opposite faction occupied their possessions,—some taking one and some another,—and thus Dante's house was occupied.

"But after five years or more had elapsed, and the city was more rationally governed, it is said, than it was when Dante was sentenced, persons began to question their rights, on different grounds, to what had been the property of the exiles, and they were heard. Therefore Madonna Gemma was advised to demand back Dante's property, on the ground that it was her dowry. She, to prepare this business, required certain writings and documents which were in one of the chests, which, in the violent plunder of effects, she had sent away, nor had she ever since removed them from the place where she had deposited them. For this purpose, this Andrea said, she had sent for him, and, as Dante's nephew, had entrusted him with the keys of these chests, and had sent him with a lawyer to search for the required papers ; while the lawyer searched for these, he, Andrea, among other of Dante's writings, found many sonnets, canzoni, and such similar pieces. But among them what pleased him the most was a sheet in which, in Dante's handwriting, the seven first cantos of the *Commedia* were written ; and therefore he took it and carried it off with him, and read it over and over again ; and although he understood but little of it, still it appeared to him a very fine thing ; and therefore he determined, in order to know what it was, to carry it to an esteemed man of our city, who in those times was a much celebrated reciter of verses, whose name was Dino, the son of Messer Lambertuccio Frescobaldi.

" It pleased Dino marvellously ; and having made copies of it for several of his friends, and knowing that the composition was merely begun, and not completed, he thought that it would be best to send it to Dante, and at the same time to beg him to follow up his design, and to finish it. And having inquired, and ascertained that Dante was at this time in the Lunigiana, with a noble man of the name of Malaspina, called the Marquis Moroello, who was a man of understanding, and who had a singular friend-ship for him, he thought of sending it, not to Dante himself, but to the Marquis, in order that he should show it to him : and so Dino did, begging him that, as far as it lay in his power, he would exert his good offices to induce Dante to continue and finish his work.

" The seven aforesaid cantos having reached the Marquis's hands, and having marvellously pleased him, he showed them to Dante ; and having heard from him that they were his composition, he entreated him to continue the work. To this it is said that Dante answered : ' I really supposed that these, along with many of my other writings and effects, were lost when my house was plundered, and therefore I had given up all thoughts of them. But since it has pleased God that they should not be lost, and He has thus restored them to me, I shall endeavour, as far as I am able, to proceed with them according to my first design.' And recalling his old thoughts, and resuming his interrupted work, he speaks thus in the beginning of the eighth canto : ' My wondrous history I here renew '." [1]

The question as to why Dante, a man of great learning, chose to write the *Commedia* in Italian, instead of in Latin, exercised the minds of many wise men of his day, Boccaccio tells us. His own opinion on the subject he gives as follows :—

[1] *Comento*, ii. 129-32 (trans. by Bunbury) ; cf. *Vita di Dante*, ed. cit. § 14, pp 65-7.

"In reply to this question," he says, "two chief reasons, amongst many others, come to my mind. The first of which is, to be of more general use to his fellow-citizens and other Italians; for he knew that if he had written metrically in Latin as the other poets of past times had done, he would only have done service to men of letters, whereas, writing in the vernacular, he did a deed ne'er done before, and there was no bar in any incapacity of the men of letters to understand him; and by showing the beauty of our idiom and his own excelling art therein, he gave delight and understanding of himself to the unlearned who had hitherto been abandoned of every one. The second reason which moved him thereto was this. Seeing that liberal studies were utterly abandoned, and especially by princes and other great men, to whom poetic toils were wont to be dedicated, wherefore the divine works of Virgil and the other illustrious poets had not only sunk into small esteem, but were well-nigh despised by the most; having himself begun, according as the loftiness of the matter demanded, after this guise—

> 'Ultima regna canam, fluido contermina mundo,
> Spiritibus quae lata patent, quae praemia solvunt
> Pro meritis cuicumque suis,' etc.,[1]

he left it there; for he conceived it was a vain thing to put crusts of bread into the mouths of such as were still sucking milk; wherefore he began his work again in style suited to modern senses, and followed it up in the vernacular."[2]

The skill exhibited by Dante in the management of the rhymes in his poem, which consists of considerably over

---

[1] "The furthest realms I sing, conterminous with the flowing universe, stretching afar for spirits, paying the rewards to each after his merits," etc.

[2] *Vita di Dante*, ed. cit. § 15, pp. 71-2 (trans. by Wicksteed). This information was obviously derived by Boccaccio from a passage in the suspect) letter of Frate Ilario (see above, p. 92 note).

fourteen thousand lines, is very remarkable. According to the author of the commentary known as the *Ottimo Comento*, who was a contemporary of Dante, the poet boasted that he had never been trammelled in his composition by the exigencies of rhyme. "I, the writer," says the commentator, "heard Dante say that never a rhyme had led him to say other than he would, but that many a time and oft he had made words say in his rhymes what they were not wont to express for other poets."

Another commentator, Benvenuto da Imola, in connection with Dante's extraordinary facility in the matter of rhymes, repeats a quaint conceit, which had been imagined, he says, by an ardent admirer of the poet :—" When Dante first set about the composition of his poem, all the rhymes in the Italian language presented themselves before him in the guise of so many lovely maidens, and each in turn humbly petitioned to be granted admittance into this great work of his genius. In answer to their prayers, Dante called first one and then another, and assigned to each its appropriate place in the poem ; so that, when at last the work was complete, it was found that not a single one had been left out."

The statistics as to the editions, manuscript and printed, of the *Divina Commedia* are interesting. The known manuscripts number between five and six hundred,[1] giving an average of about four a year for the 150 years between the date of Dante's death (1321) and that of the first printed edition (1472). None of these dates earlier than fourteen or fifteen years after Dante's death, of whose original manuscript not a trace has yet been discovered. Of printed editions there are between three and four hundred, giving an average of less than one a year for the 430

---

[1] See E. Moore, *Contributions to the Textual Criticism of the Divina Commedia ;* and Colomb de Batines, *Bibliografia Dantesca* (Parte iv.).

years between the date of the first edition (1472) and the latest.[1] The earliest probably is that printed at Foligno in 1472, in which year editions appeared also at Mantua and at Jesi. Two editions were printed at Naples shortly after, one in 1474, the other in 1477. A Venetian edition appeared also in 1477; a Milanese in 1477-78; and a second Venetian in 1478. The first Florentine edition (with the commentary of Cristoforo Landino) did not appear until 1481. At least six other editions were printed in Italy in the fifteenth century. In the next century two editions were printed at the famous Venetian press of Aldus, one in 1502 (in which the well-known Aldine anchor began to be used for the first time), the other in 1515. The first edition printed outside Italy was the counterfeit of the first Aldine, which appeared at Lyons in 1502 or 1503. Three other editions were printed in the sixteenth century at Lyons, viz. in 1547, 1551, and 1571. No other edition appeared outside Italy for nearly two hundred years, till 1768, when an edition was published at Paris. An edition with the imprint London, but actually printed at Leghorn, appeared in 1778. The earliest specimen of any length of the Italian text of the *Commedia* printed in England was a passage of twenty-seven lines—a curiosity of misprinting—from the last canto of the *Inferno* (xxxiv. 28-54), inserted by Thomas Heywood, the dramatist, in the seventh book of his *Hierarchie of the Blessed Angels*, which was published in 1635.[2] More than a hundred years later Giuseppe Baretti printed selections from the sixth canto of the *Inferno*, the eighth of the *Purgatorio*, and the thirty-third of the *Paradiso*, in his *Italian Library* (published in

---

[1] At first sight it might appear as if the popularity of the poem had decreased since the invention of printing; but it must be borne in mind that a manuscript " edition " consisted of *one copy only*, whereas a printed edition may consist of hundreds or even thousands of copies.

[2] See Paget Toynbee, *Dante in English Literature*, vol. i. pp. 129-30.

London in 1757). Not long afterwards (in 1782) William Hayley printed the first three cantos of the *Inferno*, with a translation in *terza rima*, in the notes to the third Epistle, in his *Essay on Epic Poetry*. This was followed by the complete text of the *Inferno*, which accompanied the first issue of Cary's *Hell*, published in London in two volumes in 1805-6. Two complete English editions of the *Commedia* (the first of the whole poem) were printed in London in 1808. The first (perhaps) of these, in three volumes 16mo, edited by G. B. Boschini, and dedicated to the Ladies Elizabeth and Emily Percy, daughters of the second Duke of Northumberland, contained the text only without notes. The other, in three volumes 12mo, dedicated respectively to the Countess of Lonsdale, the Countess of Dartmouth, and Mrs. Pilkington, was edited by Romualdo Zotti, who supplied notes in Italian, selected and abbreviated from various Italian commentaries. Two other editions were printed in London in 1819; one in three volumes 16mo, edited by S. E. Petronj ; the other in three volumes 12mo, a reissue, with the notes recast, of Zotti's edition of 1808. In 1822-23 was published the diminutive edition of the *Commedia*, in two volumes 32mo (dated respectively 1823 and 1822), dedicated to the second Earl Spencer, the great book collector, which forms part of the well-known series of " Diamond Classics " issued by William Pickering, and printed by Corrall, this being the first complete edition of the *Commedia* issued in England in which no foreigner's name appears. In 1824 a French translation of the *Inferno*, dedicated to the Princess Augusta, second daughter of George III, by J. C. Tarver, accompanied by the Italian text, was printed at Windsor, of which a second impression, with a reconstructed title-page, was issued in 1826. In 1826-27 John Murray published the first instalment, in two volumes 8vo, of Gabriele Rossetti's famous

Comento Analitico on the *Commedia*, consisting of the text of the *Inferno*, with the commentary. The work, the first volume of which is dedicated to John Hookham Frere, and which numbers among its subscribers Brougham, Scott, Isaac D'Israeli, Henry Hallam, and Samuel Rogers, is announced on the title-page as being in six volumes, but no more than the first two ever saw the light. In 1827 appeared the first English printed edition of the *Commedia* complete in one volume. The text, beautifully printed by the Whittinghams at their Chiswick Press, was edited by Pietro Cicchetti. The editor claims that this volume, which is in 12mo, and consists of 610 pages, is the first single-volume of the *Commedia* in this small *format*— a claim which shows that his acquaintance with the bibliography of the subject was limited, since at least half a dozen single volume editions in small *format* were published in Italy and France during the sixteenth century. In 1839 and 1840 two single-volume editions were published in Edinburgh in 24mo, neither of which, singularly enough, is in the British Museum. In 1842-43 was published in London by Pietro Rolandi, in four volumes 8vo, under the editorship of Giuseppe Mazzini, Ugo Foscolo's edition of the *Commedia*, containing the Italian text and various illustrative matter, the first instalment of which had been published by Pickering during Foscolo's lifetime in 1825. In 1849 the well-known translation of the *Inferno* by John A. Carlyle, accompanied by the Italian text, was published by Chapman and Hall ; and from this date onwards English editions of the *Commedia* or of one or other of the divisions of the poem, for the most part accompanied by translations, have followed each other fast, the grand total at the present date amounting to twenty-six, exclusive of reprints and reimpressions. The most important text of the *Commedia* published in England is that included in the volume, known as the Oxford Dante, issued at Oxford in 1894 (second edition, 1897; third edition, 1904), which contains the whole of the works of Dante.[1] Two editions of the text alone were published in 1900 (one in London,[2] the other at Oxford)[3] in commemoration of the six hundredth anniversary of Dante's journey through the three kingdoms of the other world. The latest of all are the beautiful edition, in three volumes (*Inferno*, 1902 ; *Purgatorio*, 1904 ; *Paradiso*, 1905), printed at the Ashendene Press by C. H. St. John Hornby ; and the sumptuous reprint, in one large folio volume, of the text of the Oxford Dante (comprising the whole works) issued from the same press in 1909.[4]

The *Commedia* has been translated, in whole or in part, into almost every known literary language. Besides English, there are versions of the whole poem in Bohemian, Catalan, Danish, Dutch, French, German, Greek, Hungarian, Latin, Polish, Portuguese, Roumanian, Russian, Spanish, Swedish, and Welsh. The *Inferno* has been rendered into Hebrew; and various selections into Armenian, Basque, Icelandic, Norwegian, Sanskrit, and even Volapük. Versions in French, Spanish, and Catalan were already in existence in the fifteenth century, and a Latin translation was made as early as the fourteenth century, in 1381 as is supposed. The first German translation of the *Commedia* did not appear until the eighteenth century, in 1767-69,

---

[1] *Tutte le opere di Dante Alighieri, nuovamente rivedute nel testo dal* Dr. E. Moore; *con Indice dei Nomi Propri e delle Cose Notabili compilato da* Paget Toynbee (Clarendon Press).

[2] *La Commedia di Dante Alighieri. Il testo Wittiano riveduto da* Paget Toynbee ('Per il sesto centenario del viaggio di Dante MCCC . . . MDCCCC' (Methuen and Co.).

[3] *La Divina Commedia di Dante Alighieri nuovamente riveduta nel testo dal* Dr. E. Moore, *con indice dei nomi propri compilato da* Paget Toynbee (Clarendon Press).

[4] See Paget Toynbee, *The Earliest Editions of the Divina Commedia printed in England*, in *Athenæum*, 2 Jan. 1904.

several years after the completion of the earliest English version.

Renderings of detached passages from the *Commedia* occur in English literature within sixty years or so of Dante's death, in the works of Chaucer, who introduces a translation of St. Bernard's prayer to the Virgin, from the thirty-third canto of the *Paradiso*, in the *Prologue to the Second Nun's Tale*; and in the *Monk's Tale* a rendering of the story of Ugolino, from the thirty-third canto of the *Inferno*; besides shorter passages in others of the *Tales*, and in *Troilus and Cressida*, the *Legend of Good Women*, and elsewhere.[1] With the exception of a few lines by Sir John Harington and Milton, the first English translation from the *Commedia*, other than mere incidental renderings, was the version of the Ugolino episode, published by Jonathan Richardson, the artist, in 1719 in his *Discourse on the Dignity, Certainty, Pleasure and Advantage of the Science of a Connoisseur.* The same piece was translated by the poet Gray some twenty years later; and five more versions of it appeared before the end of the eighteenth century. The earliest recorded English translation of the whole poem was one by William Huggins, the translator of Ariosto, who at his death in 1761 left the work in manuscript, with directions that it should be printed and published, which, however, was never done. About the same time Dr. Burney made a translation of the *Inferno*, which likewise never saw the light. In 1782 William Hayley published his *terza rima* translation of the first three cantos of the *Inferno* mentioned above.[2] In the same year appeared the first complete English translation (that is, the first published translation) of the *Inferno*. This was by Charles Rogers, in blank verse. Rogers' version was followed in

---

[1] See Paget Toynbee, *Dante in English Literature*, vol. i. pp. 1 ff.
[2] See above, p. 215.

1785 by a rendering, in six-line stanzas, by Henry Boyd, who seventeen years later, in 1802, published a translation of the whole of the *Commedia* in the same metre—the first complete English version to see the light.[1] In 1805 Cary published the first instalment of his famous blank verse translation, consisting of the first seventeen cantos of the *Inferno*, the other seventeen cantos being published in the following year. A fourth translation of the *Inferno*, in blank verse, by Nathaniel Howard, appeared in 1807; and a fifth, also in blank verse, by Joseph Hume, in 1812. In 1814 was published the first edition of Cary's translation of the whole of the *Commedia*, of which a second edition was issued in 1819, and a third in 1831. In 1833 Ichabod Charles Wright published a translation of the *Inferno*, in bastard *terza rima*, which was followed by the *Purgatorio* in 1836, and the *Paradiso* in 1840, in the same metre. In 1844 appeared the fourth, and last edition corrected by himself, of Cary's translation. Since that date twenty other English translations of the *Commedia* have been published. Of these, nine are in *terza rima*, four in blank verse, five in prose, one in heroic couplets, and one in nine-line stanzas. There have been, besides, eighteen independent translations of the *Inferno* alone, of which eight are in *terza rima*, five in blank verse, three in prose, one in rhymed quatrains, and one in Spenserian stanzas. Also there have been six independent translations of the *Purgatorio*, three in prose, one in Marvellian stanzas, one in octosyllabic *terza rima*, and one in blank verse; and one independent translation, in prose, of the *Paradiso*. Reckoning the totals for each *cantica* of the poem, this gives in all forty-four English translations of the *Inferno*, twenty-nine of the *Purgatorio*, and twenty-four of

[1] See Paget Toynbee, *English Translations of Dante in the Eighteenth Century*, in *Modern Language Review*, vol. i. pp. 9-24.

the *Paradiso*. A classification of these according to metre gives, for the *Inferno*, seventeen in *terza rima*, twelve in blank verse, eight in prose, and seven in what, for convenience, may be called experimental metres;[1] for the *Purgatorio*, ten in *terza rima*, eight in prose, five in blank verse, and six in experimental metres;[2] for the *Paradiso*, nine in *terza rima*, six in prose, five in blank verse, and four in experimental metres.[3]

From these figures it appears that during the last century and a quarter the *Commedia* has been translated into English on an average once in about every five years. If the independent translations of the several divisions of the poem be included in the reckoning, it will be found that an English translation of one or other of the three *cantiche* has been produced on an average once in about every sixteen months of the same period.

Next after the Ugolino episode, from the thirty-third canto of the *Inferno*, of which there are altogether more than seventy English versions, the two most popular passages of the *Commedia* with English translators have been the episode of Francesca da Rimini, from the fifth canto of the *Inferno*, and the first two *terzine* of the eighth canto of the *Purgatorio*. Of the Francesca da Rimini episode there are twenty-three separate versions independent of translations of the *Inferno*, of which only one belongs to the eighteenth century, as against seven of the Ugolino. The most famous version is that by Lord Byron, in "third rhyme," to use his own term, which was composed in 1820, but not published until ten years later. Of the first six lines of the eighth canto of the *Purgatorio*, the last line of

---

[1] Including bastard *terza rima*, six-line stanzas, nine-line stanzas, heroic couplets, and rhymed quatrains.

[2] Including bastard *terza rima*, six-line stanzas, nine-line stanzas, heroic couplets, and Marvellian stanzas.

[3] Including bastard *terza rima*, six-line stanzas, nine-line stanzas, and heroic couplets.

which is famous in English literature as having inspired the first line of Gray's *Elegy*, there are sixteen independent translations. Among these are versions by Peacock in *Headlong Hall* (1816); by Byron in the third canto of *Don Juan* (1821); and by Samuel Rogers in his *Italy* (1830).

This record [1] constitutes a remarkable tribute on the part of the English-speaking [2] races to the transcendent genius of Dante. Not as yet, it seems, need Dante fear

" Di perder viver tra coloro
Che questo tempo chiameranno antico," [3]

as he expressed it to the spirit of his ancestor Cacciaguida six hundred years ago.

Commentaries on the *Commedia* began to make their appearance in Italy at a very early date. Four at least, on the *Inferno*, were written within three or four years of Dante's death; viz. one, in Latin, by Graziolo de' Bambaglioli (d. before 1343), Chancellor of Bologna, composed in 1324 (published in 1892 by Antonio Fiammazzo),[4] of which an Italian translation (published in 1848 by Lord Vernon) [4] was made in the fourteenth century [5]; one, in Italian, by Dante's son, Jacopo (d. before 1349), written

---

[1] For details, see Paget Toynbee, *Chronological List of English Translations from Dante, from Chaucer to the Present Day*, in *Annual Report of the Cambridge* (U.S.A.) *Dante Society* for 1906; see also *English Translations of Dante's Works*, in *Bulletin Italien*, tom. vi. pp. 285-8 (1906).

[2] Translations (three of the *Commedia*, and one of the *Inferno*) by Americans are included in the record.

[3] *Paradiso*, xvii. 119-20:—
" To be as one forgotten among those
Who shall regard as ancient these our days."

[4] See *Appendix* D, where the titles of the printed editions of the early commentaries referred to above are given *in extenso*.

[5] See Luigi Rocca, *Di alcuni Commenti della Divina Commedia composti nei primi vent' anni dopo la morte di Dante*. Firenze, 1891, pp. 43-77. The identification of this work as a translation of the commentary of Graziolo de' Bambaglioli is due to Dr. Moore (see his *Studies in Dante*, vol. iii. p. 345 *n*. 2).

before 1325 (published by Lord Vernon in 1848),[1] which is considered by some to be earlier than that of Graziolo[2]; one, in Latin, by Guido da Pisa, written probably about 1324 (as yet unpublished)[3], of which a fourteenth century Italian translation exists (also unpublished)[4]; and one, in Italian, by an anonymous author, probably a native of Siena, written between 1321 and 1337 (published in 1865 by Francesco Selmi).[5] The first commentary on the whole of the *Commedia* was written in Italian between 1323 and 1328 by Jacopo della Lana (d. after 1358), of Bologna; this was first printed in the edition of the *Commedia* published at Venice by Vendelin da Spira in 1477, in which, however, it was erroneously attributed to Benvenuto da Imola; it was printed a second time in the following year in the edition of the *Commedia* published by Nidobeato at Milan; and was reprinted at Milan in 1865, and at Bologna in 1866-7, by Luciano Scarabelli.[6] Lana's commentary, of which more than sixty MSS. are known, was twice translated into Latin in the fourteenth

[1] See *Appendix* D.

[2] See Rocca, *op. cit.* pp. 63 ff. Another authority, F. P. Luiso, holds that the *Chiose* printed by Lord Vernon were not written in that shape by Jacopo di Dante, but are a distorted translation of a Latin original. He considers, on the other hand, that the Latin *Chiose di Dante le quali fece el figliuolo co le sue mani*, preserved in a MS. in the Laurentian library at Florence, of which he published a portion (on the *Purgatorio*) at Florence in 1904, represent the work of Jacopo, and were written probably in his father's lifetime, and were possibly to some extent inspired by the poet himself. See, however, an article by M. Barbi in *Bullettino della Società Dantesca Italiana*, N.S. xi. pp. 195-229 (1904).

[3] See Moore, *Studies in Dante*, vol. iii. pp. 349, 357, 363.

[4] See Colomb de Batines, *Bibliografia Dantesca*, vol. ii. p. 300.

[5] See *Appendix* D. Some authorities, including Selmi, think that this commentary was written in Dante's lifetime, before 1320; Rocca, however, shows (*op. cit.* pp. 109-10, 117), that it must have been written later than 1321, the date of Dante's death, and before 1337.

[6] See *Appendix* D.

century, the author of one of these versions being Alberico da Rosciate (d. 1354), a celebrated lawyer of Bergamo.[1] Eight more commentaries belong to the fourteenth century; viz. that known as the *Ottimo Comento*, written in Italian by Andrea Lancia (*c.* 1290–*c.* 1360), a Florentine notary, about 1334[2] (published in 1827-9 by Alessandro Torri)[3]; the Latin commentary of Dante's son, Pietro (d. 1364), written in 1340-1, which exists in two different forms,[4] only one of which has been published (by Lord Vernon in 1845)[3]; that written in Latin by an unknown monk of Monte Cassino not earlier than 1350 (published in 1865)[3]; the unfinished commentary in Italian on the *Inferno*, comprising the first sixteen cantos and part of the seventeenth, written by Boccaccio (1313-1375) for the purpose of his public lectures on Dante in Florence between 1373 and 1375[5] (first published in 1724 by Lorenzo Ciccarelli)[3]; the Latin commentary (of which a fourteenth century Italian version exists in MS.)[6] composed between 1373 and 1380 by Benvenuto da Imola (*c.* 1338-1390), part of which he delivered as public lecturer on Dante at Bologna in 1375[7] (published in 1887 by William Warren Vernon, under the editorship of G. F. Lacaita)[3]; the Italian commentary, formerly attributed to Boccaccio, composed in 1375 (published in 1846 by Lord Vernon)[3]; that in Italian by Francesco da Buti (1324-1406), of which

---

[1] See Rocca, *op. cit.*, pp. 127-227.   [2] See Rocca, *op. cit.* pp. 228-342.

[3] See *Appendix D.*   [4] See Rocca, *op. cit.* pp. 343-407.

[5] See Paget Toynbee, *Boccaccio's Commentary on the Divina Commedia*, in *Modern Language Review*, vol. ii. pp. 97-120.

[6] See Batines, *op. cit.* vol. iii. p. 315.

[7] See Paget Toynbee, *Benvenuto da Imola and his Commentary on the Divina Commedia*, in *Dante Studies and Researches*, pp. 216-37. M. Barbi has recently shown that the Latin commentary which passes under the name of Stefano Talice da Ricaldone is little more than a transcription of Benvenuto's lectures at Bologna. See *Bullettino della Società Dantesca Italiana*, N.S. xv. pp. 213-36 (1908).

the first draft appears to have been completed in 1385, and which was finally completed in 1395,[1] composed for delivery as public lectures at Pisa (published in 1858-62 by Crescentino Giannini)[2]; and the commentary in Italian, written at the end of the fourteenth or beginning of the fifteenth century[3] by an unknown Florentine (commonly referred to as "Anonimo Fiorentino") (published in 1866-74 by Pietro Fanfani).[2]

To the beginning of the fifteenth century belongs the Latin commentary written by Giovanni dei Bertoldi (c. 1350-1445), commonly known as Giovanni da Serravalle, Bishop of Fermo, which was composed between February 1416 and January 1417. This commentary[4] (published

---

[1] The reading of the date of the completion of the commentary in the colophon at the end of the *Paradiso* is uncertain; but at any rate the work was not completed before 1393, for in the comment on *Paradiso*, vi. 1-9, Buti gives a list of Emperors, which he concludes with these words: "lo centesimo tredecimo è ora Vinceslao re di Boemia . . . lo quale non è anco coronato, benchè corra 1393 dalla incarnazione".

[2] See *Appendix* D.

[3] The MS. from which Fanfani, the editor, printed the commentary professes to have been written in 1343, but this date, which appears to have been added by a later hand, is obviously incorrect, for the author borrows freely from Boccaccio's commentary, which was not begun till thirty years afterwards.

[4] A copy of this commentary was presented in 1443 by Humphrey, Duke of Gloucester, to the University of Oxford, where it was seen in the public library a hundred years later by John Leland, the antiquary, during his tour through England in 1536-42. The commentary was accompanied by a prose translation of the *Commedia* in Latin (begun in January 1416 and completed in May of the same year). It was probably a MS. of this translation which was seen by Leland in the Cathedral library at Wells (founded and endowed by Bishop Bubwith) during the tour above-mentioned (see G. L. Hamilton's notes on Serravalle in *Annual Report of the Cambridge* (U.S.A.) *Dante Society*, 1902; and Paget Toynbee, *Dante in English Literature*, vol. i. pp. xviii. 21-2, 29-30). Only three complete MSS. of Serravalle's work are known; one of these is in the Vatican, another in the British Museum, and a third in the Escorial (see A. Farinelli, *Dante in Ispagna*, p. 70 n).

at Prato in 1891)[1] has a special interest for Englishmen as having been written (during the Council of Constance, 1414-1418) at the instigation of two English Bishops, Nicholas Bubwith, of Bath and Wells, and Robert Hallam, of Salisbury, by one who had himself been in England,[2] and who made, for the first time, the explicit statement that Dante visited this country and studied at Oxford— [3] a statement (unhappily not otherwise authenticated) prompted probably by a desire to please his English colleagues, one of whom, Hallam, had been Chancellor of the University of Oxford.[4] Three other commentaries belong to this century, one, on the *Inferno* only, by Guiniforto delli Bargigi (1406–*c.* 1460), of Pavia, written about 1440 (published in 1838 by G. Zacheroni)[5]; another, in Latin, by Stefano Talice da Ricaldone (d. *c.* 1520), written in 1474, and supposed at one time to have been delivered as lectures at Saluzzo,[6] but now regarded as a more or less faithful transcription of Benvenuto da Imola's lectures at Bologna[7] (privately printed, by order of the King of Italy, at Turin in 1886; published in 1888 at Milan under the editorship of V. Promis and C. Negroni)[1]; and the third, in Italian, written in 1480 by Cristoforo Landino (1434-1504), of Florence, which first saw the light in the celebrated first Florentine edition of the

---

[1] See *Appendix* D.

[2] In his comment on *Inferno*, xx. 126, he says he passed through the Straits of Gibraltar " quando redibam de regno Anglie ".

[3] See above, p. 93.   [4] From 1403 to 1405.

[5] See *Appendix* D. Zacheroni unfortunately did not print Guiniforto's work in full, all the theological portions of the commentary being omitted.

[6] See vol. i. pp. xiii, xvi, of the Milan edition (1888) of the commentary.

[7] See the article by M. Barbi referred to above (p. 223 n. 7), and also Rocca, *op. cit.* p. 137.

Commedia (published in 1481),[1] and has many times been reprinted.[2]

In the sixteenth century the only commentaries of importance were those (in Italian), of Alessandro Vellutello (*c.* 1519–*c.* 1590), of Lucca, first published at Venice in 1544,[3] and three times reprinted[4]; of Giovan Battista Gelli (1498-1563), of Florence, whose lectures on the *Commedia* before the Florentine Academy (delivered at various times between 1541 and 1563) were successively printed at Florence in a series of issues between 1547 and 1561,[5] and have recently (1887) been collected and published by C. Negroni[6]; and of Bernardino Daniello (d. *c.* 1560), of Lucca, whose commentary was printed at Venice in 1568,[3] and has not been reprinted.

In the seventeenth century, during which only three editions of the *Commedia* were printed in Italy,[7] as against some forty in the previous century, the interest in Dante was at its lowest ebb. It is not surprising, consequently, that during this period no commentaries on

---

[1] See *Appendix D*. This edition, a copy of which was sold recently for £1000, was illustrated with plates from designs by Botticelli.

[2] No less than fifteen times in the fifteenth and sixteenth centuries, viz. at Brescia in 1487, and at Venice in 1484, 1491 (two editions), 1493, 1497, 1507, 1512, 1516, 1520, 1529, 1536, 1564, 1578, 1596 (the commentary of Vellutello being printed with it in the last three editions).

[3] See *Appendix D*.

[4] At Venice, in the so-called " edizioni del naso " (from the big-nosed portrait of Dante), in 1564, 1578, 1596.

[5] See Batines, *op. cit.* vol. ii. pp. 655-60.

[6] See *Appendix D*. It appears from a remark of Gelli that his contemporary Pier Francesco Giambullari (1495-1555), who published in 1544 a work *De'l sito, forma, e misure dello inferno di Dante*, also wrote a commentary on part of the *Commedia*. In his *Lettura Terza, Lezione Prima*, Gelli quotes Giambullari's opinion, " secondo che scrive in uno comento ch' egli faceva sopra questo poeta, non condotto da lui se non a pochi canti del Purgatorio, per esserci stato tolto con non piccola perdita de la morte " (ed. Negroni, vol. i. p. 318). This commentary has not been preserved.

[7] Vicenza, 1613; Padua, 1629; Venice, 1629.

the poem were produced. In the eighteenth century, however, when a marked reaction took place, two notable commentaries made their appearance which retained their popularity down to the middle of the next century. The earlier of these, by Pompeo Venturi (1693-1752), a Jesuit of Siena, was first published at Lucca in 1732, and was reprinted more than twenty times in the next hundred years (between 1739 and 1850).[1] The other was the celebrated commentary of Lombardi, first published at Rome in 1791, with the title *La Divina Commedia di Dante Alighieri novamente correta spiegata e difesa da F. B. L. M. C.* (i.e. Francesco Baldassare Lombardi, Minor Conventuale), a voluminous work, which has been seven times reprinted in full,[2] and four times in an abbreviated form.[3] To the eighteenth century also belong the valuable indices to the *Commedia*, the first of their kind, compiled by Giovanni Antonio Volpi (1686-1766), of Padua, which were first published in the third volume of the edition of the poem issued at Padua in 1726-27,[4] and have been many times reprinted.

In the nineteenth century commentaries on the *Commedia* began to abound. The best known of the earlier ones are, that of Niccolò Giosafatte Biagioli (1772-1830),

---

[1] Three editions have been printed at Venice (1739, 1751, 1772), one at Verona (1749), nine at Florence (1771, 1813, 1819, 1821, 1826, 1827, 1830, 1837, 1839), four at Bassano (1815, 1820, 1826, 1850), two at Leghorn (1817, 1818), one at Pisa (1819), one at Turin (1830), one at Palermo (1834), and one at Paris (1841).

[2] Two more editions were printed at Rome (1815, 1820), one at Padua (1822), two at Florence (1830, 1838), one at Naples (1830), and one at Prato (1847).

[3] These were issued respectively at Rome (1806, 1810), Jena (1807), and Naples (1839).

[4] The indices are there described as "indici ricchissimi, che spiegano tutte le cose difficili, e tutte l' Erudizioni di esso Poema, e tengono la vece d' un' intero Comento".

first published in Paris in 1818-19, and reprinted more than a dozen times between 1819 and 1868[1]; and the still more popular commentary of Paolo Costa, first published at Bologna in 1819-21, which has been reprinted more than thirty times.[2] Others worthy of mention belonging to the first half of the century are the once famous "Comento analitico" of Gabriele Rossetti (1783-1854), projected in six volumes, but of which only the first two volumes (on the *Inferno*) were published (London, 1826-27);[3] the commentary projected by Ugo Foscolo (1778-1827) in five volumes, of which only one, containing the *Discorso sul testo*, appeared in his lifetime (London, 1825), the remaining portion of the work so far as completed being published twenty years later (London, 1842-43) under the editorship of Mazzini; and that of Niccolò Tommaseo, first published at Venice in 1837, and several times reprinted.[4] Of more recent Italian commentaries the following may be mentioned, all of which more or less hold their own at the present day; viz. those of Brunone Bianchi (Florence, 1854, 1857, 1863, etc.; tenth edition, 1890) (based on that of Costa, of which Bianchi had previously published several editions, with additions of his

---

[1] Six editions were printed at Milan (1819, 1820, 1829, 1838, 1845, 1851), eight at Naples (1838, 1845, 1854, 1855, 1858, 1860, 1862, 1868), and one at Palermo (1856).

[2] Three more were printed at Bologna (two in 1826, one in 1832-3), nine at Milan (1827, 1840, 1850, 1855, 1857, 1862, 1863, 1873, 1888), nine at Florence (1827, 1830, 1836, 1839, 1840-2, 1844, 1846, 1847, 1849), four at Naples (1830, 1837, 1839, 1849-50), one at Monza (1837), two at Colle (1841, 1844), one at Voghera (1841-2), two at Prato (1850, 1852), and three at Venice (two in 1852, one in 1856-7).

[3] In this work Rossetti developed his extravagant theories as to the esoteric anti-papal significance of the *Commedia*, which he afterwards more fully expounded in his works *Sullo Spirito Antipapale che produsse la Riforma* (London, 1832), and *Il Mistero dell' Amor Platonico del Medio Evo* (London, 1840).

[4] At Milan, in 1854, 1856, 1865, 1869.

own); Pietro Fraticelli (Florence, 1852, 1860, 1864, etc.; reprinted eight or nine times before 1900) (based on Venturi, Lombardi, Costa, and Bianchi); G. A. Scartazzini (Leipzig, 1874-90; minor editions, Milan, 1893, 1896, 1903); and Tommaso Casini (Florence, 1887, 1889, 1892, etc.; fifth edition, 1903); to which may be added those of Antonio Lubin (Padua, 1881); Giuseppe Campi (Turin, 1888-93); Giacomo Poletto (Rome, 1894); and Francesco Torraca (Rome-Milan, 1905-7).

English commentaries, like English translations, came late into the field. The earliest made their appearance in the form of notes to the translations of Henry Boyd (1785, 1802), H. F. Cary (1805-6, 1814, 1819, 1831, 1844), Nathaniel Howard (1807), Joseph Hume (1812); I. C. Wright (1833-40, 1845, 1854), and John Dayman (1843, 1865).[1] The first English commentary properly so called was that published anonymously in London in 1822 by John Taaffe, an Irishman domiciled in Italy, under the title of *A Comment on the Divine Comedy of Dante Alighieri*, in the publication of which Byron and Shelley interested themselves, but of which only the first portion (on *Inferno*, i.-viii.) ever saw the light.[2] Among recent commentaries in the form of notes to translations of the *Commedia*, the most important are those of C. B. Cayley (1855),[3] J. W. Thomas (1859-66), H. W. Longfellow (1865-7),[4] A. J. Butler (1880-92),[5] E. H. Plumptre (1886-87), F. K. H. Haselfoot (1887),[6] and C. E. Norton (1891-92)[7]; and of commentaries proper, W. W. Vernon's

---

[1] See Paget Toynbee, *Chronological List of English Translations from Dante*, in *Annual Report of the Cambridge* (U.S.A.) *Dante Society*, 1906.

[2] See Paget Toynbee, *Dante in English Literature*, vol. ii. pp. 340 ff.

[3] Issued as a supplement to his translation (1851-4).

[4] Frequently reprinted.

[5] Second editions, 1891 (*Paradiso*), 1892 (*Purgatorio*).

[6] Second edition, 1899.   [7] Second edition, 1902.

"Readings" on the *Inferno* (1894), *Purgatorio* (1889), and *Paradiso* (1900)[1]; and H. F. Tozer's "English Commentary on the *Divina Commedia*" (1901).[2]

Other works on the *Commedia* (or including the *Commedia*) which should be mentioned here are, the *Vocabolario Dantesco* of L. Blanc (Leipzig, 1852), translated into Italian by G. Carbone (Florence, 1859)[3]; the *Dizionario della Divina Commedia* of Donato Bocci (Turin, 1873); the *Dizionario Dantesco* of Giacomo Poletto (Siena, 1885-7); the *Concordance of the Divina Commedia* of E. A. Fay (Boston, Mass. 1888); the *Enciclopedia Dantesca* of G. A. Scartazzini (Milan, 1896-8); the *Dante Dictionary* of Paget Toynbee (Oxford, 1898); and the *Indice dei Nomi Propri e delle Cose Notabili* of the same author, appended to the Oxford Dante (Oxford, 1894).[4]

---

[1] Second editions, 1897 (*Purgatorio*), 1906 (*Inferno*), 1909 (*Paradiso*).
[2] See *Chronological List of English Translations from Dante* (loc. cit.).
[3] Often reprinted. [4] Second edition, 1897; third edition, 1904.

DANTE ALIGHIERI
From the painting by Andrea del Castagno, in the Museo Nazionale at Florence

CHAPTER III

Latin Works—The *De Monarchia*—The *De Vulgari Eloquentia*—The *Letters*—The *Eclogues*—The *Quaestio de Aqua et Terra*—Apocryphal Works.

IN addition to his Italian works Dante wrote several works in Latin.

De Monarchia.—The most important of these and the best known is the *De Monarchia*, a treatise on monarchy, which has been described as "the creed of Dante's Ghibellinism". Its subject is the relations between the Empire and the Papacy; it is a plea for the necessity of a universal temporal monarchy, coexistent with the spiritual sovereignty of the Pope. The work is divided into three books,[1] in the first of which Dante treats of the necessity of monarchy; in the second he discusses the question how far the Roman people were justified in assuming the functions of monarchy, or the imperial power; in the third he inquires to what extent the function of the monarchy, i.e. the Empire, depends immediately upon God.

[1] The division of the books into chapters was made by Dante himself, as is evident from the passages in which he refers to previous or subsequent chapters (e.g. i. 8, l. 33; ii. 6, l. 10; ii. 8, ll. 106-7; iii. 16, l. 1). The numeration of the chapters is due to modern editors, who unfortunately have not all adopted a uniform system. Witte, for instance, divides Book i. into sixteen chapters, Book ii. into thirteen, and Book iii. into sixteen; whereas Fraticelli and Torri divide Book i. into eighteen, Book ii. into eleven, and Book iii. into fifteen; while Giuliani adopts yet another system. (For a comparative table of the various arrangements, see *Table* xxxiii. in the *Dante Dictionary*.)

Both Villani and Boccaccio include the *De Monarchia* in their lists of Dante's works. The former says briefly: "Dante also composed the *Monarchia*, in which he treated of the function of the Pope and of the Emperors".[1] Boccaccio, on the other hand, speaks of the book at some length, and relates how, soon after Dante's death, it was publicly condemned to be burned by the Papal Legate in Lombardy, who would also have burned Dante's bones if he had not been prevented:—

"This illustrious writer also, when the Emperor Henry VII came into Italy, composed a book in Latin prose, entitled *Monarchia*, which he divided into three books, corresponding to the three questions which he determines in it. In the first book he proves by logical argument that the existence of the Empire is necessary to the well-being of the world; and this is the first question. In the second book, drawing his arguments from history, he shows that Rome of right gained the imperial title; which is the second question. In the third book he proves by theological arguments that the authority of the Empire proceeds direct from God, and not through the medium of any vicar, as the clergy would seem to hold; and this is the third question.

"This book, a few years after the death of the author, was condemned by Messer Beltrando, Cardinal of Il Poggetto,[2] and Papal Legate in Lombardy, during the pontificate of John XXII. And the occasion of this was because Lewis, Duke of Bavaria, elected by the German electors King of the Romans, coming to Rome for his coronation, contrary to the wishes of the aforesaid Pope John, when he was in Rome, made a Minor Friar, named

---

[1] Bk. ix. ch. 136.

[2] Bertrand du Pouget, created Cardinal by his uncle, Pope John XXII, in 1316.

Piero della Corvara, Pope, contrary to the ordinances of the Church, and made many cardinals and bishops; and had himself crowned in Rome by this Pope. And when afterwards questions arose in many cases as to his authority, he and his following, having discovered this book, began to make use of many of the arguments it contained, in defence of his authority and of themselves; for which cause the book, which up till then had hardly been known, became very famous. But later, when the said Lewis was gone back to Germany, and his followers, and especially the clerics, had declined and were scattered, the said Cardinal, there being none to oppose him, seized the aforesaid book, and publicly condemned it to the flames, as containing heretical matter. And he strove to deal with the bones of the author after the same fashion, to the eternal infamy and confusion of his memory; but in this he was opposed by a valiant and noble knight of Florence, Pino della Tosa by name, who happened to be then at Bólogna, where this matter was under consideration; and with him was Messer Ostagio da Polenta, both of whom were regarded as influential persons by the aforesaid Cardinal." [1]

Critics are by no means agreed as to the date when the *De Monarchia* was composed. Some hold that Dante wrote it before his exile from Florence, chiefly on the ground that it contains no reference to his exile, it being the only work of Dante, with the exception of the *Vita Nuova*

---

[1] *Vita di Dante*, ed. Macrì-Leone, § 16, pp. 72-3. The whole of Boccaccio's account of the *De Monarchia* is omitted from the edition of the *Vita di Dante* published, together with the *editio princeps* of the *Vita Nuova*, at Florence in 1576 with the *imprimatur* of the Florentine Inquisitor General. This suppression was noticed by Milton, who remarks on the fact in his Commonplace Book (see Paget Toynbee, *Dante in English Literature*, vol. i. p. 122).

(written in his youth), and the *Quaestio de Aqua et Terra* (written just before his death), in which he does not refer to his being an exile.[1] Others maintain that it was written as late as 1317-18, or even later, on the ground that in many of the MSS. there is a passage which contains a direct mention of the *Paradiso*.[2] Unless this is a later interpolation either by Dante himself, or by some copyist (which seems the more probable), it follows necessarily that the treatise must have been written after the *Paradiso*, and consequently towards the close of Dante's life. On the whole, the most probable view is that it was written, as Boccaccio says it was, about the time when the Emperor Henry VII visited Italy, perhaps in 1311 or 1312.[3]

---

[1] The chief upholder of this theory was Karl Witte—see the *Prolegomena* to his edition (Vienna, 1874) of the *De Monarchia*, pp. xxxiii-xlix.

[2] The passage in question, which occurs in the middle of the twelfth chapter of the first book runs as follows:—

"Libertas arbitrii . . . est maximum donum humanae naturae a Deo collatum, sicut in Paradiso Comedie jam dixi".

This is an unmistakable reference to *Paradiso*, v. 19-24:—

> " Lo maggior don che Dio per sua larghezza
> Fesse creando, ed alla sua bontate
> Più conformato, e quel ch' ei più apprezza,
> Fu della volontà la libertate,
> Di che le creature intelligenti,
> E tutte e sole furo e son dotate."

[3] There is a passage at the beginning of the second book, which, according to the reading of the most important MS., as well as of all the early printed editions, contains an undoubted reference to the Emperor Henry VII. In his rebuke to the opposition offered to the Emperor Dante speaks of " Reges et principes in hoc unico concordantes, ut adversentur Domino suo et uncto suo Romano Principi " (ii. 1, ll. 25-7). This reference to the Emperor as " the Lord's anointed " can only be to Henry VII. To no other of the successors of Frederick II, contemporary with himself, would Dante have dreamed of applying this term. In a passage of the *Convivio*, where he describes Frederick as " the last Emperor of the Romans," he emphatically declines to recognize Rudolf and Adolf and Albert (the im-

The arguments of the *De Monarchia* are admirably summarised in Bryce's *Holy Roman Empire*[1] :—

Book I.—Monarchy is first proved to be the true and rightful form of Government. Men's objects are best attained during universal peace : this is possible only under a monarch (i. 1-7). And as he is the image of the divine unity, so man is through him made one, and brought most near to God (i. 8). There must, in every system of forces, be a *primum mobile;* to be perfect, every organization must have a centre, into which all is gathered, by which all is controlled (i. 9). Justice is best secured by a supreme arbiter of disputes, himself untempted by ambition, since his dominion is already bounded only by ocean (i. 10-11). Man is best and happiest when he is most free; to be free is to exist for one's own sake. To this noblest end does the monarch and he alone guide us ; other forms of government are perverted, and exist for the benefit of some class ; he seeks the good of all alike, being to that very end appointed (i. 12-15). Abstract arguments are then confirmed from history. Since the world began there has been but one period of perfect peace, and but one of perfect monarchy, that, namely, which existed at our Lord's birth, under the sceptre of Augustus (i. 16).

Book II.—Since then the heathen have raged, and the kings of the earth have stood up; they have set themselves against their Lord, and His anointed the Roman

mediate predecessors of Henry VII) as Emperors at all: "Federigo di Soave, ultimo Imperador de' Romani, ultimo dico per rispetto al tempo presente, non ostante che Ridolfo e Adolfo e Alberto poi eletti sieno appresso la sua morte e de' suoi discendenti" (iv. 3, ll. 39-43). Now Henry VII was crowned at Aix on 6 January, 1309; consequently, if the above be the true reading, as there can be hardly a doubt that it is, the book must have been written later than that date (see Paget Toynbee, *Dante Studies and Researches*, pp. 302-3).

[1] Reproduced (with references added) by kind permission of the author.

prince (ii. 1). The universal dominion, the need for which has been thus established, is then proved to belong to the Romans. Justice is the will of God, a will to exalt Rome shown through her whole history. Her virtues deserved honour : Virgil is quoted to prove those of Aeneas, who by descent and marriage was the heir of the three continents : of Asia through Assaracus and Creusa ; of Africa by Electra (daughter of Atlas and mother of Dardanus) and by Dido ; of Europe by Dardanus and Lavinia. God's favour was approved in the fall of the shields to Numa, in the miraculous deliverance of the capitol from the Gauls, in the hailstorm after Cannae. Justice is also the advantage of the state : that advantage was the constant object of the virtuous Cincinnatus, and the other heroes of the republic. They conquered the world for its own good, and therefore justly, as Cicero attests ; so that their sway was not so much the command as the protection of the whole earth (ii. 2-6). Nature herself, the fountain of all right, had, by their geographical position and by the gift of a genius so vigorous, marked them out for universal dominion :—

> Excudent alii spirantia mollius aera,
> Credo equidem : vivos ducent de marmore vultus ;
> Orabunt causas melius, coelique meatus
> Describent radio, et surgentia sidera dicent :
> Tu regere imperio populos, Romane, memento ;
> Hae tibi erunt artes ; pacisque imponere morem,
> Parcere subjectis, et debellare superbos (ii. 7).[1]

Finally, the right of war asserted, Christ's birth, and death under Pilate, ratified their government. For Christian doctrine requires that the procurator should have been a lawful judge, which he was not unless Tiberius

---

[1] *Aeneid*, vi. 848-54.

was a lawful Emperor. Else Adam's sin and that of his race was not duly punished in the person of the Saviour (ii. 8-13).

Book III.—The relations of the imperial and papal power are then examined, and the passages of Scripture (tradition being rejected), to which the advocates of the Papacy appeal, are elaborately explained away (iii. 1-3). The argument from the sun and moon does not hold, since both lights existed before man's creation, and at a time when, as still sinless, he needed no controlling powers. Else *accidentia* would have preceded *propria* in creation. The moon, too, does not receive her being nor all her light from the sun, but so much only as makes her more effective. So there is no reason why the temporal should not be aided in a corresponding measure by the spiritual authority (iii. 4) This difficult text disposed of, others fall more easily; Levi and Judah, Samuel and Saul, the incense and gold offered by the Magi[1]; the two swords, the power of binding and loosing given to Peter (iii. 5-9). Constantine's Donation was illegal: no single Emperor or Pope can disturb the everlasting foundations of their respective thrones : the one had no right to bestow, nor the other to receive, such a gift (iii. 10). In giving the imperial crown to Charles the Great, Leo the Third[2] exceeded his powers: *usurpatio juris non facit jus* (iii. 11). It is alleged that all things of one kind are reducible to one individual, and so all men to the Pope. But Emperor and Pope differ in kind, and so far as they are men, are reducible only to God, on whom the Empire immediately depends ; for it existed before Peter's see, and was recog-

[1] Typifying the spiritual and temporal powers. Dante meets this by distinguishing the homage paid to Christ from that which His Vicar can rightfully demand.

[2] [Dante actually, by an error, says Hadrian crowned Charles the Great.]

nized by Paul when he appealed to Cæsar. The temporal
power of the Papacy can have been given neither by
natural law, nor divine ordinance, nor universal consent :
nay, it is against its own Form and Essence, the life of
Christ, who said "My kingdom is not of this world" (iii.
12-15).

Man's nature is twofold, corruptible and incorruptible :
he has therefore two ends, active virtue on earth, and the
enjoyment of the sight of God hereafter; the one to be
attained by practice conformed to the precepts of philosophy, the other by the theological virtues.   Hence two
guides are needed, the Pontiff and the Emperor, the latter
of whom, in order that he may direct mankind in accordance with the teachings of philosophy to temporal
blessedness, must preserve universal peace in the world.
Thus are the two powers equally ordained of God, and
the Emperor, though supreme in all that pertains to the
secular world, is in some things dependent on the Pontiff,
since earthly happiness is subordinate to eternal.   " Let
Cæsar, therefore, show towards Peter the reverence wherewith a firstborn son honours his father, that, being illu-
mined by the light of his paternal favour, he may the
more excellently shine forth upon the whole world, to the
rule of which he has been appointed by Him alone who
is of all things, both spiritual and temporal, the King and
Governor " [1] (iii. 16).

The *De Monarchia* was twice translated into Italian in
the fifteenth century; viz. by an anonymous writer in
1461, and by Marsilio Ficino, the Florentine Platonist, in
1467.[2]   It was first printed in the original Latin at Basle

[1] Ed. 1904, pp. 276-80.
[2] See Torri's edition, pp. xli-ii, 118-21. Ficino's translation accompanies
the Latin text in the editions of Fraticelli, by whom it was first printed
in 1839. There are three English translations of the *De Monarchia*, viz

in 1559 (in a collection of treatises on subjects connected with the Roman Empire),[1] by a Protestant publisher, Joannes Oporinus (Johann Herbst), and was in all probability seen through the press by an Englishman, John Foxe, the martyrologist, who was employed as reader of the press in the printing-office of Oporinus, and who quotes the work in his *Book of Martyrs*.[2] Curiously enough, Oporinus thought the treatise was not written by the author of the *Divina Commedia*, but by a fifteenth century writer of the same name.[3]

Eight manuscripts of the *De Monarchia* have been preserved, three of the fourteenth century, four of the fifteenth, and one of the sixteenth.[4]

De Vulgari Eloquentia :—Besides the *De Monarchia* Dante wrote in Latin prose a treatise on the vulgar tongue (*De Vulgari Eloquentia*), which is mentioned among his writings by both Villani and Boccaccio. The former says (in a passage which is omitted from some manuscripts) :—

" Dante also wrote a short work, entitled *De Vulgari Eloquentia*, which he intended to be in four books, but only two of these are in existence, perhaps owing to his premature death ; in this work, in vigorous and elegant

by F. J. Church, in *Dante : an Essay*, by R. W. Church, 1879 (pp. 177-308) ; by P. H. Wicksteed, in *Translation of the Latin Works of Dante*, 1904 (pp. 127-279) ; and by Aurelia Henry, 1904.

[1] *Andreæ Alciati Jureconsulti clariss. De Formula Romani Imperii Libellus. Accesserunt non dissimilis argumenti Dantis Florentini De Monarchia libri tres. Radulphi Carnotensis De translatione Imperii libellus. Chronica M. Jordanis, Qualiter Romanum Imperium translatum sit ad Germanos. Omnia nunc primum in lucem edita.*

[2] See Paget Toynbee, *John Foxe and the Editio Princeps of Dante's De Monarchia*, in *Athenæum*, 14 April, 1906.

[3] In his *Epistola Dedicatoria* he says: " Sunt autem quos adjunximus, primùm Dantis Aligherii, non vetustioris illius Florentini poetae celeberrimi, sed philosophi acutissimi atque doctiss. viri, et Angeli Politiani familiaris quondam, de Monarchia libri tres " (p. 51).

[4] See the *Codicum Elenchus* in Witte's edition, pp. lvii-viii.

Latin, and with admirable arguments, he condemns all the vernacular dialects of Italy".[1]

Boccaccio says :—

"Subsequently, not long before his death, Dante composed a little book in Latin prose, which he entitled *De Vulgari Eloquentia*, wherein he purposed to give instruction, to such as wished to learn, in the art of composing in rime; and though it appears from the work itself that he intended to devote four books to the subject, either because he was surprised by death before he had completed them, or because the others have been lost, only two books are now to be found."[2]

The work consists of a dissertation on the Italian language as a literary tongue, in the course of which Dante passes in review the fourteen dialects of Italy. It also contains a consideration of the metre of the *canzone*, thus forming to a certain extent an "art of poetry". Like the *Convivio*, the *De Vulgari Eloquentia* is incomplete. It was originally planned, as both Villani and Boccaccio observe, to consist of at least four books, as appears from the fact that Dante twice reserves points for consideration in the fourth book.[3] In its unfinished state it consists of two books only; the first, which is introductory, is divided into nineteen chapters; the second, into fourteen, the last of which is incomplete, the work breaking off abruptly in the middle of the inquiry as to the structure of the stanza. The division into numbered chapters, as in the case of the *Convivio*, is due to Dante himself, as is evident from the fact that on one occasion he refers back to a previous chapter.[4]

The exact date of the composition of the *De Vulgari Eloquentia* is disputed. It was certainly written after

[1] Bk. ix. ch. 136.   [2] *Vita di Dante*, ed. cit. § 16, p. 74.
[3] "In quarto hujus operis" (ii. 4, l. 13; 8, l. 83).
[4] "In tertio hujus libri capitulo" (ii. 8, ll. 61-2).

Dante's exile, references to which occur in both books of the treatise.[1] It is probably an earlier work than the *De Monarchia*, and perhaps earlier than the *Convivio;* but there is a strong argument for placing it after the latter in a passage in that work in which Dante speaks of a book which, God willing, he intends to compose upon the vulgar tongue.[2] On the other hand, John I, Marquis of Montferrat, who died in 1305, is spoken of as being still alive; as are Azzo VIII of Este, who died in 1308, and Charles II of Naples, who died in 1309.[3] It appears probable, therefore, that the treatise was written between 1302 and 1305, and consequently before the *Convivio*.[4]

The contents of the *De Vulgari Eloquentia* are briefly as follows[5]:—

Book I.—*Chap.* 1. Introductory. Wherein the vulgar tongue, or vernacular, differs from a learned or literary language, such as Latin.—*Chap.* 2. That man alone, as distinguished from angels and animals, is endowed with speech.—*Chap.* 3. For what reasons man had need of speech.—*Chap.* 4. The origin of human speech. Adam the first speaker; his first utterance the name of God.—*Chap.* 5. Adam's first utterance addressed to God, in the Garden of Eden.—*Chap.* 6. That the Hebrew tongue, the language of all mankind down to the building of the Tower of Babel, was the language spoken by Adam.—

---

[1] " Nos autem cui mundus est patria, velut piscibus aequor, quamquam Sarnum biberimus ante dentes, et Florentiam adeo diligamus ut, quia dileximus, exilium patiamur injuste . . ." (i. 6, ll. 17-21 ; cf. i. 17, ll. 35-8 ; ii. 6, ll. 36-9).

[2] " Un libro ch' io intendo di fare, Dio concedente, di Volgare Eloquenza " (i. 5, ll. 67-9).

[3] *V. E.* i. 12, ll. 36-9.

[4] It is, of course, possible that Dante may have had the two works on hand concurrently.

[5] The arguments at the head of the chapters in A. G. Ferrers Howell's translation have occasionally been utilised in this analysis.

Chap. 7. Of the building of the Tower of Babel, and
of the confusion of tongues. That the children of Shem,
who took no part in the building of Babel, and from
whom was descended the people of Israel, alone retained
the use of the Hebrew tongue.—*Chap.* 8. Of the inhabitants and languages of Europe, and of their boundaries;
viz. the Teutons, English, and others, in the North of
Europe, who used the affirmation *iò*; the Greeks in the
East of Europe and part of Asia; and the Spaniards,
French, and Italians in the South, whose affirmations were
respectively *oc, oïl*, and *sì*.—*Chap.* 9. Of the language of
the South of Europe, which was originally one and the
same, but eventually was split up into three, as indicated
by the affirmations *oc, oïl*, and *sì*. Of the cause of variation in language. That no vernacular is invariable,
whence the necessity for the invention of "grammar" (i.e.
literary language with fixed rules).—*Chap.* 10. Of the
respective claims to precedence of the languages of *sì, oïl*,
and *oc*. Classification of the principal dialects of Italy,
according as they belong to the west or east side of
the Apennines. The number of dialects fourteen, but the
varieties of idiom in Italy alone more than a thousand, if
every variation be reckoned.—*Chaps.* 11-15. Examination
of the several dialects of Italy, in the search for a language
worthy to be called the Italian tongue.—*Chap.* 11. Rejection of the dialects of Rome, the March of Ancona,
Spoleto, Milan, Bergamo, Aquileia, Istria, the Casentino,
Prato, and Sardinia.—*Chap.* 12. Of Sicily as the birth-
place of Italian poetry. Of the degeneracy of the princes
of Italy as compared with Frederick II and his son
Manfred. Rejection of the local Sicilian dialect (as distinguished from the language used by Sicilian poets), and
of the Apulian dialect.—*Chap.* 13. Rejection of the
Tuscan dialects (of Florence, Pisa, Lucca, Siena, and

Arezzo); of the Umbrian (of Perugia, Orvieto, and Città di Castello); and of the Genoese. Of certain Tuscan poets (including Dante himself) who rose superior to their local dialect.—*Chap.* 14. Of the two types of dialect on the east side of the Apennines; viz. the soft dialect peculiar to Romagna, and especially to Forlì, and the harsh dialect characteristic of Brescia, Verona, Vicenza, Padua, and Treviso. All of these rejected, together with the Venetian dialect.—*Chap.* 15. Examination of the dialect of Bologna, which, though superior to all other local dialects, is yet by no means worthy to be ranked as the language of Italy, as is evident from the fact that it was rejected by the most distinguished poets of Bologna, such as Guido Guinicelli, Onesto, and others. Rejection of the frontier dialects of Trent, Turin, and Alessandria.— *Chap.* 16. No single dialect having been found to conform to the required conditions, a standard must be sought for, which is declared to be the "illustrious, cardinal, courtly, and curial" vernacular, common to all the cities of Italy, and peculiar to none.—*Chap.* 17. Explanation of the term "illustrious" as applied to the common language of Italy.—*Chap.* 18. Explanation of the terms "cardinal," "courtly," and "curial," as applied to the same.—*Chap.* 19. This "illustrious, cardinal, courtly, and curial" language declared to belong to the whole of Italy, and to be the Italian vulgar tongue. The author's intention (only fulfilled in part) to treat first of this "illustrious" language, and of those considered worthy to use it; and then to discuss in detail the lower forms of the vernacular language.

Book II.—*Chap.* 1. That the "illustrious" language is equally fitted for prose and verse. Consideration of its use in verse. Ought it to be used by every one who writes verse? No, but only by those who write with knowledge and genius, since the best language is suited only to the best thoughts.—*Chap.* 2. Of the subjects worthy to be treated of in the "illustrious" language. These decided to be Arms, Love, and Virtue. Of the poets, Provençal and Italian (including Dante himself), who have sung of these subjects.—*Chap.* 3. Of the different forms of vernacular poems: canzoni, ballate, and sonnets. The canzone the most excellent form, and consequently that in which the most excellent subjects (named above) should be treated of. Of the preëminence of the canzone. —*Chap.* 4. Of the form of the canzone. Definition of poetry. Of the choice of subject, and of the style in which it should be treated of, whether in the tragic, comic, or elegiac. Of the tragic style.—*Chap.* 5. Of the different lines permissible in the canzone. The line of eleven syllables the most stately on several grounds, and consequently to be preferred. Examples of this line from Provençal and Italian poets (including Dante himself).— *Chap.* 6. Of construction, that is, of the arrangement of words according to rule. Of the various kinds of construction. The most illustrious kind that which combines taste, elegance, and loftiness. Examples of the use of this kind by Provençal and Italian poets (including Dante). List of Latin writers, in verse and prose, who might have furnished other examples. Denunciation of those who cry up Guittone d' Arezzo as a model, his style being plebeian both in vocabulary and construction.—*Chap.* 7. Of the different classes of words, viz. "childish," "feminine," "manly," "sylvan," "urban," etc. Of those whose use is admissible in the canzone. Instances of these.—*Chap.* 8. Of the meanings of the term canzone. Definition of the canzone in the technical sense as used by the author. One of Dante's own canzoni quoted as an example.— *Chap.* 9. Of the stanza; and of the three essential points in the art of the canzone. Definition of the stanza.— *Chap.* 10. Of the structure of the stanza in relation to the musical setting. Explanation of the various terms employed. —*Chap.* 11. Of the relation between the several parts of the stanza in regard to the number of lines and syllables. Three of Dante's own canzoni quoted in illustration.— *Chap.* 12. Of the arrangement of different kinds of lines in the stanza. Canzoni of Provençal and Italian poets (including Dante) quoted in illustration. Rules as to the order of sequence of lines of different lengths in the " foot " and in the " verse " (in the technical sense of these terms as used by Dante).—*Chap.* 13. Of the unrimed stanza; and of the rimed stanza. Rules as to the arrangement of rimes in the " foot " and in the " verse ". Of three things to be avoided in the matter of rime. Two sestine of Dante's quoted in illustration.—*Chap.* 14. Of the number of lines and syllables in the stanza; and of the length of the stanza in relation to the subject [in the midst of which the treatise comes abruptly to an end].

The *De Vulgari Eloquentia* made its first appearance in print in the Italian translation of Trissino, published (anonymously) at Vicenza in 1529. The original Latin text was first printed about fifty years later (in 1577) at Paris, by Jacopo Corbinelli, a Florentine, who came to France in the train of Catherine de Medicis. A second Italian translation was made at the beginning of the seventeenth century by Celso Cittadini of Siena (d. 1627), the manuscript of whose version, which has never been published, and which was first brought to light in 1824, is preserved in the Imperial Library at Schönbrunn.[1] Be-

[1] See the introduction (pp. lxxxv ff.) to Rajna's critical edition, *Il Trattato De Vulgari Eloquentia* (Florence, 1896). Rajna, who prints specimens of Cittadini's version (pp. ccxii-xv), shows that this translation was made from Corbinelli's edition of the Latin text, with the help of Trissino's version (p. xcvi). An English translation, by A. G. Ferrers Howell, was published in 1890, and reissued in a revised form in 1904, in *Translation of the Latin Works of Dante* (pp. 3-115).

fore the publication of the Latin text by Corbinelli the genuineness of the treatise, as printed in Italian by Trissino, was by no means generally admitted. The Latin text has been many times reprinted. A critical edition, by Pio Rajna, was published at Florence, under the auspices of the *Società Dantesca Italiana*, in 1896; a revised text by the same editor was published in 1897.

Only three manuscripts of the *De Vulgari Eloquentia* are known to be in existence, two of which (preserved respectively at Grenoble and at Milan) belong to the fourteenth century or beginning of the fifteenth. The Grenoble manuscript (which has been reproduced in facsimile) formed the base of Corbinelli's edition of the Latin text; while the Milanese (or Trivulzian) manuscript was the original from which Trissino made his Italian version.

Latin Letters.—Dante wrote several letters in Latin, mostly political, some of which have been already quoted.[1] Those commonly accepted as genuine are ten in number, viz. :—

Epist. i.[2] To Niccolò Albertini da Prato, Cardinal of Ostia (written after July, 1304), thanking him on behalf of the Florentine Bianchi for his attempts to make peace in Florence, and bring about the return of the exiles, and begging him to persevere in his efforts, and, further, promising in obedience to his wishes to abstain from hostilities against the Neri.

This letter, together with five others (*Epistolae* ii, iii, v, vi, vii), is preserved in a MS. in the Vatican (*Palatine*

---

[1] See above, pp. 93-9, 195-6. Such as we possess were mostly discovered in the last century through the exertions of Karl Witte, who in 1827 printed at Padua (in *Dantis Alligherii Epistolae quae exstant*) the letters which had up to that date been brought to light.

[2] According to the numeration of the *Epistolae* in the Oxford Dante (pp. 403-20).

1729), which also contains the *De Monarchia*. This MS., which was taken from Heidelberg on the capture of the city by Tilly in 1622, was presented by Maximilian of Bavaria to Pope Gregory XV in that year. It belongs to the end of the fourteenth century, being dated 1394. The above letter, which was first printed by Torri in 1842,[1] is not expressly assigned to Dante in the MS., but is commonly ascribed to him on internal evidence.

Epist. ii. To Guido and Oberto, Counts of Romena (written *circ.* 1304), condoling with them on the death of their uncle, Count Alessandro of Romena, chief of the Ghibellines of Arezzo.

This letter is preserved in the Vatican MS. (*Palatine* 1729) already mentioned (see above). It was first printed by Torri in 1842.[2] It is assigned to Dante in the title supplied by the copyist, but is considered by some authorities to be not by Dante, but by another hand, though not necessarily a forgery.

Epist. iii. To the Marquis Moroello Malaspina (written *circ.* 1307), with a canzone (*Canz.* xi. " Amor, dacchè convien pur ch' io mi doglia "), describing how the writer had been overcome by a tempestuous passion for a lady he had met in the valley of the Arno.

This letter, like the two previous ones, is preserved in the Vatican MS. mentioned above. It was first printed (with considerable emendations) by Witte in 1842.[3] It is assigned to Dante in the MS., and is generally accepted as authentic.

[1] *Epistole di Dante Alighieri edite e inedite,* Livorno, 1842 (pp. 2-4).
[2] *Op. cit.* p. 8.
[3] In *Dante Alighieri's Lyrische Gedichte, übersetzt und erklärt von K. L. Kannegiesser und K. Witte,* Leipzig, 1842 (Zweiter Theil, pp. 235-36). A critical text was printed by O. Zenatti, in *Dante e Firenze* (pp. 431-2); but see *L' Epistola di Dante a Moroello Malaspina,* by F. Novati, in *Dante e la Lunigiana* (pp. 507-42).

Epist. iv. To a Pistojan exile, commonly supposed to be Cino da Pistoja (written *circ.* 1308), in reply to his inquiry whether the soul "can pass from passion to passion," with a sonnet (perhaps *Son.* xxxvi. " Io sono stato con Amore insieme ").

This letter is preserved in a MS. (which belonged to Boccaccio) in the Laurentian Library at Florence (xxix. 8). It was first printed by Witte in 1827.[1] The letter is headed in the MS. " Exulanti Pistoriensi Florentinus exul immeritus," the two exiles being commonly identified with Cino da Pistoja and Dante. In this same MS. are preserved two other letters of Dante (*Epistolae* viii, ix), as well as the letter of Frate Ilario to Uguccione della Faggiuola.[2]

Epist. v. To the Princes and Peoples of Italy on the advent of the Emperor Henry VII into Italy (written in 1310), exhorting them to receive him as the Imperial successor of Caesar and Augustus, and the representative of justice and mercy.[3]

This letter, like the first three, is preserved in the Vatican MS. above mentioned. The Latin original, which was not discovered until 1838, was first printed by Torri in 1842.[4] There exists an early Italian translation of it, attributed to Marsilio Ficino (1433-1499), which was first printed at Rome in 1754. In the title the writer is described as " humilis Italus Dantes Aligherius Florentinus et exul immeritus ".

Epist. vi. To the people of Florence (dated 31 March, 1311), expressing his indignation at their resistance to Henry VII, and fiercely denouncing them as rebels against the Empire.[5]

---

[1] *Dantis Alligherii Epistolae quae exstant*, Patavii, 1827 (pp. 14-16).
[2] See above, p. 92 note.   [3] See above, p. 93.
[4] *Op. cit.* pp. 28-32.   [5] See above, pp. 93-6.

This letter, like the preceding, is preserved in the Vatican MS. It was first printed by Torri in 1842.[1] In the title the writer is described as " Dantes Aligherius Florentinus et exul immeritus ". This is one of the three letters of Dante mentioned by Villani.[2]

Epist. vii. To the Emperor Henry VII (written on 16 April, 1311), urging him to come without delay, and crush the rebellious Florentines.[3]

This letter, like the two preceding ones, is preserved in the Vatican MS. The Latin original was first printed by Witte in 1827[4] from a MS. at Venice. There exists an early Italian translation, which was first printed by Doni in 1547 at Florence.[5] In the title the writer is described as in the preceding letter. This is one of the three letters of Dante mentioned by Villani.[6]

Epist. viii. To the Italian Cardinals in conclave at Carpentras after the death of Clement V (written after 20 April, 1314), calling upon them to elect an Italian Pope, who should restore the Papal See to Rome.[7]

This letter is preserved in the Laurentian MS. (xxix. 8), mentioned above, which contains also *Epistolae* iv, ix. It was first printed by Witte in 1827.[8] In the title the writer is described as " Dantes Aligherius de Florentia ". This letter, like the two preceding ones, is mentioned by Villani, who says :—

" This Dante, when he was in exile . . . wrote three noble letters, one of which he sent to the government of Florence, complaining of his undeserved exile; the second he sent to the Emperor Henry when he was be-sieging Brescia,[9] reproaching him for his delay, after the

---

[1] *Op. cit.* pp. 36-42.   [2] See below.   [3] See above, p. 94.
[4] *Dantis Alligherii Epistolae quae exstant*, Patavii, 1827 (pp. 30-46).
[5] In *Prose Antiche di Dante, Petrarcha, et Boccaccio*, etc., pp. 9-12.
[6] See below.   [7] See above, p. 97.
[8] *Op. cit.* pp. 53-61.   [9] Actually, Cremona.

manner of the prophets of old ; and the third he sent to the
Italian Cardinals, at the time of the vacancy of the Holy
See after the death of Pope Clement, urging them to agree
together in electing an Italian Pope.   These letters were
written in Latin, in a lofty style, fortified with admirable
precepts and authorities, and were greatly commended by
men of wisdom and discernment." [1]

Epist. ix. To a Florentine friend (written in 1316), rejecting with scorn the offer of a return to Florence under
certain degrading conditions. [2]

This letter, like the preceding, is preserved in the
Laurentian MS. (xxix. 8), which formerly belonged to
Boccaccio. It was first printed by Dionisi in 1790 at
Verona. [3]

Epist. x.   To Can Grande della Scala (written not later
than 1318), dedicating the *Paradiso* to him, with remarks
upon the interpretation of the poem, and on the subject,
form, and title of the *Divina Commedia*. [4] This letter,
which is preserved, in whole or in part, in six MSS.,
including one of the fourteenth century, [5] formed the
subject of the opening lecture on the *Divina Commedia*
delivered in Florence by Filippo Villani in 1391, when
he was appointed (next but one in succession to Boccaccio) to the readership on Dante, which had been established in 1373. [6] It was first printed, in a very corrupt
text, by G. Baruffaldi in 1700 at Venice. [7] In the title the
writer is described as "Dantes Aligherius Florentinus
natione, non moribus".

[1] Bk. ix. ch. 136.   [2] See above, pp. 98-9.
[3] In the fifth volume of his *Aneddoti* (p. 176).   [4] See above, pp. 195-6.
[5] See N. Zingarelli, *Dante*, pp. 723-4.
[6] See Scartazzini's *Companion to Dante* (translated by A. J. Butler),
pp. 359-60.
[7] In *Galleria di Minerva*, vol. iii. pp. 220-8 (see Torri's *Epistole di
Dante Alighieri* (p. 158).

Besides the above ten letters,[1] there are three short letters written in Latin, between 1310 and 1311, by the Countess of Battifolle to Margaret of Brabant, wife of the Emperor Henry VII, which were supposed by Witte to have been composed by Dante, but this attribution is not generally accepted.[2] There is another letter, which exists only in Italian, purporting to have been written by Dante to Guido Novello da Polenta at Ravenna, from Venice, on 30 March, 1314; this, however, is an undoubted forgery, probably of the sixteenth century, when it was first printed.[3] Other letters, which have been lost, are mentioned by several of Dante's early biographers; and Dante himself in the *Vita Nuova* (§ 31, ll. 5-9) refers to a letter he composed beginning, "Quomodo sedet sola civitas". Boccaccio says "he wrote many prose epistles in Latin, of which a number are still in existence".[4] Leonardo Bruni claims to have seen several letters in Dante's own handwriting (of which he gives a description),[5] among which he mentions one giving an account of the battle of Campaldino[6]; and another referring to his priorate as the origin of all his misfortunes[7]; and others which he wrote after his exile to members of the government of Florence, as well as to the people,[8] among

---

[1] There are two English translations of these letters, viz. by C. S. Latham, in *A Translation of Dante's Eleven Letters*, 1891; and by P. H. Wicksteed, in *Translation of the Latin Works of Dante*, 1904 (pp. 295-368).

[2] These letters, which are preserved in the Vatican (MS. *Palat.* 1729), were first printed by Torri, *op. cit.* pp. 64-8; their authenticity as compositions of Dante is upheld by F. Novati and others (see Novati's article *L' Epistola di Dante a Moroello Malaspina*, in *Dante e la Lunigiana* (pp. 509, 537).

[3] By Doni, in *Prose Antiche di Dante, Petrarcha, et Boccaccio*, etc., Fiorenza, 1547 (pp. 75-6).

[4] *Vita di Dante*, ed. Macrì-Leone, § 16, p. 74.

[5] See above, p. 54 note.   [6] See above, pp. 54, 57 note.

[7] See above, p. 74.   [8] See above, p. 91.

the latter being a long one, beginning, " Popule mee, quid feci tibi?"[1]   Filelfo quotes the beginnings of three Latin letters alleged to have been written by Dante (to the King of Hungary, to Pope Boniface, and to his own son at Bologna), and adds that Dante wrote many others, too numerous to mention.[2]   No trace of any of these letters has been found; and it is probable that his account of them was a mere fiction on the part of Filelfo, whose statements are by no means always to be believed, and who is known to have been guilty of literary frauds of various kinds.

Latin Eclogues.—Dante also wrote two Eclogues, in Latin hexameters, addressed to Giovanni del Virgilio, professor of poetry at the University of Bologna, who had urged Dante to write poetical compositions in Latin, and had invited him to come to Bologna to receive the poet's laurel crown.   These Eclogues were written during the last two years of Dante's life, between 1319 and 1321.[3] "Two eclogues of great beauty" are mentioned by Boccaccio among Dante's works,[4] and, though some critics reject them as spurious, there seems no sufficient reason for questioning their authenticity.   They exist in five independent manuscripts, in one of which (the Laurentian MS. xxix. 8, which also contains three of Dante's letters), written in the hand of Boccaccio, they are accompanied by a Latin commentary by an anonymous contemporary writer,[5] supposed by some to be Boccaccio

---

[1] *Vita di Dante*, ed. Brunone Bianchi, 1883, pp. xv, xvii, xxi.

[2] *Vita Dantis*, ed. 1828, pp. 111-14.

[3] See C. Ricci, *L' Ultimo Rifugio di Dante*, pp. 68 ff.

[4] *Vita di Dante*, ed. Macrì-Leone, § 16, p. 74.   They are also twice mentioned by Bruni, *Vita di Dante*, ed. cit. pp. xxv, xxvii.

[5] Edited by F. Pasqualigo, Lonigo, 1887.   For the MSS., see Wicksteed and Gardner, *Dante and Giovanni del Virgilio*, pp. 268 ff.

himself.[1]   The Eclogues were first printed at Florence, at the beginning of the eighteenth century, in a collection of Latin poems (in eleven volumes), *Carmina Illustrium Poetarum Italorum* (1719-1726); they were reprinted at Verona in 1788 by Dionisi in the fourth series of his *Aneddoti*, together with the Latin commentary, and have been many times reprinted since.   Critical editions have been published by Wicksteed and Gardner (London, 1902),[2] and G. Albini (Florence, 1903).[3]

   In the Latin *Carmen*[4] which opens his correspondence with Dante, Giovanni del Virgilio, after a complimentary reference to the *Commedia*, expresses his regret that Dante should confine himself to the composition of poems in the vernacular, instead of in Latin ; to submit such themes as his to the judgment of the vulgar herd is like casting pearls before swine (ll. 1-21).   Giovanni then suggests to Dante several subjects from contemporary history worthy of being treated in a Latin poem, for instance, the exploits and death of the Emperor Henry VII (24 August, 1313) ; the defeat of the Guelfs at Monte Catini by Uguccione della Faggiuola (29 August, 1315); the operations of Can Grande della Scala against Padua (1314-1318) ; or, finally, the siege of King Robert of Naples in Genoa, and his ultimate defeat of the Ghibellines (July 1318-February

---

[1] See G. Albini, *Dantis Eclogae* (Firenze, 1903), p. xvi.

[2] In *Dante and G. del Virgilio*, pp. 146 ff.

[3] There are three English translations of the Eclogues, viz. one (in blank verse) by Dean Plumptre, in *The Commedia and Canzoniere of Dante* (1887), vol. ii. pp. 326-41 ; and two by P. H. Wicksteed, one (in prose) in *Dante and G. del Virgilio*, pp. 147 ff. ; the other (in blank verse) in *Translation of the Latin Works of Dante* (1904), pp. 373 ff.

[4] Beginning, " Pieridum vox alma, novis qui cantibus orbem " ; the *Carmen* and Dante's two *Eclogae*, with Giovanni's *Ecloga Responsiva*, are printed in the Oxford Dante (pp. 185-90).   The *Carmen* appears from internal evidence to have been written in the spring of 1319.   (See Ricci, *op. cit.* p. 71).

1319) (ll. 26-30); such a poem would extend Dante's fame throughout the four quarters of the globe, and Giovanni himself, if thought worthy, would present him for the laurel crown (ll. 30-38). Giovanni concludes by begging Dante to send him a reply.

Ecloga i. Dante in reply sends to Giovanni a Latin eclogue,[1] in which he says that when the latter's poem reached him he (Tityrus) was in company with a friend, Meliboeus (Dino Perini of Florence),[2] who was eager to know what Mopsus (Giovanni) had to say (ll. 1-6); to which Tityrus replied that Mopsus discoursed of matters too high for his (Meliboeus') comprehension (ll. 7-23); at length, however, yielding to Meliboeus' entreaties Tityrus informs him that Mopsus has invited him to receive the laurel crown at Bologna (ll. 24-33). Meliboeus assumes that Tityrus will accept the invitation, but Tityrus gives reasons why he should decline, suggesting that it would be better for him to await his recall to Florence and receive the crown there (ll. 34-44). Meliboeus reminds him that time flies, but Tityrus assures him that when his poem dealing with the heavens and their inhabitants (the *Paradiso*) shall be finished, he will then be prepared to receive the crown, if Mopsus approve (ll. 45-51). Meliboeus thereupon recalls Mopsus' objections against vernacular poetry, and asks Tityrus how he proposes to win him over (ll. 51-7). Tityrus replies that he will send to Mopsus ten vessels of milk from his favourite ewe (i.e. ten cantos of the *Paradiso*); meanwhile let Meliboeus concern himself with his own duties (ll. 58-66).

Ecloga Responsiva.[3] Giovanni del Virgilio, adopting the pastoral style in imitation of Dante, sends back an

---

[1] Beginning, " Vidimus in nigris albo patiente lituris ".

[2] Apparently the same individual who related to Boccaccio the story of the finding of the lost cantos of the *Commedia* (see above, p. 209 note).

[3] Beginning, " Forte sub irriguos colles, ubi Sarpina Rheno."

eclogue in which he relates how, while he was in solitude at Bologna, the song of Tityrus (Dante) was borne to him by Eurus from Ravenna (ll. 1-21); and was echoed in Arcady, where the long-unheard strain was welcomed with delight by the inhabitants and by the very beasts. (ll. 22-5). Mopsus (Giovanni) then, asking himself why he too should not sing a pastoral strain instead of, as before, a city lay (his *carmen*), forthwith begins (ll. 26-32). Hailing Tityrus as a second Virgil, he bewails his hard fate as an exile, and expresses the hope that he may be granted his heart's desire to return to his own city and there be crowned (ll. 33-46); meanwhile will he consent to visit Mopsus in his cave (Bologna), where he should receive every welcome from the friends of Mopsus and from all the dwellers in Arcady, and where he need fear no danger (ll. 47-76). But perhaps Tityrus would despise the abode of Mopsus; and, besides, Iolas (Guido da Polenta) would hardly permit him to exchange his lordly roof for such humble entertainment as Mopsus could offer (ll. 77-83). Yet the invitation is dictated by admiration and love; and if Tityrus despise Mopsus, why then he will content himself with a draught of his Phrygian Muso (i.e. with the company of Albertino Mussato of Padua) (ll. 83-9) —but he must conclude, milking time is at hand, and his companions are returning with the setting sun (90-7).

Ecloga ii.[1] In response to the eclogue of Giovanni del Virgilio, Dante writes a second poem in the same style,[2] relating how, while he (Tityrus) and Alphesiboeus (Fiduccio

[1] It appears from a note of the anonymous commentator that this second eclogue (which some critics hesitate to accept as entirely from the hand of Dante) was not composed until a year after the receipt of Giovanni's eclogue, and did not reach the latter until after Dante's death (see Pasqualigo, *op. cit.* p. 13).

[2] Beginning, " Velleribus Colchis praepes detectus Eous ".

de' Milotti)[1] were conversing together in the shade one spring day at noontide, suddenly Meliboeus (Dino Perini) appeared, hot and out of breath (ll. 1-30). Greeting him with laughter, Tityrus asks him why he comes in such hot haste (ll. 31-5). Meliboeus makes no reply, but blows on his flute, which gives forth the words of the poem sent by Mopsus ("Forte sub irriguos colles," etc.) (ll. 36-43). When they have gathered its import, Alphesiboeus inquires of Tityrus if he intends to accept the invitation of Mopsus; to which Tityrus replies, "why not?" (ll. 44-8). Alphesiboeus then beseeches him not to leave his friends, and warns him of the danger he would incur if he went (ll. 49-62). Tityrus answers that for Mopsus' sake he would willingly for a time exchange their pleasant pastures for the rugged abode of his friend, were it not for his dread of the violence of Polyphemus[2] (ll. 63-75). Thereupon Alphesiboeus dilates on the cruelty of Polyphemus, and prays that Tityrus will never place himself in his power (ll. 76-87). Tityrus listens in silence, and smiles assent —and now evening has begun to fall (ll. 88-94). Meanwhile Iolas (Guido da Polenta) had been in hiding close by and had overheard the whole conversation (ll. 95-8).

Quaestio de Aqua et Terra.—The authenticity of the short physical treatise attributed to Dante, known as the *Quaestio de Aqua et Terra,* has been long disputed. Until quite recently it was held by the majority of professed Dantists to be an undoubted forgery. This work, which consists of twenty-four short sections, purports to be a scientific inquiry as to the relative levels of land and water

---

[1] So identified by the anonymous commentator, who describes him as a physician of Certaldo resident at Ravenna.

[2] Polyphemus is thought by some to indicate King Robert of Naples, the protector of the Guelfs; others hold the reference to be to a member of some Bolognese family whom Dante had offended, e.g. the Caccianimici (cf. *Inf.* xviii. 48-66) (see Ricci, *op. cit.* pp. 105 ff.).

on the surface of the globe; it claims, in fact, to be a report, written by Dante's own hand, of a public disputation held by him at Verona on Sunday, 20 January, 1320, wherein he determined the question, which had previously been propounded in his presence at Mantua, in favour of the theory that the surface of the earth is everywhere higher than that of the water.

The treatise was first published at Venice in 1508, by one Moncetti, who professed to have printed it from a manuscript copy, with corrections of his own.[1] Unfortunately he never produced the manuscript, of which nothing more has ever been heard. In spite, however, of the suspicious circumstances attending its publication, and of the fact that no such work is mentioned by any of Dante's biographers or commentators, it is difficult to believe that it could have been written by any one but Dante. The internal evidence in favour of its authenticity is overwhelmingly strong; while there seems no adequate motive for a falsification of this kind at the beginning of of the sixteenth century, when the literary forger found a

---

[1] *Quaestio florulenta ac perutilis de duobus elementis aquae et terrac tractans, nuper reperta que olim Mantuae auspicata, Veronae vero disputata et decisa ac manu propria scripta, a Dante Florentino poeta clarissimo, quam diligenter et accurate correcta fuit per reverendum Magistrum Joannem Benedictum Moncettum de Castilione Arretino Regentem Patavinum ordinis Eremitarum divi Augustini Sacraeque Theologiae doctorem excellentissimum.* At the beginning of the treatise proper, after the preliminary matter, is the following short title: *Quaestio aurea ac perutilis edita per Dantem Alagherium poetam Florentinum clarissimum de natura duorum elementorum aquae et terrae diserentem.* Only seven copies are known of the *editio princeps*, of which one is in the British Museum, one in the Cornell University Library (Fiske Collection) in America, and the remaining five in various public libraries in Italy. The work was reprinted at Naples in 1576, but this edition is also exceedingly rare (see *Athenaeum*, 16 October, and 13 November, 1897; and 8 July, 1905). A facsimile of the *editio princeps*, with translations in Italian, French, Spanish, English, and German, was published (by L. Olschki) at Florence in 1905.

more promising field in the imitation of classical works. One of the latest writers on the subject, Dr. E. Moore, who has gone very carefully into the whole matter, unhesitatingly believes it to be a genuine work of Dante, "corrupted possibly in some of its details, but still in all essential points the production of the same mind and pen to which we owe the *Divina Commedia*, the *De Monarchia*, and the *Convivio*."[1] A critical text of the *Quaestio*, edited by Dr. C. L. Shadwell, to whom the rehabilitation of the treatise is largely due, is printed in the third edition (1904) of the Oxford Dante. This text was reissued in a revised form, together with an English translation, in 1909.[2]

Analysis of the *Quaestio de Aqua et Terra* :—

The treatise opens with the author's statement that while he was at Mantua a debate arose as to whether water "within its own natural circumference" is in any part higher than the land ; he then states his reasons for attempting a solution of the question, and his resolve to commit his conclusions to writing (§§ 1-2). Five of the chief arguments of those who upheld the affirmative view are first set out (§§ 3-7); but the author holds this opinion to be contrary both to observation and to reason, and states his intention of proving first, that water cannot in any part of its circumference be higher than the land ; and secondly, that the land is everywhere higher than the surface of the sea ; he will then deal with the objections to these conclusions, after which he will show what is the

---

[1] *Studies in Dante*, ii. 356.

[2] Five English translations of the treatise have been published ; viz. by C. H. Bromby, *A Question of the Water and of the Land*, 1897 ; by A. C. White, in *Annual Report of the Cambridge* (U.S.A.) *Dante Society* for 1903 ; by P. H. Wicksteed, in *Translation of the Latin Works of Dante*, 1904 (pp. 389-423) ; by S. P. Thompson, in the volume containing facsimile reprint of the *editio princeps*, Florence, 1905 (pp. 59-86); and by C. L. Shadwell, in *Dante's Quaestio de Aqua et Terra*, Oxford, 1909.

final cause of this elevation of the land, and lastly he will refute the five arguments in favour of the contrary opinion already stated (§§ 8-9). Water in its own circumference can only be higher than the land either by being excentric, or by being concentric, but in some part irregularly elevated or gibbous (§ 10); in proof of his first proposition the author demonstrates that water can neither be excentric nor gibbous (§§ 11-14); proof of the author's second proposition (§ 15); opponent's arguments against these conclusions (§ 16), and author's reply (§ 17); opponent's answer to author's objections and author's fresh arguments (§§ 18-19). Having now established his position that earth is everywhere higher than water, the author proceeds to examine into the cause of this elevation, which he finally refers to the influence of the stars (§§ 20-21); as to further inquiry, let men cease to search into matters that are too high for them (§ 22). The author next refutes the arguments in favour of the contrary view stated at the outset (§ 23), and concludes with the record of his own name and of the place and date of the dissertation (§ 24).

Apocryphal Works.—Besides the spurious letters mentioned above, and sundry apocryphal sonnets and canzoni, Dante has been credited with the authorship of certain religious poems in *terza rima*, namely a translation of the seven Penitential Psalms, and a poem of eighty-three *terzine*, known as his *Professione di Fede*, which consists of a paraphrase of the Apostle's Creed, the ten Commandments, the *Pater Noster*, and the *Ave Maria*, together with reflections on the seven Sacraments, and seven Deadly Sins. The *Professione di Fede*, sometimes spoken of as Dante's *Credo*,[1] is contained in more than forty

---

[1] For the circumstances in which this *Credo* is alleged to have been composed, see above, pp. 150-2.

manuscripts, in the majority of which it is attributed to Dante, though in a few it is assigned to Antonio da Ferrara. It was first printed at Rome in the fifteenth century (*circ.* 1476),[1] and was reprinted as an appendix to the edition of the *Divina Commedia* published at Venice by Vendelin da Spira in 1477. It has been many times reprinted since.[2] The *Sette Salmi Penitenziali*, which are contained in numerous manuscripts, were first printed in the fifteenth century (*c.* 1475) at Venice.[3] They were reprinted with the Latin originals and annotations, together with the *Professione di Fede*, by Quadrio at Milan in 1752, who published a second edition, with additional matter, at Bologna in 1753, which has frequently been reprinted. An *Ave Maria*, in twenty-four *terzine*, quite distinct from that contained in the *Professione di Fede*, was printed in a limited edition at Bologna, in 1853, from a fourteenth century manuscript[4]; and another *Credo* was printed at Mantua in 1871.[5]

Whatever may be said as to the genuineness or otherwise of the *Professione di Fede*, the *proemio* of which, at any rate, can hardly have been written by Dante, it seems at least possible that the *Sette Salmi Penitenziali* may have been his composition, perhaps as an early exercise in the use of *terza rima*, a metre which he was the

---

[1] Two fifteenth century editions (Rome, *circ.* 1476; and Florence, *circ.* 1490) are in the British Museum.

[2] It is included, together with the *Sette Salmi Penitenziali*, in the Oxford Dante (pp. 193-202). The *Professione di Fede* has been translated into English by Dean Plumptre, in *The Commedia and Canzoniere of Dante* (vol. ii. pp. 318-25).

[3] Two fifteenth century editions, both printed at Venice, are in the British Museum.

[4] *Ave Maria inedita di Dante Alighieri*, edited by A. Bonucci (100 copies).

[5] *Un nuovo Credo di Dante Alighieri*, published by A. Manardi on the occasion of the inauguration of Dante's statue at Mantua on 30 July, 1871.

first to introduce. It is not to be supposed that Dante acquired the complete mastery of this metre, which he displays from the outset in the *Divina Commedia*, without considerable previous practice. In the *Commedia* itself the increase of skill in the handling of the *terza rima*, and in the avoidance of repetition in the rimes, is easily perceptible to a close observer as the poem advances. Quadrio, who pointed out the many Dantesque phrases which occur in the *Sette Salmi*, and who had no hesitation in accepting them as genuine works of Dante, regarded them as examples of the "elegiac" style,[1] as distinguished from the tragic and comic, of which Dante speaks in the *De Vulgari Eloquentia*.[2]

[1] See his *Prefazione*.   [2] Bk. ii. ch. 4.

APPENDIX A

GENEALOGICAL TABLE OF THE FAMILY OF DANTE ALIGHIERI

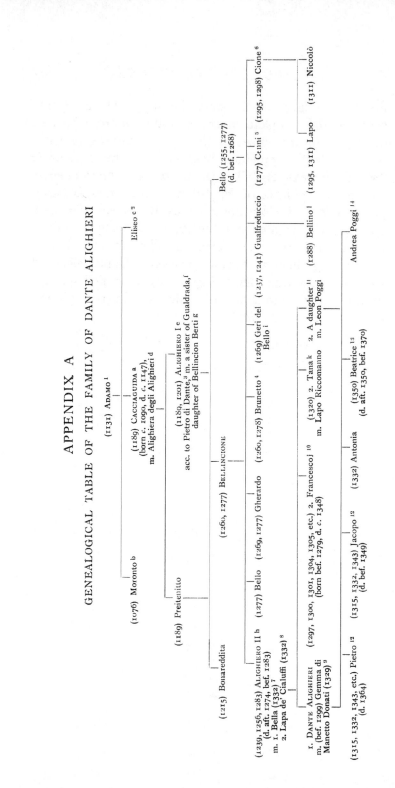

Note.—The dates attached to the names are those of documents in which the individuals in question are mentioned.

a *Par.* xv. 89, 135. b *Par.* xv. 136. c *Par.* xv. 136. l *Son.* liii*. 10. k *Son.* liii*. 10. l *Son.* liii*. 11.

j *Son.* liii*. 10. k *Son.* liii*. 10. l *Son.* liii*. 11.

[1] In a document dated 28 April, 1131, mention is made of " Cacciaguida filius Adami " (see Davidsohn, *Geschichte von Florenz*, i. 440 *n.*). [2] Eliseo had a grandson (Arrigo), and great-grandsons (Bonaccorso and Eliseo), exiled from Florence in 1268; and great-great-grandsons (Bonaccorso, d. 1303, and Guidotto), returned to Florence in 1280. [3] See above, p. 41 *n.* [4] Brunetto fought at Montaperti (4 Sept. 1260), where he was in charge of the Carroccio. [5] Cenni, i.e. Bencivenni. [6] Cione, i.e. Uguccione, was alive in 1298; his sons are mentioned, together with Dante, in the *Riforma di Baldo d' Aguglione* (2 Sept. 1311), viz. " *De Sextu Porte Sancti Petri.* . . . Filii domini Cionis del Bello et Dante Allighierii." [7] Bella's family is unknown; it is conjectured that she was the daughter of Durante di Scolaio degli Abati, in which case Dante's Christian name (a contraction of Durante) was doubtless derived from his maternal grandfather. Bella is mentioned as deceased in a document dated 16 May, 1332: " dominae Bellae olim matris dicti Dantis, et olim aviae dictorum Jacobi et domini Pieri " (see Scherillo, *Alcuni Capitoli della Biografia di Dante*, p. 29). [8] Lapa was alive in 1332, as appears from the document of 16 May, 1332, quoted in the previous note: " dominae Lapae matris dicti Francisci, et filiae olim Chiarissimi Cialuffi, et uxoris olim Alaghierii supradici". [9] Gemma is mentioned in a deed dated 24 Aug. 1329: " domine Gemme vidue uxori olim dantis allagherii et filie quondam domini Manctti domini Donati " (see *Bullettino della Società Dantesca Italiana*, N.S. 1902, ix. 184). [10] Francesco is mentioned in at least twenty documents between 1297 and 1343 (see *Bullettino della Società Dantesca Italiana*, N.S. 1907, xiv. 124-36). [11] This sister of Dante's is conjectured to be the " donna giovane e gentile . . . la quale era meco di propinquissima sanguinità congiunta " of *Vita Nuova*, § 23, ll. 86, 94-6; the " Donna pietosa e di novella etate, Adorna assai di gentilezze umane," of *Canz.* ii. 1-2. [12] Pietro and Jacopo are mentioned in the second decree of banishment against Dante (6 Nov. 1315): " Dantem Adhegerii et filios "; as well as (by name) in documents of 1332 and 1342. Many documents relating to Pietro's life at Verona (1332-1364) have been preserved (see *Bullettino della Società Dantesca Italiana*, N.S. 1906, xiii. 41-7). [13] Beatrice was alive in 1350 as a nun at Ravenna (" suora Beatrice figliuola che fu di Dante Allighieri monaca nel monastero di San Stefano dell' Uliva di Ravenna "), when Boccaccio was commissioned to present her with ten gold florins on behalf of the Capitani di Or San Michele of Florence; she died before 1370, in which year there is a record of the payment of a bequest of hers of three gold ducats to the convent where she had lived (see *Giornale Dantesco*, vii. 339-40). [14] Andrea Poggi supplied Boccaccio with information about Dante's habits and manner of life (see above, pp. 39, 209-11).

[Besides the authorities mentioned above, see L. Passerini, *Della Famiglia di Dante*, in *Dante e il suo Secolo* (pp. 53-78); Frullani e Gargani, *Della Casa di Dante*; G. L. Passerini, *La Famiglia Alighieri*; and A. Bartoli, *Della Vita di Dante Alighieri*, in *Storia della Letteratura Italiana* (vol. v. pp. 1-21, 97-110).]

d *Par.* xv. 137-8. e *Par.* xv. 91-4. f *Inf.* xvi. 37. g *Par.* xv. 112; xvi. 99. h *Son.* liii*. 8; liii*. 14; liv*. 1. i *Inf.* xxix. 27.

APPENDIX B

LETTER OF FRATE ILARIO TO UGUCCIONE DELLA FAGGIUOLA[1]

"To the most illustrious and magnificent Lord, Uguccione della Faggiuola, among the Princes of Italy the foremost and most eminent, Frate Ilario, a humble monk of the monastery of Corvo, at the mouth of the Magra, sendeth greeting in His name who verily is the salvation of all men.

"In the words of our Saviour in the Gospel, 'A good man out of the good treasure of his heart, bringeth forth that which is good'. Wherefrom we learn two things,—firstly, that by what cometh out of a man we may judge of that which is in his heart; and secondly, that by our speech, which was given to us for this purpose, we may make manifest that which is in our own hearts. As it is written, 'By their fruits ye shall know them'. And albeit this was said of the unrighteous, yet it may be understood much more generally of the righteous, inasmuch as these are ever more ready to make known their thoughts, and the others to hide them. Nor is it only the desire of glory which moves the good that is within us to bring forth fruit, but the very commandment of God, which forbids us to leave idle the gifts that are given to us. For God and Nature abhor that which is idle; wherefore the tree that bringeth not forth fruit in due season is cast into the fire. Truly, therefore, this man, whose work, together with mine own exposition thereon, I now purpose to send to you, above all men of Italy appears to have observed from his youth up this precept as to the bringing forth

---

[1] See above, p. 92 note.

of the treasure of the heart; seeing that, according as I have
been informed—and it is a marvel to hear—he tried, even when
a child, to express himself upon subjects such as had never
been told of before. And, greater marvel still, he set himself
to discuss in the vulgar tongue matters which could scarce be
expounded by the most accomplished scholars even in Latin—
in the vulgar tongue, I say, not in unadorned prose, but in the
music of verse. But leaving his praises to his works, where
without doubt every wise man will most plainly perceive them,
I come briefly to my present purpose.

" Know, then, that this man, when he was on his way to cross
the mountains, and was passing through the diocese of Luni,
whether from reverence for the place, or from some other
motive, betook himself to the monastery mentioned above.
And when I saw him, and as yet neither I nor the other monks
knew who he was, I enquired what he sought. As he returned
no reply, but only kept his eyes fixed on the buildings of the
monastery, I again asked him what he sought. Whereupon,
looking at me and my brother monks, he said ' Peace '. This
made me burn more and more to know what manner of man
he was; so drawing him apart from the others I entered into
conversation with him, and at last recognised who he was; for
though I had never set eyes on him before that day, his fame
had long ago reached me. Now when he noted that my whole
attention was set on him, and that I was interested in what he
was saying, he drew forth from his bosom with a friendly air
a small book, which he frankly offered to me. ' This,' he said,
' is part of a work of mine, which perhaps you have never seen.
I leave it to you as a memento, that you may the better keep
me in mind.' So saying he handed me the book, which I
gratefully accepted; and pressing it to my bosom I opened it,
and in his presence lovingly fixed my gaze upon it. And when
I caught sight of words in the vulgar tongue, and exhibited some
degree of astonishment, he asked what was the cause of my
hesitation. To which I replied that I was surprised at the na-

ture of the language; for not only did it seem to me a difficult, nay, an inconceivable, task to express such an arduous theme in the vulgar tongue; but also it appeared not altogether fitting that such weighty matters should be clothed in a popular dress. 'Your opinion,' he replied, 'is certainly in accordance with reason. When at the outset the seed (sent to me perchance from heaven) began to germinate in the form of this undertaking, I made choice of the language most appropriate for it. And not only did I make choice of it, but I made a beginning with it, in the usual poetical style, as follows :—

> Ultima regna canam fluvido contermina mundo,
> Spiritibus quae lata patent, quae praemia solvunt
> Pro meritis cuicunque suis.

"'But when I came to consider the condition of the present time, I observed that the songs of illustrious poets were rejected as things almost of no worth; and this because the nobles, for whom in better times such things were written, to their shame be it said, had abandoned the liberal arts to men of low estate. For this reason I laid aside the poor lyre which I had ventured to use, and made ready another, better adapted to the intelligence of the public of to-day. For it is vain to put solid food to the lips of sucklings.' After saying this he added very kindly that if I had leisure for such a task I might furnish this work of his with a running commentary, and send it to you along with my notes. If I have not always succeeded in unravelling his hidden meaning, at any rate I have laboured faithfully and in an ungrudging spirit; and I now, in obedience to the behest of this devoted friend of yours, despatch to you the work in question, as requested. Any ambiguities that may be discovered in it you must set down to my insufficiency, for be assured that the text itself is in every respect to be regarded as unimpeachable. If at any time your Highness should enquire for the other two parts of this work, with the intention of uniting them together into a single whole, you may ask for the second part, which is the sequel to this, from the eminent

Marquis Moroello ; and the third and last part will be found in the hands of the most illustrious Frederick, King of Sicily. For as the author assured me was his intention—after surveying the whole of Italy, he made choice of you three, in preference to all others, to be the patrons of this threefold work of his."

(The original of this letter, with an Italian translation, is printed by Fraticelli in his *Vita di Dante*, pp. 346-9, 357-9; a critical text is given by Rajna, *op. cit.*[1] pp. 126-8).

---

[1] See above, p. 92 note.

APPENDIX C

EXTRACTS from letters from Seymour Kirkup to Gabriele Rossetti, concerning the discovery of the Giotto portrait of Dante in the Bargello, and Kirkup's drawing from it.[1]

I

FLORENCE, 12 *September*, 1840.

. . . We have made a discovery of an original portrait of Dante in fresco by Giotto! Although I was a *magna pars* in this undertaking, the Jacks in Office have not allowed me yet to make a copy. *Sono tanto gelosi*, most likely afraid I should publish it and prevent some friends of their own reaping all the profit they hope from that speculation.

I was the person who first mentioned to Sig. Bezzi, a Piedmontese and friend of Carlo Eastlake's, the existence of the portrait under the whitewash of three centuries. We were joined by an American, and we three undertook at our expense to employ a restorer to uncover the walls of the old chapel in the palace of the Podestà in search of the portrait—mentioned by F. Villani, Filelfo, L. Aretino, Vasari, Cinelli, etc. Nothing but the constancy and talent of Sig. Bezzi could have overcome the numberless obstacles and refusals we met with. He wrote and spoke with the persuasions of an advocate, and persevered with the obstinacy and activity of an Englishman (which I believe he now is). He alone was the cause of success. We should have had no chance without him. At last, after uncovering enough of three walls to ascertain it was not

[1] These extracts are reprinted from *Gabriele Rossetti: A Versified Autobiography* (pp. 144-54), by kind permission of Mr. W. M. Rossetti, and Messrs. Sands and Co.

there, the Government took the task into their own hands, on our terms, with the same restorer, and in the fifth wall they have succeeded. The number of walls is six, for the chapel has been divided into two—(magazines of wine, oil, bread, etc. for the prisoners).

The precise date of the painting is not known. The poet looks about twenty-eight—very handsome—*un Apollo colle fattezze di Dante.* The expression and character are worthy of the subject, and much beyond what I expected from Giotto. Raphael might own it with honour. Add to which it is not the mask of a corpse of fifty-six—a ruin—but a fine, noble image of the Hero of Campaldino, the Lover of Beatrice. The costume very interesting—no beard or even a lock of hair. A white cap, over which a white *capuccio*, lined with dark red showing the edge turned back. A parchment book under his arm—perhaps the *Vita Nuova.*

It is in a group of many others—one seems Charles II of Naples. Brunetto Latini and Corso Donati are mentioned by the old authors.

II

FLORENCE, 14 *September*, 1841.

By the time you receive this, I hope that the portrait of Dante, for you, will be in London. The gentleman who has taken charge of it was in such haste to leave the country (from the consequences of a fatal duel) that I had not an opportunity for writing.

You will receive, in fact, three portraits. They are as follows :—

No. 1. A drawing in chalk, on light-brown paper, of the face as large as the original. I had intended to write a memorandum on it, but in my hurry it was forgotten. Perhaps you would have the kindness to add it, if you think it worth while, viz. :—

" Drawn by S. K., and traced with talc, on the original fresco by Giotto, discovered in the Chapel of the Palazzo del Podestà, Florence, on the 21st July, 1840, before it was retouched."

No. 2. A small sketch in water-colours, giving the colours of the dress, and the heads supposed to be of Corso Donati and Brunetto Latini.

No. 3. A lithography by the painter and restorer Marini, who uncovered the painting. This is made on a tracing by himself.

I thought it useful to send you these in order to give you a better idea of this very interesting discovery—Dante, under thirty years of age. With respect to No. 1, it is fixed with glue-water, and will not rub out with common usage. The only thing it is liable to is the cracking or bending of the paper, which sometimes in a face alters the expression.

Since I drew it, I have had the mortification to see the original retouched, and its beauty destroyed. You will perceive that the eye is wanting. A deep hole in the wall was found exactly on that spot, as if done on purpose. It was necessary to fill it that it might not extend further; not content, they ordered Sig. Marini to paint the eye on it, and he has daubed over the face in many parts, to the ruin of its expression and character. It is now fifteen years older, a mean pinched expression, and an effeminate character, compared to what it was. It is not quite so bad as the lithography I send you, but not far from it. When I saw what was done, I asked a young man, his assistant, if it was done with colours in *tempera*, and he assured me, with a boast, that it was in *bon fresco*. If so, Dante is gone for good. But I have still hopes that he spoke only of the eye, and many of my friends think it can only be accomplished on the old, and hard painting by some distemper-colour of a glue, size, or egg; and, if so, a damp cloth fixed on it for half an hour will bring it all away without injuring the original fresco. I mean to take my time, and perhaps some day I may restore Dante to himself a second time. I had the principal part in the late discovery.

The lithography I send you is exceedingly unlike and incorrect, though a tracing. In shading and finishing he has totally lost and changed the outline, if he ever had it. It is vulgar, old, and effeminate—the contrary in every respect to the original. The Florentines of to-day cannot draw, nor even trace. Think of what such a hand would do, if allowed to paint over it! and that has been the case. . . . When I mentioned to you that my drawing was a secret, I only meant that, if known here that I obtained access to make a tracing by bribery, it would compromise those who had assisted me. You are welcome to show it to whom you please, and *do whatever you wish with it.* But I recommend you not to give it away, for it is the *only* copy that has been made to my knowledge before the fresco was retouched,[1] except the miserable lithography which I send; and, if so bad a copy was produced by the help of tracing, and from the original in its pure state, nothing very good is to be expected in future. The eye in the said lithography was, of course, added by the copier. You will perceive by my drawing that the outline (the eye lash) remained, which was fortunate, as it gives the exact situation of the feature.

III

FLORENCE, 5 *February*, 1843.

. . . The three pomegranates in Giotto's fresco are so uncertain in their appearance, from injury and time, that I was doubtful about them, but a word from you decides the question in my mind. They are chipped and much obliterated; and, from there seeming a sort of double outline, and no shade or colour but the yellow drapery on which they are painted, I took them for an embroidery on the breast of the Barone. Some remains of fingers and stalk, however, had led the Florentines to consider them as *melograni,* and they were puzzling their brains to find a meaning.

---

[1] Another drawing, the original of which is now in Berlin, was made by Perseo Faltoni, who acted as assistant to Marini, the "restorer" of the fresco (see T. Paur, *Dante's Porträt,* in *Jahrbuch der Deutschen Dante-Gesellschaft,* vol. ii. pp. 301-2; and K. Witte's note, p. 440). A reproduction of this drawing is given by F. X. Kraus in *Dante, Sein Leben und Sein Werk,* p. 166.

APPENDIX D

CHRONOLOGICAL LIST OF EARLY (CENT. XIV-XVI) COMMENTARIES ON THE *COMMEDIA*, WITH TITLES OF THE PRINTED EDITIONS REFERRED TO IN THE TEXT[1]

1. GRAZIOLO DE' BAMBAGLIOLI; in Latin (1324): *Il commento più antico e la più antica versione latina dell' inferno di Dante, dal codice di Sandaniele del Friuli.* Udine, 1892 (published by A. Fiammazzo).

2. Italian translation of the preceding[2] (Cent. xiv): *Comento alla Cantica dell' Inferno di Dante Allighieri di autore anonimo, ora per la prima volta dato in luce.* Firenze, 1848 (published by Lord Vernon).

3. JACOPO DI DANTE; in Italian (before 1325): *Chiose alla Cantica dell' Inferno di Dante Allighieri attribuite a Jacopo suo figlio, ora per la prima volta date in luce.* Firenze, 1848 (published by Lord Vernon).

4. GUIDO DA PISA; in Latin (about 1324), unpublished; Italian translation (Cent. xiv.) of the same, also unpublished.

5. Anonymous; in Italian (between 1321 and 1337): *Chiose Anonime alla prima cantica della Divina Commedia, di un contemporaneo del Poeta, pubblicate per la prima volta.* Torino, 1865 (published by F. Selmi).

6. JACOPO DELLA LANA; in Italian (between 1323 and 1328): printed at Venice in the 1477 edition of the *Commedia*,[3] and at Milan in the 1478 edition of the *Commedia*; reprinted (by L. Scarabelli) at Milan in 1865, and at Bologna in 1866-7:

---

[1] See above, pp. 221-6. [2] See above, p. 221 note 5.
[3] In which it is erroneously attributed to Benvenuto da Imola.

271

Comedia di Dante degli Allagherii col commento di Jacopo della Lana Bolognese; two Latin translations (Cent. xiv) of the same, one by Alberico da Rosciate of Bergamo, unpublished.

7. ANDREA LANCIA; in Italian (about 1334): *L' Ottimo Commento della Divina* Commedia. *Testo inedito d' un contemporaneo di Dante.* Pisa, 1827-9 (published by A. Torri).

8. PIETRO DI DANTE; in Latin (1340-1): *Petri Allegherii super Dantis ipsius genitoris comoediam Commentarium, nunc primum in lucem editum.* Florentiae, 1845 (published by Lord Vernon).

9. Anonymous; in Latin (after 1350): *Il Codice Cassinense della Divina Commedia per la prima volta letteralmente messo a stampa.* Monte Cassino, 1865.

10. GIOVANNI BOCCACCIO; in Italian (1373-5): first published at Naples (with the false imprint of Florence) in 1724 by Lorenzo Ciccarelli: *Il Commento di Giovanni Boccacci sopra la Divina Commedia di Dante Alighieri, con le Annotazioni di Ant. Maria Salvini. Prima impressione;* reprinted at Florence in 1831-2 by Ignazio Moutier; and again at Florence in 1844 by Pietro Fraticelli; latest edition, by Gaetano Milanesi, published at Florence by Felice Le Monnier in 1863.

11. BENVENUTO DA IMOLA; in Latin (1373-80): *Benevenuti de Rambaldis de Imola Comentum super Dantis Alligherii Comœdiam nunc primum integre in lucem editum.* Florentiæ, 1887 ("sumptibus Gulielmi Warren Vernon, curante Jacopo Philippo Lacaita"); Italian translation (Cent. xiv) of the same, unpublished; another (very untrustworthy) by Giovanni Tamburini, published at Imola in 1855-6: *Benvenuto Rambaldi da Imola illustrato nella vita e nelle opere, e di lui Commento Latino sulla Divina Commedia di Dante Allighieri voltato in Italiano.*[1]

12. Anonymous; in Italian (1375): *Chiose sopra Dante.*[2]

---

[1] On this so-called translation, see C. E. Norton: *Review of a translation into Italian of the Commentary. by Benvenuto da Imola on the Divina Commedia.* Cambridge, Mass., 1861.

[2] Formerly attributed to Boccaccio, hence commonly known as *Il Falso Boccaccio.*

Testo inedito ora per la prima volta pubblicato. Firenze, 1846 (published by Lord Vernon).

13. FRANCESCO DA BUTI; in Italian (completed 1385 and 1395): *Commento di Francesco da Buti sopra la Divina Commedia di Dante Allighieri.* Pisa, 1858-62 (published by Crescentino Giannini).

14. Anonymous; in Italian (about 1400): *Commento alla Divina Commedia d'Anonimo Fiorentino del Secolo XIV*[1] *ora per la prima volta stampato.* Bologna, 1866-74 (published by Pietro Fanfani).

15. GIOVANNI DA SERRAVALLE; in Latin (February 1416-January 1417): *Fratris Johannis de Serravalle Ord. Min. Episcopi et Principis Firmani Translatio et Comentum totius libri Dantis Aldigherii, cum textu italico Fratris Bartholomaei a Colle ejusdem Ordinis, nunc primum edita.* Prato, 1891 (edited by M. da Civezza and T. Domenichelli).

16. GUINIFORTO DELLI BARGIGI[2]; in Italian (*Inferno* only) (about 1440): *Lo Inferno della Commedia di Dante Alighieri col Comento di Guiniforto delli Bargigi tratto da due manoscritti inediti del secolo decimo quinto.* Marsilia-Firenze, 1838 (published by G. Zacheroni).

17. STEFANO TALICE DA RICALDONE; in Latin[3] (1474): *La Commedia di Dante Alighieri col Commento inedito di Stefano Talice da Ricaldone.* Torino, 1886; Milano, 1888 (published by order of the King of Italy, edited by Vincenzo Promis and Carlo Negroni).

18. CRISTOFORO LANDINO; in Italian (1480): *Comento di Christophoro Landini fiorentino sopra la Comedia di Danthe Alighieri poeta fiorentino.* Firenze, 1481.[4]

19. ALESSANDRO VELLUTELLO; in Italian (1544): *La Comedia*

---

[1] So described by the editor because the MS. from which it was printed is dated (but obviously in error) 1343.

[2] Otherwise known as Guiniforte Barziza.

[3] This is in reality little more than a transcript of Benvenuto da Imola's lectures at Bologna (see above, p. 225).

[4] Many times reprinted (see above, p. 226 note 2).

di Dante Aligieri con la nova espositione di Alessandro Vellutello.
Vinegia, 1544.[1]

20. GIOVAN BATTISTA GELLI ; in Italian (between 1541 and 1563) : originally printed at Florence in several volumes between 1547 and 1561 ; first collected edition : *Letture edite e inedite di Giovan Batista Gelli sopra la Commedia di Dante.*[2] Firenze, 1887 (edited by Carlo Negroni).

21. BERNARDINO DANIELLO ; in Italian (before 1560) : *Dante con l' espositione di M. Bernardino Daniello da Lucca, sopra la sua Comedia dell' Inferno, del Purgatorio, et del Paradiso ; nuovamente stampato, et posto in luce.* Venetia, 1568.

---

[1] Three times reprinted (see above, p. 226 note 4).

[2] In his various *Letture* (twelve in all) Gelli commented on *Inferno*, i.-xxv., and on portions of *Inferno*, xxvi., *Purgatorio*, xvi., xxvii., and *Paradiso*, xxvi.

APPENDIX E

BIBLIOGRAPHICAL NOTE OF THE EARLIEST BIOGRA-PHIES AND BIOGRAPHICAL NOTICES OF DANTE

1. GIOVANNI VILLANI (*d.* 1348): in his *Cronica* or *Istorie de' suoi tempi* (ix. 135 [1]); first printed at Venice, 1537. [English translation by P. H. Wicksteed (Hull, 1898).]

2. GIOVANNI BOCCACCIO (1313-1375): *Vita di Dante* [2]; first printed at Venice, 1477 (prefixed to the edition of the *Divina Commedia*, published by Vindelin da Spira). [English translation by J. R. Smith (New York, 1901); and by P. H. Wicksteed (London, 1904).]

Boccaccio also inserted brief biographical notices of Dante in his *Comento sopra la Commedia* (Lezione prima), first printed at Naples (with the imprint of Florence), 1724; and in his *De Genealogia Deorum* (xv. 6), first printed at Venice, 1472 (Italian translation by Giuseppe Betussi, first printed at Venice, 1547).

3. ANTONIO PUCCI (*circ.* 1310-*circ.* 1390): in his *Centiloquio*, in *terza rima* (cap. 55) (written in 1373); first printed at Florence, 1772-1775 (in vols. iii.-vi. of *Delizie degli Eruditi Toscani*, published by Padre Ildefonso da San Luigi).

4. BENVENUTO DA IMOLA (*circ.* 1338-1390): in Latin, pre-

---

[1] In modern editions of Villani this chapter is numbered 136.

[2] Boccaccio's *Vita di Dante* exists in two forms, one of which, commonly known as the *Compendio*, is shorter than the other. The latest writer on the subject (E. Rostagno : *La Vita di Dante, Testo del così detto Compendio attribuito a Giovanni Boccaccio.* Bologna, 1899) argues, with some probability, that the so-called *Compendio* is Boccaccio's first draft of his work.

fixed to his Commentary on the *Divina Commedia* ; first printed at Florence, 1887.

5. MELCHIORRE[1] STEFANI (*d.* 1403); in his *Storia Fiorentina* (Lib. vi. rub. 340); first printed at Florence, 1759 (by Mehus, in his *Vita Ambrosii Traversarii*).[2]

6. FILIPPO VILLANI (*d.* 1404): in Latin, in his *Liber de Civitatis Florentiæ famosis Civibus* (ii. § 2); first printed at Florence, 1826.

7. FRANCESCO DA BUTI (1324-1406): prefixed to his Commentary on the *Divina Commedia* ; first printed at Pisa, 1858.

8. ANTONIO CARTOLARIO: in Latin,[3] appended to *De Vita ac Moribus Philosophorum veterum* ; first printed at Florence, 1759 (by Mehus, in his *Vita Ambrosii Traversarii*)[4] (anonymous Italian translation, printed at Venice, 1521).[5]

9. DOMENICO DI BANDINO (*circ.* 1340-*circ.* 1414): in Latin, in Book v. of his *Fons memorabilium Universi*[6] (completed about 1412); first printed at Florence, 1759 (by Mehus, in his *Vita Ambrosii Traversarii*).

10. SIMONE SERDINI DA SIENA (otherwise known as Il Saviozzo) (*circ.* 1360-*circ.* 1419): biographical details in his poem in *terza rima* on the *Divina Commedia* (written in 1404)[7] ; first printed at Paris, 1577 (in the *editio princeps* of Dante's *De Vulgari Eloquentia*, edited by Jacopo Corbinelli, pp. 76-81).

11. GIOVANNI DEI BERTOLDI (otherwise known as Giovanni

---

[1] In the *Delizie degli Eruditi Toscani* (vol. iii. ff.) the author's name is given as Marchionne di Coppo Stefani.

[2] See A. Solerti: *Le Vite di Dante, Petrarca e Boccaccio, scritte fino al secolo decimosesto*, p. 81.

[3] Based on Benvenuto da Imola.

[4] See A. Solerti: *Le Vite di Dante, Petrarca e Boccaccio, scritte fino al secolo decimosesto*, p. 76.

[5] See Haym, *Biblioteca Italiana*, 1781, p. 157 note 5.

[6] See Tiraboschi: *Storia della Letteratura Italiana*, vi. Pte. 2, pp. 1141-5 (ed. Milan, 1824).

[7] See Carlo del Balzo: *Poesie di mille Autori intorno a Dante Alighieri*, iii. 224-241 (Rome, 1891); and Moore: *Dante and his Early Biographers*, pp. 88 *n.* 3, 113-15.

da Serravalle) (*circ.* 1350-1445) : in Latin, prefixed to his Commentary on the Divina Commedia (completed 16 January, 1417)[1] ; first printed at Prato, 1891.

12. LEONARDO BRUNI (otherwise known as Leonardo Aretino) (1369-1444): *Vita di Dante ;* first printed at Perugia, 1671 ; and at Florence, 1672. [English translations by P. H. Wicksteed (Hull, 1898); and J. R. Smith (New York, 1901).]

13. SECCO POLENTONE (*circ.* 1375-*circ.* 1448): in Latin, in his *De Scriptoribus illustribus latinæ linguæ*[2]; first printed at Florence, 1747 (by Mehus in his edition of Manetti's lives of Dante, Petrarch, and Boccaccio).

14. ʼSANTʼ ANTONINO (1389-1459) ; Archbishop of Florence, 1446) : in Latin, in his *Opus Historiale :* first printed at Nuremberg, 1484.[3]

15. GIANNOZZO MANETTI (1396-1459): in Latin, *Vita Dantis* (originally written in Italian) ; first printed at Florence, 1747.

16. FLAVIO BIONDO (1388-1463): in Latin, in his *Historiarum ab inclinato Romano Imperio Libri xxxi* (Dec. ii. lib. ix.) (completed about 1440) ; first printed at Venice, 1484 ; a compendium of Biondo's work was made, in Latin, by Enea Silvio Piccolomini (1405-1464; Pope Pius II, 1458), and translated into Italian by Lucio Fauno ("Le Historie del Biondo, da la declinatione dello Imperio di Roma, insino al tempo suo, che vi corsero circa mille anni. Ridotte in compendio da Papa Pio, e tradotte per Lucio Fauno," Venice, 1543).[4]

---

[1] See Moore: *op. cit.* 110-13. Of this work but four MSS. are known, only three of which are complete; one of these is in the British Museum, another in the Vatican Library, and the third in the Escorial (see A. Farinelli, *Dante in Ispagna*, p. 70 *n.*).

[2] See Tiraboschi: *Storia della Letteratura Italiana*, vi. Pte. 2, pp. 1145-7 (ed. Milan, 1824). Polentone's work exists in two forms, the one much shorter than the other—the notice of Dante is printed in both forms by A. Solerti, in *Le Vite di Dante, etc.* pp. 154-5.

[3] Tiraboschi mentions an edition of Venice, 1480; but this is unknown to Hain, Brunet, and Proctor.

[4] See *Bullettino della Società Dantesca Italiana*, No. 8 (1892), pp. 21-2, 25 ; and Haym: *Biblioteca Italiana*, 1781, p. 29 note 7.

17. Anonymous Notice, in *Cronica Generale del* 1321 *al* 1470, at Ferrara; first printed at Milan (s.a.) (by A. Solerti, in *Le Vite di Dante, Petrarca e Boccaccio, scritte fino al secolo decimosesto*).[1]

18. FILIPPO DI CINO RINUCCINI (1392-1462); *Vita di Dante*;[2] first printed at Florence, 1779 (in *Delizie degli Eruditi Toscani*, vi. 245 ff.).[3]

19. GIOVANNI MARIO FILELFO (1426-1480): in Latin, *Vita Dantis*; first printed at Florence, 1828.

20. CRISTOFORO LANDINO (1434-1504): prefixed to his Commentary on the *Divina Commedia*; first printed at Florence, 1481.

21. JACOPO FILIPPO FORESTI (commonly known as Filippo da Bergamo) (1434-1520): in Latin, in his *Supplementum Chronicarum orbis ab initio mundi usque ad annum* 1482[4]; first printed at Venice, 1483 (anonymous Italian translation, printed at Venice, 1488; and another, by F. Sansovino, Venice, 1581).[5]

22. HARTMANN SCHEDEL (*d. circ.* 1500): in Latin, in his *Liber Chronicarum*[6] (the famous *Nuremberg Chronicle*, the printing of which was completed under the author's supervision on 12 July, 1493); first printed at Nuremberg, 1493.

23. Anonymous Notice, in Latin, in the Supplement to the first Venice edition (5 September, 1494) of the *Speculum Historiale* of Vincent of Beauvais.[7]

---

[1] No. xvi. p. 157.

[2] Written *circ.* 1450; based on Vellutello and Leonardo Bruni.

[3] See A. Solerti: *Le Vite di Dante, etc.*, p. 97.

[4] The text of this notice is printed in the *Modern Quarterly of Language and Literature* for March, 1898 (p. 52), where reference is made to an article in the *Historisches Jahrbuch* by Prof. Grauert, who shows that the *Speculum* notice (No. 23) was borrowed from that in the *Nuremberg Chronicle* (No. 22), and that that was borrowed from the notice in the *Supplementum* of Filippo da Bergamo, which in its turn was based on two passages in the *De Genealogia Deorum* of Boccaccio. (See above, No. 2.)

[5] See Haym: *Biblioteca Italiana*, 1781, p. 36 note 5.

[6] See above, note 4.

[7] See Paget Toynbee: *A Biographical Notice of Dante in the* 1494 *edition of the Speculum Historiale* (in *Eng. Hist. Rev.*, April 1895); and supplementary article on the same, in *Mod. Quart. Lang. Lit.*, March 1898 (see above, note 4).

24. JOHANN TRITHEIM (1462-1516): in Latin, in his *De Scriptoribus Ecclesiasticis* (c. 79)[1]; first printed at Basle, 1494.

25. RAFAELLO MAFFEI DI VOLTERRA (commonly known as Rafaello Volterrano) (1451-1522): in Latin,[2] in his *Commentariorum Urbanorum Libri xxxviii*; first printed at Rome, 1506.

26. PAOLO GIOVIO (1485-1552): in Latin, in his *Elogia Virorum literis illustrium*; first printed at Florence, 1549.

27. FRANCESCO MAUROLICO (fl. *circ.* 1550): in Latin, in his supplement to the *De Poetis Latinis* of P. Crinito and P. Sampieri; first printed at Messina, 1865.[3]

28. GIAMPIETRO FERRETTI (1482-1557): in Latin, in his *Vitae virorum illustrium civitatis Ravennae*; first printed at Ravenna, 1864.[4]

29. GIROLAMO DELLA CORTE (fl. *circ.* 1560): in his *Storia di Verona lib. xxii*[5] *fino al* 1560; first printed at Verona, 1596.[6]

30. BERNARDINO DANIELLO DA LUCCA (*d. circ.* 1560): prefixed to his Commentary on the *Divina Commedia*; first printed at Venice, 1568.

31. ALESSANDRO VELLUTELLO (*circ.* 1519-*circ.* 1590): prefixed to his Commentary on the *Divina Commedia*; first printed at Venice, 1544.

32. LODOVICO DOLCE (1508-1568); prefixed to his edition of the *Divina Commedia*; first printed at Venice, 1555.

33. MATHIAS FLACH FRANCOWITZ (known as Flaccus Illyricus) (*d.* 1575); in his *Catalogus Testium Veritatis*; first printed at Basle, 1562.[7]

---

[1] See A. Solerti: *Le Vite di Dante, etc.* p. 197.

[2] See Père Hardouin: *Doutes sur l'âge du Dante*, pp. 25-6 (ed. Paris, 1847); and Tiraboschi: *Storia della Letteratura Italiana*, vii. p. 1166.

[3] See A. Solerti: *Vite di Dante, etc.* p. 199.

[4] See A. Solerti: *Vite di Dante, etc.* pp. 200-1.

[5] Actually only xx.

[6] See *Bullettino della Società Dantesca Italiana*, No. 8 (1892), pp. 24-5; and Haym: *Biblioteca Italiana*, 1781, p. 73, n. 8.

[7] See Edward Leigh: *A Treatise of Religion and Learning, and of Religious and Learned Men* (1656), p. 177; and Paget Toynbee: *Dante in English Literature from Chaucer to Cary*, vol. i. p. 148.

34. JACOPO CORBINELLI (fl. 1570-1590); in the *editio princeps* of Dante's *De Vulgari Eloquentia* (pp. 81-2), printed at Paris, 1577.

35. MARCANTONIO NICOLETTI (1536-1596); in his *Vite degli scrittori volgari illustri libri iv*; first printed at Milan (s.a.) (by A. Solerti, in *Le Vite di Dante, Petrarca e Boccaccio, scritte fino al secolo decimosesto*).[1]

36. JEAN PAPIRE MASSON (1544-1611): in Latin, in his *Vitae trium Hetruriae procerum Dantis, Petrarchae, Boccacii;* first printed at Paris, 1587.

37. FRANCESCO BOCCHI (1548-1618): in Latin, in his *Elogia Florentinorum Doctrinis Insignium* (i. § 20); first printed at Florence, 1609.

38. ALESSANDRO ZILIOLI (fl. 1600-1630); in his *Istoria delle Vite de' Poeti Italiani;* first printed at Milan (s.a.) (by A. Solerti, in *Le Vite di Dante, Petrarca e Boccaccio, scritte fino al secolo decimosesto*).[2]

The above lives and notices of Dante (with the exception of Nos. 3, 10, 26, 29, 33), many of which were previously more or less inaccessible, as being either in MSS. or in rare early editions, have recently been printed, some for the first time, by Angelo Solerti in his collection of the lives of Dante, Petrarch, and Boccaccio, down to the end of the sixteenth century, published at Milan under the title of *Le Vite di Dante, Petrarca e Boccaccio, scritte fino al secolo decimosesto* (s.a.).

Information as to the credibility and sources of many of these notices of Dante will be found in *Storia della Letteratura Italiana* (vol. v.), by Adolfo Bartoli (Florence, 1884); *Dante and his Early Biographers,* by Edward Moore (London, 1890); *Studi Danteschi,* by Vittorio Imbriani (Florence, 1891); *Alcuni Capitoli della Biografia di Dante,* by Michele Scherillo (Turin, 1896); and in the volume of Solerti mentioned above.

In addition to these, the reader may be referred to the *Vita di Dante* of Count Cesare Balbo (first published at Turin in

---

[1] No. xxxi. pp. 222-33.   [2] No. xxxii. pp. 234-6.

1839; reissued at Florence by Le Monnier, with additional notes by Emmanuele Rocco, in 1853), of which an English translation, with modifications and additions, by Mrs. F. J. Bunbury, was published in London in two volumes in 1852; the *Vita di Dante* of Melchior Missirini (published at Florence in 1840); the *Storia della Vita di Dante* by Pietro Fraticelli (first published at Florence in 1861), which is based upon the *Memorie per servire alla vita di Dante*, collected by Giuseppe Pelli (first published at Venice in 1758, in second part of vol. iv. of Antonio Zatta's edition of *Le Opere di Dante*; second and enlarged edition published at Florence in 1823); the *Companion to Dante* (London, 1893) of G. A. Scartazzini, which is a translation (with modifications), by A. J. Butler, of the same author's *Dante-Handbuch* (Leipzig, 1892), which in its turn is a *rifacimento* of the author's own *Prolegomeni della Divina Commedia* (Leipzig, 1890); and, lastly, to the first part of Nicola Zingarelli's exhaustive volume upon Dante in the *Storia Letteraria d' Italia* (Milan, 1903), of which a compendium (*La Vita di Dante in Compendio*), was published at Milan in 1905.

References to numerous other works (many of them by English writers), including the valuable monographs by Isidoro Del Lungo, will be found in the bibliographical sections[1] of the above-mentioned works of Scartazzini, as well as, under various headings, in the same writer's *Enciclopedia Dantesca* (Milan, 1896-9).

[1] Omitted from the English edition.

INDEX

A

Abati; Ghibelline family of Florence, 37 *n.*, 38; Dante's mother perhaps member of, 37 *n.*, 38.

Abati, Bocca degli; his treachery at Montaperti, 24.

Abati, Durante degli; maternal grandfather (as is supposed) of Dante, 38.

Abati, Scolaio degli; maternal great-grandfather (as is supposed) of Dante, 38.

Accursius (d. 1260); proposed monument to, in Duomo at Florence, 112.

Adamo; great-great-great-grandfather of Dante, 40.

Adamo, Maestro; burnt alive for coining, 84 *n.*

Adimari family of Florence; their hostility to Dante, 43 *n.*, 149; Dante's relations with, 147-9.

Adolf (Emperor, 1292-1298); not recognized as Emperor by Dante, 234-5 *n.*

Aguglione, Baldo d' (d. c. 1315); his *Riforma*, 95.

Aix; coronation of Henry VII at, 235 *n.*

Alberico da Rosciate. *See* Rosciate.

Albert I (Emperor, 1298-1308); reference to, in *Convivio*, 175, 235 *n.*; not recognized as Emperor by Dante, 234-5 *n.*

Albertino Mussato. *See* Mussato.

Albini, G.; critical edition of Dante's *Eclogues*, 253.

Aldobrandi, Tegghiaio; Florentine Guelf, 21.

Aldus (Aldo Manuzio) (1450-1515); editions of *D. C.* printed by, 214.

Alfraganus; Dante's astronomical authority, 48 *n.*, 67.

Alighieri, Alighiera degli; Dante's great-great-grandmother, 40, 41.

Alighieri, Alighiero degli; Dante's great-grandfather, 40, 41; his wife and sons, 41.

Alighieri, Alighiero degli; Dante's father, 37, 38; a notary, 38; mention of, in documents, 38 *n.*; twice married, 38; his children, 38; position of, in Florence, 39; character of, 39; alluded to by Forese Donati, 39; eldest son of Bellincione, grandson of Cacciaguida, 42.

Alighieri, Antonia; Dante's daughter, 70; identified by some with Beatrice Alighieri, 71 *n.*

Alighieri, Beatrice; Dante's daughter, 70; with Dante at Ravenna, 71, 99; a nun in the convent of Santo Stefano dell' Uliva, 71; visited by Boccaccio there, 71; her bequest to the convent, 71; identified by some with Antonia Alighieri, 71 *n.*

Alighieri, Bellincione degli; Dante's grandfather, 37, 41; his sons, 42.

Buckingham, Duke of (1592-1628); anecdote of Dante quoted to, by Lord Keeper Williams, 125 *n.*

Bulletin Italien, 221 *n.*

Bullettino della Società Dantesca Italiana. See Società Dantesca.

Bunbury, Mrs. F. J.; account of Bargello in 1852, 132 *n.;* translation from Boccaccio's *Vita di Dante*, 207-8; from his *Comento*, 209-11; translation of Balbo's *Vita di Dante*, 281.

Buonconte da Montefeltro. See Montefeltro.

Buonconvento; death of Henry VII at, 96.

Buondelmonti, Buondelmonte dei; murder of, 5-7, 8, 34.

Burnetto; Dante's uncle, 37 *n.*, 42; in charge of Florentine Carroccio at Montaperti, 42.

Burney, Charles (1726-1814); translated *Inferno*, 218.

Burning alive; punishment of, 84 *n.*

Buti, Francesco da (1324-1406); commentary on the *D. C.*, 48 *n.*, 223, 224, 273, 276; date of, 224; mentions tradition that Dante joined Franciscan Order, 48 *n.;* lectures at Pisa on *D. C.*, 224; notice of Dante, 276.

Butler, A. J.; translation of *D. C.* with notes, 220; translation of Scartazzini's *Dante Handbuch*, 250 *n.*, 281.

Byron, Lord (1788-1824); translated Francesca da Rimini episode from *D. C.*, 220; version of *Purg.* viii. 1-6 in *Don Juan*, 221; interest in publication of Taaffe's *Comment on D. C.*, 229.

C

Cacciaguida; great-great-grandfather of Dante, 38 *n.*, 40; mention of, in documents, 40 *n.;* his father Adamo, 40; his history related in the *Commedia*, 40-1; baptized in San Giovanni, 40, 42; his brothers Moronto and Eliseo, 40; his wife Alighiera, 40; military services and death, 40; situation of his house in Florence, 40-1; his sons Preitenitto and Alighiero, 40-1; descendants, 41-2; "foretells" Dante's exile, 88, 90, 91.

Caccianimici family of Bologna; member of, supposed to figure as Polyphemus in poetical correspondence between Dante and G. del Virgilio, 256 *n.*

Calendars, Arabian and Syrian; utilized by Dante in *V. N.*, 47 *n.*, 48 *n.*, 67, 165, 170.

Calimala; street in Florence connecting Mercato Vecchio and Mercato Nuovo, 31 *n.*

Cambridge (U.S.A.) Dante Society; *Annual Reports*, 82 *n.*, 91 *n.*, 161 *n.*, 221 *n.*, 224 *n.*

Cammino, Gherardo da (d. 1306); reference to, in *Convivio*, 175.

Campaldino, battle of (1289); Tuscan Ghibellines defeated by Florentine Guelfs, 53-62, 67; Dante takes part in, 53-4, 57, 61, 62, 74; alleged account of, by Dante, 57 *n.*, 251; Villani's account of, 57-60; Buonconte da Montefeltro killed in, 60, 61-2; reminiscences of, in *D. C.*, 61, 62.

Campi, G.; commentary on *D. C.*, 229.

Can Grande. See Scala.

Canaccio, Bernardo; friend of Dante at Ravenna, 100 *n.;* his epitaph on Dante, 105-6; supposed until recently to have been written by Dante

dates of composition, 198; scheme of, 198-206; Boccaccio's story of lost cantos of *Paradiso*, 206-8; and of unfinished *Inferno*, 209-11; why written in Italian, 211-12; Dante and his rhymes, 213; statistics of MSS., 213; of printed editions, 213-14, 226; *editio princeps*, 172, 191, 214; French editions, 214; selections printed in England, 214-15; English editions, 215-17; translations, 217-18; English translations, 218-221; statistics of, 219-20; lectures on, by Boccaccio, 223; by Benvenuto da Imola, 223, 225; by Buti, 223-4; by Filippo Villani, 250; commentaries on, 41 *n.*, 70, 98 *n.*, 101 *n.*, 103 *n.*, 131 *n.*, 146-7, 221-9, 271-4; Cent. XIV, 221-4, 271-3; Cent. XV, 224-6, 273; Cent. XVI, 226, 273-4; Cent. XVIII, 227; Cent. XIX, 227-9; English commentaries, 229-30; indices, 227, 230; dictionaries, 230; concordance, 230; the work quoted, 21, 22, 24, 27, 30, 36, 37, 38, 39, 40, 41, 42, 48 *n.*, 51, 55, 56, 61-3, 64, 69, 71, 84, 89, 90, 91, 92, 97, 100, 101 *n.*, 129 *n.*, 138, 140, 146, 175 *n.*, 196 *n.*, 197, 211, 221, 234 *n.*

Compagni, Dino (c. 1260-1326); his *Chronicle* quoted, 77-8.

Conrad the Salic (Emperor, 1024-1039); progenitor of Swabian Emperors, 2.

Conrad III (Emperor, 1138-1152); defeats Henry of Bavaria at Weinsberg, 2.

Conradin of Hohenstaufen (1251-1268); intrigues of Guelfs with, 28.

Constance, Council of (1414-1418); G. da Serravalle at instigation of two English bishops writes commentary on *D. C.* at, 225.

Convito; incorrect title of Dante's *Convivio* first used by Biscioni, 173 *n.*, 191.

Convivio ; reference to Dante's exile in, 88-9, 91, 175, 177; Kirkup makes drawing of Giotto's portrait of Dante in copy of 1531 edition of, 134 *n.*; reference to *V. N.* in, 161; Biscioni's edition, 172, 173 *n.*, 191; account of the work, 173-92; correct title of, 173 *n.*, 191; *editio princeps* of, 173 *n.*, 191; Cent. XVI editions, 173 *n.*, 191; MSS. of, 173 *n.*, 191-2; attempts to identify missing canzoni in, 174; division into chapters, 174; Villani's account of, 174; Boccaccio's, 174-5; date of work, 175; perhaps composed at Bologna, 175; meaning of name, 175; wherein it differs from *V. N.* 175, 176; reason why written in Italian, 175, 177-8; analysis of work, 176-91; English translations of, 176 *n.*, 192 *n.;* printed editions of, 191; critical editions, 191; supposed reference to *De Vulg. Eloq.* in, 241; the work quoted, 42 *n.*, 48 *n.*, 65-6, 66 *n.*, 69 *n.*, 88-9, 161, 173 *n.*, 174 *n.*, 175 *n.*, 197 *n.*, 234-5 *n.*

Corbinelli, Jacopo (fl. 1570-1590); printed *editio princeps* of *De Vulg. Eloq.*, 245, 246, 276, 280; first printed Serdini's notice of Dante, 276; his notice of Dante, 280.

Cordeliers; Franciscans so called, 48 *n.*

Cornell University Library; copy of *editio princeps* of *Quaestio de Aqua et Terra* in, 257 *n.*

Corrall, C.; printer of Pickering's diminutive edition of *D. C.*, 215.

Corsi, Domenico Maria (Cardinal, 1686-1697); restores Dante's tomb at Ravenna, 107; engraving of tomb as restored by him, 107 *n.*

Corso Donati. *See* Donati.

Costa, Paolo; commentary on *D. C.*, 228; editions of, 228 *n.*

Credo, Dante's; alleged origin of, 150-2; MSS. of, 259-60: assigned by some to Antonio da Ferrara, 260; editions of, 260; English translation of, 260 *n.;* another *Credo*, 260 *n.*

294 INDEX

Cremona; besieged by Henry VII, 94.
Cronica Generale dal 1321 *al* 1470; anonymous notice of Dante in, 278.

D

D' Ancona e Bacci; *Manuale della Letteratura Italiana*, 72 *n.*
Daniello, Bernardino (d. c. 1560); commentary on *D. C.*, 226, 274, 279; notice of Dante, 279.
Danish; translation of *D. C.* in, 217.
Dante Alighieri. *See* Alighieri, Dante.
Dante, Jacopo di. *See* Alighieri, Jacopo.
Dante, Pietro di. *See* Alighieri, Pietro.
Dante da Majano (fl. 1290); replies to Dante's first sonnet, 159; reply translated by Rossetti, 159 *n.*
Dante e il suo Secolo, 98 *n.*
Dante e la Lunigiana, 247 *n.*
" Dantinus" at Padua, doubtfully identified with Dante, 91 *n.*
Dartmouth, Countess of (Frances Finch, 1761-1838); second English edition of *D. C.* dedicated to, 215.
Davidsohn, R.; *Geschichte von Florenz*, 40 *n.*
Dayman, J.; notes on *D. C.*, 229.
Del Balzo, C.; *Poesie di Mille Autori intorno a Dante Alighieri*, 276 *n.*
Del Lungo, I.; *Beatrice nella Vita e nella Poesia del Secolo xiii*, 43 *n.*, 46 *n.; Dante ne' tempi di Dante*, 51 *n.; Dell' Esilio di Dante*, 71 *n.*, 84 *n.*, 95 *n.*, 98 *n.*, 112 *n.*, 113 *n.*, 115 *n.; Dal Secolo e dal Poema di Dante*, 74 *n; Dino Compagni e la sua Cronica*, 97 *n.;* monographs on Dante, 281.
Delizie degli Eruditi Toscani, 275, 276 *n.*, 278.
Della Corte, Girolamo (fl. c. 1560); notice of Dante, 279.
Della Torre, A.; critical text of Dante's letter to Florentine friend, 99 *n.*
Dino Compagni. *See* Compagni.
Dino Perini. *See* Perini.
Dionisi, Giovanni Giacomo (1724-1808); first printed Dante's letter to Florentine friend, 250; reprinted Dante's *Eclogues* in his *Aneddoti*, 253.
D'Israeli, Isaac (1766-1848); anecdote of Dante in *Curiosities of Literature*, 156-7; subscriber to Rossetti's *Comento Analitico alla D. C.*, 216.
Divina Commedia. See Commedia.
Dolce, Lodovico (1508-1568); notice of Dante, 279.
Domenichelli, T.; joint editor of Serravalle's commentary on *D. C.*, 273.
Domenico di Michelino (1417-1491); his representation of Dante, 143; formerly attributed to Orcagna, 143 *n.;* notice of, by William Barker, 143 *n.;* inscription on, translated by Ed. Wright, 143 *n.*
Dominican Schools of Santa Maria Novella, 66 *n.*
Donati family of Florence; their houses back to back with those of Alighieri, 67 *n.;* leaders of Black Party, 76; feud with Cerchi, 77-81.
Donati, Corso (d. 1308); Podestà of Pistoja, 58; at battle of Campaldino, 58, 59, 61, 67, 76; leaders of Blacks in Florence, 76, 80, 83; Giotto's portrait of, 131, 268, 269.
Donati, Forese (d. 1296); friend of Dante, 39, 51, 67; poetical correspondence with Dante, 39, 51, 86.

Franciscan Order; tradition that Dante joined it for a time, 48 *n.*; salutation of, given by Statius and returned by Virgil in Purgatory, 48 *n.*

Francowitz, Mathias Flach (d. 1575); notice of Dante, 279.

Frangipani of Rome; Dante's reputed descent from, 37.

Fraticelli, P.; *Vita di Dante*, 67 *n.*, 72 *n.*, 73 *n.*, 266, 281; commentary on *D. C.*, 229; edition of *De Monarchia*, 231 *n.*, 238 *n.*; chapter divisions in, 231 *n.*; first printed Ficino's translation, 238 *n.*; edition of Boccaccio's commentary on *D. C.*, 272.

Frederick II (Emperor, 1212-1250); helps to repel Guelfs from Florence, 7-10; called by Dante the last Emperor of the Romans, 234 *n.*

Frederick II (King of Sicily, 1296-1337); *Paradiso* said to have been dedicated to, 92 *n.*, 266.

French; translations of *D. C.* in, 217.

Frere, John Hookham (1769-1846); Rossetti's *Comento Analitico alla D. C.* dedicated to, 216.

Frescobaldi, Dino; sends first seven cantos of *Inferno* to Moroello Malaspina, 210-11.

Frullani e Gargani; *Della Casa di Dante*, 40 *n.*

G

Gabrielli, Cante de'; Podestà of Florence, 83; sentences Dante to banishment, and afterwards to death, 83-4, 88, 98.

Gaddi, Taddeo (c. 1300-1366); portrait of Dante in Santa Croce, 141; destroyed by Vasari, 141.

Gaetana (Tana) Alighieri. *See* Alighieri.

Galleria di Minerva, 250 *n.*

Gardner, E. *See* Wicksteed and Gardner.

Gargani, G. *See* Frullani.

Gargonza; meeting of exiled Whites at, 90.

Garrow, Joseph (fl. 1840); translation of *V. N.*, 173 *n.*

Gelli, Giovan Battista (1498-1563); lectures on *D. C.*, 226, 274; statement as to commentary on *D. C.* by Giambullari, 226 *n.*

Gemma Donati. *See* Donati.

Genoa; Henry VII at, 95; King Robert of Naples besieged in, 253.

Gentucca; Dante's attachment to, 71, 97; identified as wife of Cosciorino Fondora of Lucca, 97 *n. See* Morla.

Geri del Bello; first cousin of Dante's father, 41; murder of, by one of Sacchetti, 42, 147; Dante's meeting with, in Hell, 42; his murder avenged, 42.

German; translations of *D.C.* in, 217; translation of Dante's lyrical poems in, 247 *n.*

Gherardesca, Ugolino della (d. 1289); leader of Pisan Guelfs, 55; imprisonment and death in Tower of Famine at Pisa, 55, 62.

Ghibellines; expelled from Florence, 14-15; retire to Siena, 15-16; helped by King Manfred, 16-17; victorious at Montaperti, 21-5; hold council at Empoli, 27; return to Florence, 27-8; masters of Tuscany, 28; downfall after death of Manfred, 28-35; defeated at Campaldino, 53-60.

Giambullari, Pier Francesco (1495-1555); commentary on *D. C.*, 226 *n.*; quoted by Gelli, 226 *n.*; *De 'l sito, forma, e misure dello Inferno*, 226 *n.*

I

J

Leland, John (c. 1500-1552); saw copies of G. da Serravalle's commentary on *D. C.* at Oxford and Wells, 224 *n.*

Leo X (Pope, 1513-1521); authorizes removal of Dante's remains from Ravenna, 113-14, 117.

Leon Poggi. *See* Poggi.

Leonardo Aretino. *See* Bruni, Leonardo.

Letters of Dante; mentioned by Bruni, 54 *n.*, 57 *n.*, 86 *n.*, 91 *n.*, 95 *n.*, 251; by Villani, 249-50; by Boccaccio, 251; by Filelfo, 252; account of, 246-52; discovered mostly through exertions of Witte, 246 *n.;* Witte's editions of, 246 *n.*, 247, 248, 249; numeration of, in Oxford Dante, 246 *n.;* Torri's edition, 247, 248, 249, 251 *n.;* doubtful letters, 251-2; English translations, 251 *n.;* to Cino da Pistoja, 50, 248; to Princes and Peoples of Italy, 93, 248; to Florentines, 93-4, 95-6, 248-9; to Emperor Henry VII, 94, 249; to Italian Cardinals, 97, 249-50; to friend in Florence, 98-9, 250; critical text of, 99 *n.;* to Can Grande, 195-6, 250; utilized by F. Villani, 250; to Niccolò da Prato, 246-7; to Counts of Romena, 247; to Moroello Malaspina, 247; letters quoted, 54 *n.*, 93-4, 195-6.

Lindsay, Lord (1812-1880); account of Giotto's portrait of Dante in *History of Christian Art,* 129, 130, 133 *n.*

Liverpool; Rossetti's picture of " Dante's Dream " in Walker Art Gallery, 170 *n.*

Livorno; edition of *V. N.* published at, 167 *n.*; edition of *D. C.* printed at, with false imprint of London, 214; editions of Venturi's commentary on *D. C.* published at, 227 *n.;* Torri's edition of Dante's letters, 247 *n.*, 248 *n.*, 249 *n.*, 251 *n.*

Lombardi, Francesco Baldassare; commentary on *D. C.*, 227; editions of, 227.

Lombardi, Pietro (d. c. 1515); Venetian architect entrusted by Bembo with restoration of Dante's tomb at Ravenna, 106-7; part of his work still existent, 107.

London; edition of *D. C.* with false imprint of, 214; earliest editions of *D. C.* printed in, 215-16; Rossetti's *Comento Analitico alla D. C.*, 216, 228; Foscolo's *Discorso sul testo della D. C.*, and edition of *D. C.*, 216, 228; centenary edition of *D. C.*, 217.

Longfellow, H. W.; translation of *D. C.*, with notes, 229.

Lonsdale, Countess of (Augusta Fane, 1761-1838); second English edition of *D. C.* dedicated to, 215.

Lowell, J. R.; quoted, 104.

Lubin, A.; commentary on *D. C.*, 229.

Lucan; quoted in *V. N.*, 66.

Lucca; Dante's attachment to lady of, 71, 97; captured by Uguccione della Faggiuola, 97; Dante at, 97; Venturi's commentary on *D. C.* first published at, 227.

Luiso, F. P.; *Chiose di Dante le quali fece el figluolo*, 70 *n.*, 222 *n.; Tra Chiose e Commenti Antichi alla D. C.*, 70 *n.*

Luni, Bishop of; Dante's negotiations with, on behalf of Malaspini, 92.

Lunigiana; Dante in, 91-2.

Lyell, Charles (1767-1849); *Poems of the Vita Nuova and Convito of Dante,* 136 *n.*, 160 *n.;* letter from Kirkup as to mask of Dante, 136 *n.;* translation of Dante's lyrical poems, 160 *n.*

Lyons; editions of *D. C.* printed at, 214; first edition of *D. C.* printed outside Italy, executed at, 214.

Lyrical Poems of Dante, 45, 49, 50, 51-2, 71, 158-60, 165 *n.*; mention of, by Villani, 159; by Boccaccio, 159-60; earliest printed editions, 160; English translations, 160 *n.*; Santi's edition, 174 *n.*

Lysistratus Sicyonius (c. 320 B.C.); according to Pliny the first who took cast of human face, 135 *n.*

M

Macrì-Leone, F.; edition of Boccaccio's *Vita di Dante*, 45 *n.*, 68 *n.*, 69 *n.*, and *passim.* See Boccaccio.

Maffei, Rafaello (1451-1522); notice of Dante, 279.

Maghinardo da Susinana (d. 1302); though Ghibelline by birth supports the Florentine Guelfs, 56 *n.*

Malaspina Currado (d. c. 1294); "foretells" Dante's visit to the Malaspini in Lunigiana, 91-2.

Malaspina, Franceschino (d. bet. 1313 and 1321); Dante's host at Sarzana, 91-2.

Malaspina, Moroello (d. c. 1315); *Purgatorio* said to have been dedicated to, 92 *n.*, 266; first seven cantos of *Inferno* sent to, by Dino Frescobaldi, 210-11; Dante with, in Lunigiana, 211; urges Dante to complete *Inferno*, 211; letter of Dante to, 247; F. Novati on, 247 *n.*

Malaspini; Dante's relations with, 91-2.

Malavolti, Catalano de'; Guelf, appointed joint Podestà of Florence, with Lòderingo degli Andalò, in 1266, 30 *n.*

Manardi, A.; edition of alleged *Credo* of Dante, 260 *n.*

Manetti, Giannozzo (1396-1459); mentions Giotto's portrait of Dante, 130-1; *Vita Dantis*, 131 *n.*, 277.

Manetto Portinari. See Portinari.

Manfred, King (c. 1231-1266); helps exiled Florentine Ghibellines, 16-17, 18-19; defeat of his German horsemen, 19; reinforces the Ghibelline exiles at Siena, 19-21; defeated and killed at Benevento, 28-9, 34, 35, 36.

Mantua; Dante at, 100-1, 257; edition of *D. C.* printed at, 214; statue of Dante at, 260 *n.*

Mantuans; their reverence for Virgil, 110.

Marini; helps in search for Bargello portrait of Dante, 133; retouches the portrait, 133, 269.

Martin, Theodore (1816-1909); translation of *V. N.*, 173 *n.*

Martinella; Florentine bell so called, 17, 18, 21, 24; captured with Carroccio by Sienese at battle of Montaperti, 24.

Marvellian stanzas; translation of *Purgatorio* in, 219, 220 *n.*

Masson, Jean Papire (1544-1611); *Vita Dantis*, 280.

Maurolico, Francesco (fl. c. 1550); notice of Dante, 279.

Maximilian of Bavaria (1573-1651); presents MS. of Dante's letters and *De Monarchia* to Pope Gregory XV, 247.

Mazzini, Giuseppe (1805-1872); editor of Foscolo's edition of *D. C.*, 216, 228.

Medicean Academy at Florence; urge removal of Dante's remains to Florence, 113, 114, 117 *n.*

S

Sacchetti family of Florence; feud with Alighieri, 42; Geri del Bello murdered by member of, 42, 147; one of Sacchetti murdered in revenge, 42; reconciliation between the two families, 42.

Sacchetti, Franco (c. 1335-1400); anecdotes of Dante in his *Novelle*, 147-50.

Salutati, Coluccio (d. 1406); attests friendship of Menghino Mezzano with Dante, 100 *n.*, 105 *n.;* speaks of *D. C.* as "opus divinissimum," 196 *n.*

Saluzzo; Stefano Talice da Ricaldone's so-called commentary on *D. C.*, supposed to have been delivered as lectures at, 225.

Salvadori, G.; *Sulla Vita Giovanile di Dante*, 66 *n.*

Salvani, Provenzano (d. 1269); leader of Sienese Ghibellines, 20.

San Gemignano; Dante's embassy to, 73.

San Giovanni. *See* Giovanni, San.

San Godenzo; Dante present at meeting of exiled Whites at, 90.

San Procolo, in Florence; Dante in charge of public works on, 82.

Sanskrit; selections from *D. C.* translated into, 217.

Sansovino, Francesco (1521-1586); Italian translation of Filippo da Bergamo's *Supplementum Chronicarum*, 278.

Santa Croce, in Florence; Ricci's statue of Dante in, 137 *n.;* portrait of Dante by Taddeo Gaddi, 141.

Santa Maria Novella; Dominican schools of, at Florence, probably attended by Dante, 66 *n.*

Santa Maria Nuova; hospital at Florence endowed by Folco Portinari, 47.

Santi, A.; *Canzoniere di Dante*, 174 *n.*

Santi, Friar Antonio; conceals Dante's remains, 116.

Sarzana; Guido Cavalcanti exiled to, 81-2; Dante at, 91.

Saviozzo, Il. *See* Serdini.

Savonarola, Michele (d. c. 1460); anecdote of Dante, 145.

Sayer, E.; translation of *Convivio*, 192 *n.*

Scala, Bartolommeo della (lord of Verona, 1301-1304); Dante's host at Verona, 91.

Scala, Can Grande della (lord of Verona, 1308-1329); Dante's host at Verona, 99, 144; sonnet of Quirini to, urging him to publish Dante's *Paradiso*, 108; stories of Dante and, 144-6, 154; *Paradiso* dedicated to, 195, 250; Dante's letter to, explaining subject and aim of *D. C.*, 195-6, 250, cantos of *Paradiso* submitted to, by Dante, 208; missing cantos sent to, by Dante's sons, 208; his operations against Padua suggested to Dante by G. del Virgilio as subject for Latin poem, 253.

Scaligers of Verona. *See* Scala.

Scarabelli, L.; editor of Jacopo della Lana's commentary on *D. C.*, 222, 271.

Scartazzini, G. A.; commentary on *D. C.*, 229; *Enciclopedia Dantesca*, 230, 281; *Companion to Dante*, 250 *n.*, 281; *Dante-Handbuch*, 281; *Prolegomeni della D. C.*, 281.

Schedel, Hartmann (d. c. 1500); notice of Dante in *Nuremberg Chronicle*, 278.

Scherillo, M.; *Alcuni Capitoli della Biografia di Dante*, 38 *n.*, 280; *La Forma Architettonica della Vita Nuova*, 166 *n.*

Schönbrunn; MS. of Cittadini's translation of *De Vulg. Eloq.* preserved at, 245.

20 *

A CATALOG OF SELECTED
DOVER BOOKS
IN ALL FIELDS OF INTEREST

A CATALOG OF SELECTED DOVER
BOOKS IN ALL FIELDS OF INTEREST

CONCERNING THE SPIRITUAL IN ART, Wassily Kandinsky. Pioneering work by father of abstract art. Thoughts on color theory, nature of art. Analysis of earlier masters. 12 illustrations. 80pp. of text. 5⅜ x 8½.   23411-8

ANIMALS: 1,419 Copyright-Free Illustrations of Mammals, Birds, Fish, Insects, etc., Jim Harter (ed.). Clear wood engravings present, in extremely lifelike poses, over 1,000 species of animals. One of the most extensive pictorial sourcebooks of its kind. Captions. Index. 284pp. 9 x 12.   23766-4

CELTIC ART: The Methods of Construction, George Bain. Simple geometric techniques for making Celtic interlacements, spirals, Kells-type initials, animals, humans, etc. Over 500 illustrations. 160pp. 9 x 12. (Available in U.S. only.)   22923-8

AN ATLAS OF ANATOMY FOR ARTISTS, Fritz Schider. Most thorough reference work on art anatomy in the world. Hundreds of illustrations, including selections from works by Vesalius, Leonardo, Goya, Ingres, Michelangelo, others. 593 illustrations. 192pp. 7⅛ x 10¼.   20241-0

CELTIC HAND STROKE-BY-STROKE (Irish Half-Uncial from "The Book of Kells"): An Arthur Baker Calligraphy Manual, Arthur Baker. Complete guide to creating each letter of the alphabet in distinctive Celtic manner. Covers hand position, strokes, pens, inks, paper, more. Illustrated. 48pp. 8¼ x 11.   24336-2

EASY ORIGAMI, John Montroll. Charming collection of 32 projects (hat, cup, pelican, piano, swan, many more) specially designed for the novice origami hobbyist. Clearly illustrated easy-to-follow instructions insure that even beginning papercrafters will achieve successful results. 48pp. 8¼ x 11.   27298-2

THE COMPLETE BOOK OF BIRDHOUSE CONSTRUCTION FOR WOOD-WORKERS, Scott D. Campbell. Detailed instructions, illustrations, tables. Also data on bird habitat and instinct patterns. Bibliography. 3 tables. 63 illustrations in 15 figures. 48pp. 5¼ x 8½.   24407-5

BLOOMINGDALE'S ILLUSTRATED 1886 CATALOG: Fashions, Dry Goods and Housewares, Bloomingdale Brothers. Famed merchants' extremely rare catalog depicting about 1,700 products: clothing, housewares, firearms, dry goods, jewelry, more. Invaluable for dating, identifying vintage items. Also, copyright-free graphics for artists, designers. Co-published with Henry Ford Museum & Greenfield Village. 160pp. 8¼ x 11.   25780-0

HISTORIC COSTUME IN PICTURES, Braun & Schneider. Over 1,450 costumed figures in clearly detailed engravings–from dawn of civilization to end of 19th century. Captions. Many folk costumes. 256pp. 8⅜ x 11¾.   23150-X

STICKLEY CRAFTSMAN FURNITURE CATALOGS, Gustav Stickley and L. & J. G. Stickley. Beautiful, functional furniture in two authentic catalogs from 1910. 594 illustrations, including 277 photos, show settles, rockers, armchairs, reclining chairs, bookcases, desks, tables. 183pp. 6½ x 9¼.   23838-5

AMERICAN LOCOMOTIVES IN HISTORIC PHOTOGRAPHS: 1858 to 1949, Ron Ziel (ed.). A rare collection of 126 meticulously detailed official photographs, called "builder portraits," of American locomotives that majestically chronicle the rise of steam locomotive power in America. Introduction. Detailed captions. xi+ 129pp. 9 x 12.   27393-8

AMERICA'S LIGHTHOUSES: An Illustrated History, Francis Ross Holland, Jr. Delightfully written, profusely illustrated fact-filled survey of over 200 American light-houses since 1716. History, anecdotes, technological advances, more. 240pp. 8 x 10¾.
                                              25576-X

TOWARDS A NEW ARCHITECTURE, Le Corbusier. Pioneering manifesto by founder of "International School." Technical and aesthetic theories, views of industry, eco-nomics, relation of form to function, "mass-production split" and much more. Profusely illustrated. 320pp. 6⅛ x 9¼. (Available in U.S. only.)   25023-7

HOW THE OTHER HALF LIVES, Jacob Riis. Famous journalistic record, expos-ing poverty and degradation of New York slums around 1900, by major social reformer. 100 striking and influential photographs. 233pp. 10 x 7⅞.   22012-5

FRUIT KEY AND TWIG KEY TO TREES AND SHRUBS, William M. Harlow. One of the handiest and most widely used identification aids. Fruit key covers 120 deciduous and evergreen species; twig key 160 deciduous species. Easily used. Over 300 photographs. 126pp. 5⅜ x 8½.   20511-8

COMMON BIRD SONGS, Dr. Donald J. Borror. Songs of 60 most common U.S. birds: robins, sparrows, cardinals, bluejays, finches, more–arranged in order of increasing complexity. Up to 9 variations of songs of each species.
                                              Cassette and manual 99911-4

ORCHIDS AS HOUSE PLANTS, Rebecca Tyson Northen. Grow cattleyas and many other kinds of orchids–in a window, in a case, or under artificial light. 63 illus-trations. 148pp. 5⅜ x 8½.   23261-1

MONSTER MAZES, Dave Phillips. Masterful mazes at four levels of difficulty. Avoid deadly perils and evil creatures to find magical treasures. Solutions for all 32 exciting illustrated puzzles. 48pp. 8¼ x 11.   26005-4

MOZART'S DON GIOVANNI (DOVER OPERA LIBRETTO SERIES), Wolfgang Amadeus Mozart. Introduced and translated by Ellen H. Bleiler. Standard Italian libretto, with complete English translation. Convenient and thoroughly portable–an ideal companion for reading along with a recording or the performance itself. Introduction. List of characters. Plot summary. 121pp. 5¼ x 8½.   24944-1

TECHNICAL MANUAL AND DICTIONARY OF CLASSICAL BALLET, Gail Grant. Defines, explains, comments on steps, movements, poses and concepts. 15-page pictorial section. Basic book for student, viewer. 127pp. 5⅜ x 8½.   21843-0

THE CLARINET AND CLARINET PLAYING, David Pino. Lively, comprehensive work features suggestions about technique, musicianship, and musical interpretation, as well as guidelines for teaching, making your own reeds, and preparing for public performance. Includes an intriguing look at clarinet history. "A godsend," *The Clarinet*, Journal of the International Clarinet Society. Appendixes. 7 illus. 320pp. 5⅜ x 8½. 40270-3

HOLLYWOOD GLAMOR PORTRAITS, John Kobal (ed.). 145 photos from 1926-49. Harlow, Gable, Bogart, Bacall; 94 stars in all. Full background on photographers, technical aspects. 160pp. 8⅜ x 11¼. 23352-9

THE ANNOTATED CASEY AT THE BAT: A Collection of Ballads about the Mighty Casey/Third, Revised Edition, Martin Gardner (ed.). Amusing sequels and parodies of one of America's best-loved poems: Casey's Revenge, Why Casey Whiffed, Casey's Sister at the Bat, others. 256pp. 5⅜ x 8½. 28598-7

THE RAVEN AND OTHER FAVORITE POEMS, Edgar Allan Poe. Over 40 of the author's most memorable poems: "The Bells," "Ulalume," "Israfel," "To Helen," "The Conqueror Worm," "Eldorado," "Annabel Lee," many more. Alphabetic lists of titles and first lines. 64pp. 5³⁄₁₆ x 8¼. 26685-0

PERSONAL MEMOIRS OF U. S. GRANT, Ulysses Simpson Grant. Intelligent, deeply moving firsthand account of Civil War campaigns, considered by many the finest military memoirs ever written. Includes letters, historic photographs, maps and more. 528pp. 6⅛ x 9¼. 28587-1

ANCIENT EGYPTIAN MATERIALS AND INDUSTRIES, A. Lucas and J. Harris. Fascinating, comprehensive, thoroughly documented text describes this ancient civilization's vast resources and the processes that incorporated them in daily life, including the use of animal products, building materials, cosmetics, perfumes and incense, fibers, glazed ware, glass and its manufacture, materials used in the mummification process, and much more. 544pp. 6⅛ x 9¼. (Available in U.S. only.) 40446-3

RUSSIAN STORIES/RUSSKIE RASSKAZY: A Dual-Language Book, edited by Gleb Struve. Twelve tales by such masters as Chekhov, Tolstoy, Dostoevsky, Pushkin, others. Excellent word-for-word English translations on facing pages, plus teaching and study aids, Russian/English vocabulary, biographical/critical introductions, more. 416pp. 5⅜ x 8½. 26244-8

PHILADELPHIA THEN AND NOW: 60 Sites Photographed in the Past and Present, Kenneth Finkel and Susan Oyama. Rare photographs of City Hall, Logan Square, Independence Hall, Betsy Ross House, other landmarks juxtaposed with contemporary views. Captures changing face of historic city. Introduction. Captions. 128pp. 8¼ x 11. 25790-8

AIA ARCHITECTURAL GUIDE TO NASSAU AND SUFFOLK COUNTIES, LONG ISLAND, The American Institute of Architects, Long Island Chapter, and the Society for the Preservation of Long Island Antiquities. Comprehensive, well-researched and generously illustrated volume brings to life over three centuries of Long Island's great architectural heritage. More than 240 photographs with authoritative, extensively detailed captions. 176pp. 8¼ x 11. 26946-9

NORTH AMERICAN INDIAN LIFE: Customs and Traditions of 23 Tribes, Elsie Clews Parsons (ed.). 27 fictionalized essays by noted anthropologists examine religion, customs, government, additional facets of life among the Winnebago, Crow, Zuni, Eskimo, other tribes. 480pp. 6⅛ x 9¼. 27377-6

CATALOG OF DOVER BOOKS

FRANK LLOYD WRIGHT'S DANA HOUSE, Donald Hoffmann. Pictorial essay of residential masterpiece with over 160 interior and exterior photos, plans, elevations, sketches and studies. 128pp. 9¼ x 10¾. 29120-0

THE MALE AND FEMALE FIGURE IN MOTION: 60 Classic Photographic Sequences, Eadweard Muybridge. 60 true-action photographs of men and women walking, running, climbing, bending, turning, etc., reproduced from rare 19th-century masterpiece. vi + 121pp. 9 x 12. 24745-7

1001 QUESTIONS ANSWERED ABOUT THE SEASHORE, N. J. Berrill and Jacquelyn Berrill. Queries answered about dolphins, sea snails, sponges, starfish, fishes, shore birds, many others. Covers appearance, breeding, growth, feeding, much more. 305pp. 5¼ x 8¼. 23366-9

ATTRACTING BIRDS TO YOUR YARD, William J. Weber. Easy-to-follow guide offers advice on how to attract the greatest diversity of birds: birdhouses, feeders, water and waterers, much more. 96pp. 5³⁄₁₆ x 8¼. 28927-3

MEDICINAL AND OTHER USES OF NORTH AMERICAN PLANTS: A Historical Survey with Special Reference to the Eastern Indian Tribes, Charlotte Erichsen-Brown. Chronological historical citations document 500 years of usage of plants, trees, shrubs native to eastern Canada, northeastern U.S. Also complete identifying information. 343 illustrations. 544pp. 6½ x 9¼. 25951-X

STORYBOOK MAZES, Dave Phillips. 23 stories and mazes on two-page spreads: Wizard of Oz, Treasure Island, Robin Hood, etc. Solutions. 64pp. 8¼ x 11. 23628-5

AMERICAN NEGRO SONGS: 230 Folk Songs and Spirituals, Religious and Secular, John W. Work. This authoritative study traces the African influences of songs sung and played by black Americans at work, in church, and as entertainment. The author discusses the lyric significance of such songs as "Swing Low, Sweet Chariot," "John Henry," and others and offers the words and music for 230 songs. Bibliography. Index of Song Titles. 272pp. 6½ x 9¼. 40271-1

MOVIE-STAR PORTRAITS OF THE FORTIES, John Kobal (ed.). 163 glamor, studio photos of 106 stars of the 1940s: Rita Hayworth, Ava Gardner, Marlon Brando, Clark Gable, many more. 176pp. 8⅜ x 11¼. 23546-7

BENCHLEY LOST AND FOUND, Robert Benchley. Finest humor from early 30s, about pet peeves, child psychologists, post office and others. Mostly unavailable elsewhere. 73 illustrations by Peter Arno and others. 183pp. 5⅜ x 8½. 22410-4

YEKL and THE IMPORTED BRIDEGROOM AND OTHER STORIES OF YIDDISH NEW YORK, Abraham Cahan. Film Hester Street based on *Yekl* (1896). Novel, other stories among first about Jewish immigrants on N.Y.'s East Side. 240pp. 5⅜ x 8½. 22427-9

SELECTED POEMS, Walt Whitman. Generous sampling from *Leaves of Grass*. Twenty-four poems include "I Hear America Singing," "Song of the Open Road," "I Sing the Body Electric," "When Lilacs Last in the Dooryard Bloom'd," "O Captain! My Captain!"–all reprinted from an authoritative edition. Lists of titles and first lines. 128pp. 5³⁄₁₆ x 8¼. 26878-0

THE BEST TALES OF HOFFMANN, E. T. A. Hoffmann. 10 of Hoffmann's most important stories: "Nutcracker and the King of Mice," "The Golden Flowerpot," etc. 458pp. 5⅜ x 8½. 21793-0

FROM FETISH TO GOD IN ANCIENT EGYPT, E. A. Wallis Budge. Rich detailed survey of Egyptian conception of "God" and gods, magic, cult of animals, Osiris, more. Also, superb English translations of hymns and legends. 240 illustrations. 545pp. 5⅜ x 8½. 25803-3

FRENCH STORIES/CONTES FRANÇAIS: A Dual-Language Book, Wallace Fowlie. Ten stories by French masters, Voltaire to Camus: "Micromegas" by Voltaire; "The Atheist's Mass" by Balzac; "Minuet" by de Maupassant; "The Guest" by Camus, six more. Excellent English translations on facing pages. Also French-English vocabulary list, exercises, more. 352pp. 5⅜ x 8½. 26443-2

CHICAGO AT THE TURN OF THE CENTURY IN PHOTOGRAPHS: 122 Historic Views from the Collections of the Chicago Historical Society, Larry A. Viskochil. Rare large-format prints offer detailed views of City Hall, State Street, the Loop, Hull House, Union Station, many other landmarks, circa 1904-1913. Introduction. Captions. Maps. 144pp. 9⅜ x 12¼. 24656-6

OLD BROOKLYN IN EARLY PHOTOGRAPHS, 1865-1929, William Lee Younger. Luna Park, Gravesend race track, construction of Grand Army Plaza, moving of Hotel Brighton, etc. 157 previously unpublished photographs. 165pp. 8⅞ x 11¾. 23587-4

THE MYTHS OF THE NORTH AMERICAN INDIANS, Lewis Spence. Rich anthology of the myths and legends of the Algonquins, Iroquois, Pawnees and Sioux, prefaced by an extensive historical and ethnological commentary. 36 illustrations. 480pp. 5⅜ x 8½. 25967-6

AN ENCYCLOPEDIA OF BATTLES: Accounts of Over 1,560 Battles from 1479 B.C. to the Present, David Eggenberger. Essential details of every major battle in recorded history from the first battle of Megiddo in 1479 B.C. to Grenada in 1984. List of Battle Maps. New Appendix covering the years 1967-1984. Index. 99 illustrations. 544pp. 6½ x 9¼. 24913-1

SAILING ALONE AROUND THE WORLD, Captain Joshua Slocum. First man to sail around the world, alone, in small boat. One of great feats of seamanship told in delightful manner. 67 illustrations. 294pp. 5⅜ x 8½. 20326-3

ANARCHISM AND OTHER ESSAYS, Emma Goldman. Powerful, penetrating, prophetic essays on direct action, role of minorities, prison reform, puritan hypocrisy, violence, etc. 271pp. 5⅜ x 8½. 22484-8

MYTHS OF THE HINDUS AND BUDDHISTS, Ananda K. Coomaraswamy and Sister Nivedita. Great stories of the epics; deeds of Krishna, Shiva, taken from puranas, Vedas, folk tales; etc. 32 illustrations. 400pp. 5⅜ x 8½. 21759-0

THE TRAUMA OF BIRTH, Otto Rank. Rank's controversial thesis that anxiety neurosis is caused by profound psychological trauma which occurs at birth. 256pp. 5⅜ x 8½. 27974-X

A THEOLOGICO-POLITICAL TREATISE, Benedict Spinoza. Also contains unfinished Political Treatise. Great classic on religious liberty, theory of government on common consent. R. Elwes translation. Total of 421pp. 5⅜ x 8½. 20249-6

CATALOG OF DOVER BOOKS

MY BONDAGE AND MY FREEDOM, Frederick Douglass. Born a slave, Douglass became outspoken force in antislavery movement. The best of Douglass' autobiographies. Graphic description of slave life. 464pp. 5⅜ x 8½. 22457-0

FOLLOWING THE EQUATOR: A Journey Around the World, Mark Twain. Fascinating humorous account of 1897 voyage to Hawaii, Australia, India, New Zealand, etc. Ironic, bemused reports on peoples, customs, climate, flora and fauna, politics, much more. 197 illustrations. 720pp. 5⅜ x 8½. 26113-1

THE PEOPLE CALLED SHAKERS, Edward D. Andrews. Definitive study of Shakers: origins, beliefs, practices, dances, social organization, furniture and crafts, etc. 33 illustrations. 351pp. 5⅜ x 8½. 21081-2

THE MYTHS OF GREECE AND ROME, H. A. Guerber. A classic of mythology, generously illustrated, long prized for its simple, graphic, accurate retelling of the principal myths of Greece and Rome, and for its commentary on their origins and significance. With 64 illustrations by Michelangelo, Raphael, Titian, Rubens, Canova, Bernini and others. 480pp. 5⅜ x 8½. 27584-1

PSYCHOLOGY OF MUSIC, Carl E. Seashore. Classic work discusses music as a medium from psychological viewpoint. Clear treatment of physical acoustics, auditory apparatus, sound perception, development of musical skills, nature of musical feeling, host of other topics. 88 figures. 408pp. 5⅜ x 8½. 21851-1

THE PHILOSOPHY OF HISTORY, Georg W. Hegel. Great classic of Western thought develops concept that history is not chance but rational process, the evolution of freedom. 457pp. 5⅜ x 8½. 20112-0

THE BOOK OF TEA, Kakuzo Okakura. Minor classic of the Orient: entertaining, charming explanation, interpretation of traditional Japanese culture in terms of tea ceremony. 94pp. 5⅜ x 8½. 20070-1

LIFE IN ANCIENT EGYPT, Adolf Erman. Fullest, most thorough, detailed older account with much not in more recent books, domestic life, religion, magic, medicine, commerce, much more. Many illustrations reproduce tomb paintings, carvings, hieroglyphs, etc. 597pp. 5⅜ x 8½. 22632-8

SUNDIALS, Their Theory and Construction, Albert Waugh. Far and away the best, most thorough coverage of ideas, mathematics concerned, types, construction, adjusting anywhere. Simple, nontechnical treatment allows even children to build several of these dials. Over 100 illustrations. 230pp. 5⅜ x 8½. 22947-5

THEORETICAL HYDRODYNAMICS, L. M. Milne-Thomson. Classic exposition of the mathematical theory of fluid motion, applicable to both hydrodynamics and aerodynamics. Over 600 exercises. 768pp. 6⅛ x 9¼. 68970-0

SONGS OF EXPERIENCE: Facsimile Reproduction with 26 Plates in Full Color, William Blake. 26 full-color plates from a rare 1826 edition. Includes "The Tyger," "London," "Holy Thursday," and other poems. Printed text of poems. 48pp. 5¼ x 7. 24636-1

OLD-TIME VIGNETTES IN FULL COLOR, Carol Belanger Grafton (ed.). Over 390 charming, often sentimental illustrations, selected from archives of Victorian graphics—pretty women posing, children playing, food, flowers, kittens and puppies, smiling cherubs, birds and butterflies, much more. All copyright-free. 48pp. 9¼ x 12¼. 27269-9

PERSPECTIVE FOR ARTISTS, Rex Vicat Cole. Depth, perspective of sky and sea, shadows, much more, not usually covered. 391 diagrams, 81 reproductions of drawings and paintings. 279pp. 5⅜ x 8½. 22487-2

DRAWING THE LIVING FIGURE, Joseph Sheppard. Innovative approach to artistic anatomy focuses on specifics of surface anatomy, rather than muscles and bones. Over 170 drawings of live models in front, back and side views, and in widely varying poses. Accompanying diagrams. 177 illustrations. Introduction. Index. 144pp. 8⅜ x11¼. 26723-7

GOTHIC AND OLD ENGLISH ALPHABETS: 100 Complete Fonts, Dan X. Solo. Add power, elegance to posters, signs, other graphics with 100 stunning copyright-free alphabets: Blackstone, Dolbey, Germania, 97 more–including many lower-case, numerals, punctuation marks. 104pp. 8⅛ x 11. 24695-7

HOW TO DO BEADWORK, Mary White. Fundamental book on craft from simple projects to five-bead chains and woven works. 106 illustrations. 142pp. 5⅜ x 8. 20697-1

THE BOOK OF WOOD CARVING, Charles Marshall Sayers. Finest book for beginners discusses fundamentals and offers 34 designs. "Absolutely first rate . . . well thought out and well executed."–E. J. Tangerman. 118pp. 7¾ x 10⅝. 23654-4

ILLUSTRATED CATALOG OF CIVIL WAR MILITARY GOODS: Union Army Weapons, Insignia, Uniform Accessories, and Other Equipment, Schuyler, Hartley, and Graham. Rare, profusely illustrated 1846 catalog includes Union Army uniform and dress regulations, arms and ammunition, coats, insignia, flags, swords, rifles, etc. 226 illustrations. 160pp. 9 x 12. 24939-5

WOMEN'S FASHIONS OF THE EARLY 1900s: An Unabridged Republication of "New York Fashions, 1909," National Cloak & Suit Co. Rare catalog of mail-order fashions documents women's and children's clothing styles shortly after the turn of the century. Captions offer full descriptions, prices. Invaluable resource for fashion, costume historians. Approximately 725 illustrations. 128pp. 8⅜ x 11¼. 27276-1

THE 1912 AND 1915 GUSTAV STICKLEY FURNITURE CATALOGS, Gustav Stickley. With over 200 detailed illustrations and descriptions, these two catalogs are essential reading and reference materials and identification guides for Stickley furniture. Captions cite materials, dimensions and prices. 112pp. 6½ x 9¼. 26676-1

EARLY AMERICAN LOCOMOTIVES, John H. White, Jr. Finest locomotive engravings from early 19th century: historical (1804–74), main-line (after 1870), special, foreign, etc. 147 plates. 142pp. 11⅜ x 8¼. 22772-3

THE TALL SHIPS OF TODAY IN PHOTOGRAPHS, Frank O. Braynard. Lavishly illustrated tribute to nearly 100 majestic contemporary sailing vessels: Amerigo Vespucci, Clearwater, Constitution, Eagle, Mayflower, Sea Cloud, Victory, many more. Authoritative captions provide statistics, background on each ship. 190 black-and-white photographs and illustrations. Introduction. 128pp. 8⅞ x 11¾. 27163-3

LITTLE BOOK OF EARLY AMERICAN CRAFTS AND TRADES, Peter Stockham (ed.). 1807 children's book explains crafts and trades: baker, hatter, cooper, potter, and many others. 23 copperplate illustrations. 140pp. 4⅝ x 6. 23336-7

VICTORIAN FASHIONS AND COSTUMES FROM HARPER'S BAZAR, 1867–1898, Stella Blum (ed.). Day costumes, evening wear, sports clothes, shoes, hats, other accessories in over 1,000 detailed engravings. 320pp. 9⅜ x 12¼. 22990-4

GUSTAV STICKLEY, THE CRAFTSMAN, Mary Ann Smith. Superb study surveys broad scope of Stickley's achievement, especially in architecture. Design philosophy, rise and fall of the Craftsman empire, descriptions and floor plans for many Craftsman houses, more. 86 black-and-white halftones. 31 line illustrations. Introduction 208pp. 6½ x 9¼. 27210-9

THE LONG ISLAND RAIL ROAD IN EARLY PHOTOGRAPHS, Ron Ziel. Over 220 rare photos, informative text document origin (1844) and development of rail service on Long Island. Vintage views of early trains, locomotives, stations, passengers, crews, much more. Captions. 8⅞ x 11¾. 26301-0

VOYAGE OF THE LIBERDADE, Joshua Slocum. Great 19th-century mariner's thrilling, first-hand account of the wreck of his ship off South America, the 35-foot boat he built from the wreckage, and its remarkable voyage home. 128pp. 5⅜ x 8½. 40022-0

TEN BOOKS ON ARCHITECTURE, Vitruvius. The most important book ever written on architecture. Early Roman aesthetics, technology, classical orders, site selection, all other aspects. Morgan translation. 331pp. 5⅜ x 8½. 20645-9

THE HUMAN FIGURE IN MOTION, Eadweard Muybridge. More than 4,500 stopped-action photos, in action series, showing undraped men, women, children jumping, lying down, throwing, sitting, wrestling, carrying, etc. 390pp. 7⅞ x 10⅝. 20204-6 Clothbd.

TREES OF THE EASTERN AND CENTRAL UNITED STATES AND CANADA, William M. Harlow. Best one-volume guide to 140 trees. Full descriptions, woodlore, range, etc. Over 600 illustrations. Handy size. 288pp. 4½ x 6⅜. 20395-6

SONGS OF WESTERN BIRDS, Dr. Donald J. Borror. Complete song and call repertoire of 60 western species, including flycatchers, juncoes, cactus wrens, many more–includes fully illustrated booklet. Cassette and manual 99913-0

GROWING AND USING HERBS AND SPICES, Milo Miloradovich. Versatile handbook provides all the information needed for cultivation and use of all the herbs and spices available in North America. 4 illustrations. Index. Glossary. 236pp. 5⅜ x 8½. 25058-X

BIG BOOK OF MAZES AND LABYRINTHS, Walter Shepherd. 50 mazes and labyrinths in all–classical, solid, ripple, and more–in one great volume. Perfect inexpensive puzzler for clever youngsters. Full solutions. 112pp. 8⅛ x 11. 22951-3

PIANO TUNING, J. Cree Fischer. Clearest, best book for beginner, amateur. Simple repairs, raising dropped notes, tuning by easy method of flattened fifths. No previous skills needed. 4 illustrations. 201pp. 5⅜ x 8½. 23267-0

HINTS TO SINGERS, Lillian Nordica. Selecting the right teacher, developing confidence, overcoming stage fright, and many other important skills receive thoughtful discussion in this indispensible guide, written by a world-famous diva of four decades' experience. 96pp. 5⅜ x 8½. 40094-8

THE COMPLETE NONSENSE OF EDWARD LEAR, Edward Lear. All nonsense limericks, zany alphabets, Owl and Pussycat, songs, nonsense botany, etc., illustrated by Lear. Total of 320pp. 5⅜ x 8½. (Available in U.S. only.) 20167-8

VICTORIAN PARLOUR POETRY: An Annotated Anthology, Michael R. Turner. 117 gems by Longfellow, Tennyson, Browning, many lesser-known poets. "The Village Blacksmith," "Curfew Must Not Ring Tonight," "Only a Baby Small," dozens more, often difficult to find elsewhere. Index of poets, titles, first lines. xxiii + 325pp. 5⅝ x 8¼. 27044-0

DUBLINERS, James Joyce. Fifteen stories offer vivid, tightly focused observations of the lives of Dublin's poorer classes. At least one, "The Dead," is considered a masterpiece. Reprinted complete and unabridged from standard edition. 160pp. 5$\frac{3}{16}$ x 8¼. 26870-5

GREAT WEIRD TALES: 14 Stories by Lovecraft, Blackwood, Machen and Others, S. T. Joshi (ed.). 14 spellbinding tales, including "The Sin Eater," by Fiona McLeod, "The Eye Above the Mantel," by Frank Belknap Long, as well as renowned works by R. H. Barlow, Lord Dunsany, Arthur Machen, W. C. Morrow and eight other masters of the genre. 256pp. 5⅜ x 8½. (Available in U.S. only.) 40436-6

THE BOOK OF THE SACRED MAGIC OF ABRAMELIN THE MAGE, translated by S. MacGregor Mathers. Medieval manuscript of ceremonial magic. Basic document in Aleister Crowley, Golden Dawn groups. 268pp. 5⅜ x 8½. 23211-5

NEW RUSSIAN-ENGLISH AND ENGLISH-RUSSIAN DICTIONARY, M. A. O'Brien. This is a remarkably handy Russian dictionary, containing a surprising amount of information, including over 70,000 entries. 366pp. 4½ x 6⅛. 20208-9

HISTORIC HOMES OF THE AMERICAN PRESIDENTS, Second, Revised Edition, Irvin Haas. A traveler's guide to American Presidential homes, most open to the public, depicting and describing homes occupied by every American President from George Washington to George Bush. With visiting hours, admission charges, travel routes. 175 photographs. Index. 160pp. 8¼ x 11. 26751-2

NEW YORK IN THE FORTIES, Andreas Feininger. 162 brilliant photographs by the well-known photographer, formerly with *Life* magazine. Commuters, shoppers, Times Square at night, much else from city at its peak. Captions by John von Hartz. 181pp. 9¼ x 10¾. 23585-8

INDIAN SIGN LANGUAGE, William Tomkins. Over 525 signs developed by Sioux and other tribes. Written instructions and diagrams. Also 290 pictographs. 111pp. 6⅛ x 9¼. 22029-X

CATALOG OF DOVER BOOKS

ANATOMY: A Complete Guide for Artists, Joseph Sheppard. A master of figure drawing shows artists how to render human anatomy convincingly. Over 460 illustrations. 224pp. 8⅜ x 11¼. 27279-6

MEDIEVAL CALLIGRAPHY: Its History and Technique, Marc Drogin. Spirited history, comprehensive instruction manual covers 13 styles (ca. 4th century through 15th). Excellent photographs; directions for duplicating medieval techniques with modern tools. 224pp. 8⅜ x 11¼. 26142-5

DRIED FLOWERS: How to Prepare Them, Sarah Whitlock and Martha Rankin. Complete instructions on how to use silica gel, meal and borax, perlite aggregate, sand and borax, glycerine and water to create attractive permanent flower arrangements. 12 illustrations. 32pp. 5⅜ x 8½. 21802-3

EASY-TO-MAKE BIRD FEEDERS FOR WOODWORKERS, Scott D. Campbell. Detailed, simple-to-use guide for designing, constructing, caring for and using feeders. Text, illustrations for 12 classic and contemporary designs. 96pp. 5⅜ x 8½. 25847-5

SCOTTISH WONDER TALES FROM MYTH AND LEGEND, Donald A. Mackenzie. 16 lively tales tell of giants rumbling down mountainsides, of a magic wand that turns stone pillars into warriors, of gods and goddesses, evil hags, powerful forces and more. 240pp. 5⅜ x 8½. 29677-6

THE HISTORY OF UNDERCLOTHES, C. Willett Cunnington and Phyllis Cunnington. Fascinating, well-documented survey covering six centuries of English undergarments, enhanced with over 100 illustrations: 12th-century laced-up bodice, footed long drawers (1795), 19th-century bustles, 19th-century corsets for men, Victorian "bust improvers," much more. 272pp. 5⅜ x 8¼. 27124-2

ARTS AND CRAFTS FURNITURE: The Complete Brooks Catalog of 1912, Brooks Manufacturing Co. Photos and detailed descriptions of more than 150 now very collectible furniture designs from the Arts and Crafts movement depict davenports, settees, buffets, desks, tables, chairs, bedsteads, dressers and more, all built of solid, quarter-sawed oak. Invaluable for students and enthusiasts of antiques, Americana and the decorative arts. 80pp. 6½ x 9¼. 27471-3

WILBUR AND ORVILLE: A Biography of the Wright Brothers, Fred Howard. Definitive, crisply written study tells the full story of the brothers' lives and work. A vividly written biography, unparalleled in scope and color, that also captures the spirit of an extraordinary era. 560pp. 6⅛ x 9¼. 40297-5

THE ARTS OF THE SAILOR: Knotting, Splicing and Ropework, Hervey Garrett Smith. Indispensable shipboard reference covers tools, basic knots and useful hitches; handsewing and canvas work, more. Over 100 illustrations. Delightful reading for sea lovers. 256pp. 5⅜ x 8½. 26440-8

FRANK LLOYD WRIGHT'S FALLINGWATER: The House and Its History, Second, Revised Edition, Donald Hoffmann. A total revision—both in text and illustrations—of the standard document on Fallingwater, the boldest, most personal architectural statement of Wright's mature years, updated with valuable new material from the recently opened Frank Lloyd Wright Archives. "Fascinating"—*The New York Times*. 116 illustrations. 128pp. 9¼ x 10¾. 27430-6

PHOTOGRAPHIC SKETCHBOOK OF THE CIVIL WAR, Alexander Gardner. 100 photos taken on field during the Civil War. Famous shots of Manassas Harper's Ferry, Lincoln, Richmond, slave pens, etc. 244pp. 10⅝ x 8¼. 22731-6

FIVE ACRES AND INDEPENDENCE, Maurice G. Kains. Great back-to-the-land classic explains basics of self-sufficient farming. The one book to get. 95 illustrations. 397pp. 5⅜ x 8½. 20974-1

SONGS OF EASTERN BIRDS, Dr. Donald J. Borror. Songs and calls of 60 species most common to eastern U.S.: warblers, woodpeckers, flycatchers, thrushes, larks, many more in high-quality recording. Cassette and manual 99912-2

A MODERN HERBAL, Margaret Grieve. Much the fullest, most exact, most useful compilation of herbal material. Gigantic alphabetical encyclopedia, from aconite to zedoary, gives botanical information, medical properties, folklore, economic uses, much else. Indispensable to serious reader. 161 illustrations. 888pp. 6½ x 9¼. 2-vol. set. (Available in U.S. only.) Vol. I: 22798-7
Vol. II: 22799-5

HIDDEN TREASURE MAZE BOOK, Dave Phillips. Solve 34 challenging mazes accompanied by heroic tales of adventure. Evil dragons, people-eating plants, blood-thirsty giants, many more dangerous adversaries lurk at every twist and turn. 34 mazes, stories, solutions. 48pp. 8¼ x 11. 24566-7

LETTERS OF W. A. MOZART, Wolfgang A. Mozart. Remarkable letters show bawdy wit, humor, imagination, musical insights, contemporary musical world; includes some letters from Leopold Mozart. 276pp. 5⅜ x 8½. 22859-2

BASIC PRINCIPLES OF CLASSICAL BALLET, Agrippina Vaganova. Great Russian theoretician, teacher explains methods for teaching classical ballet. 118 illustrations. 175pp. 5⅜ x 8½. 22036-2

THE JUMPING FROG, Mark Twain. Revenge edition. The original story of The Celebrated Jumping Frog of Calaveras County, a hapless French translation, and Twain's hilarious "retranslation" from the French. 12 illustrations. 66pp. 5⅜ x 8½. 22686-7

BEST REMEMBERED POEMS, Martin Gardner (ed.). The 126 poems in this superb collection of 19th- and 20th-century British and American verse range from Shelley's "To a Skylark" to the impassioned "Renascence" of Edna St. Vincent Millay and to Edward Lear's whimsical "The Owl and the Pussycat." 224pp. 5⅜ x 8½. 27165-X

COMPLETE SONNETS, William Shakespeare. Over 150 exquisite poems deal with love, friendship, the tyranny of time, beauty's evanescence, death and other themes in language of remarkable power, precision and beauty. Glossary of archaic terms. 80pp. 5 3/16 x 8¼. 26686-9

THE BATTLES THAT CHANGED HISTORY, Fletcher Pratt. Eminent historian profiles 16 crucial conflicts, ancient to modern, that changed the course of civilization. 352pp. 5⅜ x 8½. 41129-X

THE WIT AND HUMOR OF OSCAR WILDE, Alvin Redman (ed.). More than 1,000 ripostes, paradoxes, wisecracks: Work is the curse of the drinking classes; I can resist everything except temptation; etc. 258pp. 5⅜ x 8½. 20602-5

SHAKESPEARE LEXICON AND QUOTATION DICTIONARY, Alexander Schmidt. Full definitions, locations, shades of meaning in every word in plays and poems. More than 50,000 exact quotations. 1,485pp. 6½ x 9¼. 2-vol. set.
Vol. 1: 22726-X
Vol. 2: 22727-8

SELECTED POEMS, Emily Dickinson. Over 100 best-known, best-loved poems by one of America's foremost poets, reprinted from authoritative early editions. No comparable edition at this price. Index of first lines. 64pp. 5$\frac{3}{16}$ x 8¼. 26466-1

THE INSIDIOUS DR. FU-MANCHU, Sax Rohmer. The first of the popular mystery series introduces a pair of English detectives to their archnemesis, the diabolical Dr. Fu-Manchu. Flavorful atmosphere, fast-paced action, and colorful characters enliven this classic of the genre. 208pp. 5$\frac{3}{16}$ x 8¼. 29898-1

THE MALLEUS MALEFICARUM OF KRAMER AND SPRENGER, translated by Montague Summers. Full text of most important witchhunter's "bible," used by both Catholics and Protestants. 278pp. 6⅝ x 10. 22802-9

SPANISH STORIES/CUENTOS ESPAÑOLES: A Dual-Language Book, Angel Flores (ed.). Unique format offers 13 great stories in Spanish by Cervantes, Borges, others. Faithful English translations on facing pages. 352pp. 5⅜ x 8½. 25399-6

GARDEN CITY, LONG ISLAND, IN EARLY PHOTOGRAPHS, 1869–1919, Mildred H. Smith. Handsome treasury of 118 vintage pictures, accompanied by carefully researched captions, document the Garden City Hotel fire (1899), the Vanderbilt Cup Race (1908), the first airmail flight departing from the Nassau Boulevard Aerodrome (1911), and much more. 96pp. 8⅞ x 11¾. 40669-5

OLD QUEENS, N.Y., IN EARLY PHOTOGRAPHS, Vincent F. Seyfried and William Asadorian. Over 160 rare photographs of Maspeth, Jamaica, Jackson Heights, and other areas. Vintage views of DeWitt Clinton mansion, 1939 World's Fair and more. Captions. 192pp. 8⅞ x 11. 26358-4

CAPTURED BY THE INDIANS: 15 Firsthand Accounts, 1750-1870, Frederick Drimmer. Astounding true historical accounts of grisly torture, bloody conflicts, relentless pursuits, miraculous escapes and more, by people who lived to tell the tale. 384pp. 5⅜ x 8½. 24901-8

THE WORLD'S GREAT SPEECHES (Fourth Enlarged Edition), Lewis Copeland, Lawrence W. Lamm, and Stephen J. McKenna. Nearly 300 speeches provide public speakers with a wealth of updated quotes and inspiration–from Pericles' funeral oration and William Jennings Bryan's "Cross of Gold Speech" to Malcolm X's powerful words on the Black Revolution and Earl of Spenser's tribute to his sister, Diana, Princess of Wales. 944pp. 5⅜ x 8⅜. 40903-1

THE BOOK OF THE SWORD, Sir Richard F. Burton. Great Victorian scholar/adventurer's eloquent, erudite history of the "queen of weapons"–from prehistory to early Roman Empire. Evolution and development of early swords, variations (sabre, broadsword, cutlass, scimitar, etc.), much more. 336pp. 6⅛ x 9¼.
25434-8

AUTOBIOGRAPHY: The Story of My Experiments with Truth, Mohandas K. Gandhi. Boyhood, legal studies, purification, the growth of the Satyagraha (nonviolent protest) movement. Critical, inspiring work of the man responsible for the freedom of India. 480pp. 5⅜ x 8½. (Available in U.S. only.) 24593-4

CELTIC MYTHS AND LEGENDS, T. W. Rolleston. Masterful retelling of Irish and Welsh stories and tales. Cuchulain, King Arthur, Deirdre, the Grail, many more. First paperback edition. 58 full-page illustrations. 512pp. 5⅜ x 8½. 26507-2

THE PRINCIPLES OF PSYCHOLOGY, William James. Famous long course complete, unabridged. Stream of thought, time perception, memory, experimental methods; great work decades ahead of its time. 94 figures. 1,391pp. 5⅜ x 8½. 2-vol. set.
Vol. I: 20381-6 Vol. II: 20382-4

THE WORLD AS WILL AND REPRESENTATION, Arthur Schopenhauer. Definitive English translation of Schopenhauer's life work, correcting more than 1,000 errors, omissions in earlier translations. Translated by E. F. J. Payne. Total of 1,269pp. 5⅜ x 8½. 2-vol. set. Vol. 1: 21761-2 Vol. 2: 21762-0

MAGIC AND MYSTERY IN TIBET, Madame Alexandra David-Neel. Experiences among lamas, magicians, sages, sorcerers, Bonpa wizards. A true psychic discovery. 32 illustrations. 321pp. 5⅜ x 8½. (Available in U.S. only.) 22682-4

THE EGYPTIAN BOOK OF THE DEAD, E. A. Wallis Budge. Complete reproduction of Ani's papyrus, finest ever found. Full hieroglyphic text, interlinear transliteration, word-for-word translation, smooth translation. 533pp. 6½ x 9¼. 21866-X

MATHEMATICS FOR THE NONMATHEMATICIAN, Morris Kline. Detailed, college-level treatment of mathematics in cultural and historical context, with numerous exercises. Recommended Reading Lists. Tables. Numerous figures. 641pp. 5⅜ x 8½.
24823-2

PROBABILISTIC METHODS IN THE THEORY OF STRUCTURES, Isaac Elishakoff. Well-written introduction covers the elements of the theory of probability from two or more random variables, the reliability of such multivariable structures, the theory of random function, Monte Carlo methods of treating problems incapable of exact solution, and more. Examples. 502pp. 5⅜ x 8½. 40691-1

THE RIME OF THE ANCIENT MARINER, Gustave Doré, S. T. Coleridge. Doré's finest work; 34 plates capture moods, subtleties of poem. Flawless full-size reproductions printed on facing pages with authoritative text of poem. "Beautiful. Simply beautiful."–*Publisher's Weekly*. 77pp. 9¼ x 12. 22305-1

NORTH AMERICAN INDIAN DESIGNS FOR ARTISTS AND CRAFTSPEOPLE, Eva Wilson. Over 360 authentic copyright-free designs adapted from Navajo blankets, Hopi pottery, Sioux buffalo hides, more. Geometrics, symbolic figures, plant and animal motifs, etc. 128pp. 8⅜ x 11. (Not for sale in the United Kingdom.) 25341-4

SCULPTURE: Principles and Practice, Louis Slobodkin. Step-by-step approach to clay, plaster, metals, stone; classical and modern. 253 drawings, photos. 255pp. 8⅛ x 11.
22960-2

THE INFLUENCE OF SEA POWER UPON HISTORY, 1660–1783, A. T. Mahan. Influential classic of naval history and tactics still used as text in war colleges. First paperback edition. 4 maps. 24 battle plans. 640pp. 5⅜ x 8½. 25509-3

CATALOG OF DOVER BOOKS

THE STORY OF THE TITANIC AS TOLD BY ITS SURVIVORS, Jack Winocour (ed.). What it was really like. Panic, despair, shocking inefficiency, and a little heroism. More thrilling than any fictional account. 26 illustrations. 320pp. 5⅜ x 8½.
20610-6

FAIRY AND FOLK TALES OF THE IRISH PEASANTRY, William Butler Yeats (ed.). Treasury of 64 tales from the twilight world of Celtic myth and legend: "The Soul Cages," "The Kildare Pooka," "King O'Toole and his Goose," many more. Introduction and Notes by W. B. Yeats. 352pp. 5⅜ x 8½.
26941-8

BUDDHIST MAHAYANA TEXTS, E. B. Cowell and others (eds.). Superb, accurate translations of basic documents in Mahayana Buddhism, highly important in history of religions. The Buddha-karita of Asvaghosha, Larger Sukhavativyuha, more. 448pp. 5⅜ x 8½.
25552-2

ONE TWO THREE . . . INFINITY: Facts and Speculations of Science, George Gamow. Great physicist's fascinating, readable overview of contemporary science: number theory, relativity, fourth dimension, entropy, genes, atomic structure, much more. 128 illustrations. Index. 352pp. 5⅜ x 8½.
25664-2

EXPERIMENTATION AND MEASUREMENT, W. J. Youden. Introductory manual explains laws of measurement in simple terms and offers tips for achieving accuracy and minimizing errors. Mathematics of measurement, use of instruments, experimenting with machines. 1994 edition. Foreword. Preface. Introduction. Epilogue. Selected Readings. Glossary. Index. Tables and figures. 128pp. 5⅜ x 8½.
40451-X

DALÍ ON MODERN ART: The Cuckolds of Antiquated Modern Art, Salvador Dalí. Influential painter skewers modern art and its practitioners. Outrageous evaluations of Picasso, Cézanne, Turner, more. 15 renderings of paintings discussed. 44 calligraphic decorations by Dalí. 96pp. 5⅜ x 8½. (Available in U.S. only.)
29220-7

ANTIQUE PLAYING CARDS: A Pictorial History, Henry René D'Allemagne. Over 900 elaborate, decorative images from rare playing cards (14th–20th centuries): Bacchus, death, dancing dogs, hunting scenes, royal coats of arms, players cheating, much more. 96pp. 9¼ x 12¼.
29265-7

MAKING FURNITURE MASTERPIECES: 30 Projects with Measured Drawings, Franklin H. Gottshall. Step-by-step instructions, illustrations for constructing handsome, useful pieces, among them a Sheraton desk, Chippendale chair, Spanish desk, Queen Anne table and a William and Mary dressing mirror. 224pp. 8⅛ x 11¼.
29338-6

THE FOSSIL BOOK: A Record of Prehistoric Life, Patricia V. Rich et al. Profusely illustrated definitive guide covers everything from single-celled organisms and dinosaurs to birds and mammals and the interplay between climate and man. Over 1,500 illustrations. 760pp. 7½ x 10⅛.
29371-8